Michel Fo

Genealogy as Critique

◆

RUDI VISKER

Translated by Chris Turner

London · New York

First published by Verso 1995
This edition © Verso 1995
Translation © Chris Turner 1995
First published as *Genealogie als kritiek: Michel Foucault*, 1990,
Boom, Meppel/Amsterdam
© Wilhelm Fink Verlag, Munich, 1991

Verso
UK: 6 Meard Street, London W1V 3HR
USA: 180 Varick Street, New York NY 10014-4606

Verso is the imprint of New Left Books

ISBN 0–86091–468–2
ISBN 1–85984–095–7

British Library Cataloguing in Publication Data
A catalogue record for this book is available from the British Library

Library of Congress Cataloging-in-Publication Data
Visker, Rudi, 1959–
[Genealogie als kritiek. English]
Michel Foucault: genealogy as critique/Rudi Visker: translated
by Chris Turner.
p.   cm.
Translation of: Genealogie als kritiek. Translated from the German
language ed. published in 1991.
Includes bibliographical references (p.   ).
ISBN 0–86091–468–2. — ISBN 1–85984–095–7 (pbk.)
1. Foucault, Michel. 2. Genealogy (Philosophy) I. Title.
II. Title: Genealogy as critique.
B2430.F724V5713 1995   95–3884
194—dc20   CIP

Typeset by Solidus (Bristol) Limited
Printed and bound in Great Britain by
Biddles Ltd, Guildford and King's Lynn

Contents

'Not Another Book on Foucault!'

'I guess you're right. I wonder what made them translate this – as if the dozens of critical outlines of Foucault in English have left anything to be said. What arrogance!'

'I hear the author prides himself on having written a book that won't save its readers time. Hopelessly old-fashioned, don't you think?'

'Pathetic. I went through some of the reviews of the original Dutch publication (1990) and looked at what the Germans had to say when the Fink translation came out. Anything but complimentary, I can tell you. What we seem to have here is another of those Habermas- or Honneth-type commentaries we were flooded with a while back. But they also claimed the book takes a Luhmannian turn near the end. And, to top it all, a very influential journal says that the author misses Foucault's point completely: he doesn't realize everything is historical!'

'But it says here he intends to talk about Foucault's quotation marks. And even his use of hyphens. You must be wrong – no doubt he's just another Derridean in disguise! I bet you anything his next book is on the capitals in Levinas.'

I hope I will be forgiven for not having resisted the temptation to listen in on this little conversation. But I thought the indiscretion of presenting in this way what was perhaps no more than a phantasy was the surest way of saving myself and my readers part of the embarrassment and as much as humanly possible of the venom one could expect from an author who in his weaker moments fears he may not have been properly understood. In a preface, one always runs the risk of adopting the ludicrous posture of telling others how they should read. Instead of laying down this law and giving in to the temptation to speak in the name of a text which, as I remember, was written so that it could speak for itself and defend itself, if only it was read to the end (a remark which I am afraid is not altogether superfluous), it seemed more appropriate to try to bridge that ambiguous gap which now separates me from the point of its conception by directing the little light from this book that still remains in me to its confused origins. For it is true that I had set out to do many things at once – none of which, however, included the plan to write another book on Foucault.

There was, on the one hand, an interest in the rise of economics as a science. I had just concluded a piece of academic research on the role of the so-called 'moral asides' in Alfred Marshall's *Principles of Economics*. Instead of following Schumpeter's advice and reducing these *obiter dicta* to all that was so typically Victorian in Marshall, I had begun to suspect that this 'impure' discourse, which was still so loquacious about everything that economic theory after its final breakthrough had decided to neglect, had played an essential role in the establishment of what, borrowing from the French, I called 'economicity' – the institution of economics as a 'régime of truth' with its own unquestioned and self-referential discursive authority. It was at that point that I had my first chance encounter with Foucault. But as I found upon *re*reading *Les Mots et les choses* (for this was one of those books we had all read), Foucault, to my surprise (for you know how we read him), proved to be on the other side of the fence. Instead of having gained an ally who could have lent me some of the fashionable philosophical jargon I needed to buttress and polish my results, I became entangled in the web of one of those problems that can change (or, indeed, mess up) one's career. As dust was gathering on my ever-growing pile of books on Habermas and Critical Theory, I found myself more and more occupied with such trivia as the fact that Foucault, not only in *The Order of Things* but, as I soon discovered, in most of his books, kept referring to the human sciences as human 'sciences'. Hence a double surprise which gradually became an obsession: not only did Foucault make it perfectly clear that economics was for him, contrary to what I was inclined (and taught) to believe, not a human science; but he also made it no secret that the human sciences were for him anything but 'sciences'. I did not understand this double move, and remained puzzled by the quotation marks under cover of which he had decided to approach the human 'sciences'. Finally, a line or two in Derrida helped to break my fascination and I decided that the work I had done on economics lent itself more appropriately to a deconstruction of the authority of science than to a direct questioning of the scientific credentials of this or that discipline.

Having 'lost' valuable research time I began devouring my Habermas literature. But *The Philosophical Discourse of Modernity* confirmed my worst fears – after that, it seemed quite unnecessary still to stage, as I had intended, a virtual dialogue between Habermas and 'the French', focusing on the pressure for transparency (*Transparenzzwang*) in Habermas, of which another piece of academic work on the crisis of forgetting in Habermas and Husserl had made me more than a little suspicious. All of a sudden, that dialogue was a fact, and no sooner had it started than it broke off with both camps engaging in trench warfare which was soon to lose its vigour and at any rate had lost it, at least on the Continent, by the time I found my earlier interest in Foucault unexpectedly renewed. Habermas's reading of Foucault in these lectures on modernity had annoyed me, as it had annoyed many a reader. But my earlier bewilderment with Foucault's critique of the scientificity of the human sciences made me perhaps a little more patient than others in taking seriously, if not Habermas's alternative programme, then at least some of his questions. At this point, things started to fit together: I decided to take over the gist of Habermas's central question to Foucault, without subscribing to the rest of the Habermassian programme. I felt that Habermas was quite entitled to question *the status of Foucault's critique* but was very unjust in his reading of the texts. A much closer and more internal reading – a deconstruction as I called it at the time – seemed to be called for. And what better place to start than with Foucault's quotation marks? Did they not make Foucault's thought unnecessarily vulnerable to the Habermassian critique? Did they not in the end threaten to jettison the one concept – discourse in its *constitutive 'incompleteness'* – which could have brought the machinery of *Critical Theory* to a standstill, as it seemed to introduce a notion of power that was unusual to the extent that it forced us to conceive of an exclusion which wasn't simply domination and hence perhaps could not be rendered transparent, since it seemed to point to an opacity at the heart of light itself . . .

No doubt today I would be less confident that, in the end, this new critical project I had hoped to forge by playing this double-agent role could still be codenamed a critique of 'objectivism'. The last pages of this book have in fact deprived me of that illusion. But not without first going through that long mourning process in which one takes one's leave of an author one has admired up to the point where the only tribute one can still pay him is that of a respectful silence. I hope to document the results of this, which have driven me back into phenomenology, elsewhere. But in the meantime I have taken the liberty of adding a few of my later essays on Foucault to the bibliography. I can only hope that, like this preface, those few references will not be seen as a sign of self-importance, but rather recognized as that gesture by which every one of us – in vain, no doubt – tries to shield himself from the infinite demands of a responsibility we all must bear, since our names, unlike our selves, are not subject to what one sometimes optimistically refers to as a process of maturation.*

Leuven, September 1994

---

* I would like to take this opportunity to thank Chris Turner for the patience that went into producing his fine translation and Jeff Bloechl for his help with my revisions.

Les gens que j'aime,
je les utilise

(MICHEL FOUCAULT,
Les Jeux du pouvoir, 1976, p. 174)

Introduction

1. Exposition: a reading of Foucault

Foucault wrote little about philosophy and the subjects with which he dealt are not those of the philosophers: madness, hospitals, the structure of the classical *epistemè*, prisons, infamy, sexuality ... And we have all read Foucault. And a good many among us claim he has had the most profound influence on our thinking.* And he is once again at the centre of a debate which fills the pages of our journals: at a point when no one is much exercised about the death of man any more – a face in the sand on the seashore, washed away by the waves – the question arises whether the critical passion to be found in his texts is well-founded. Foucault is read and quoted more than ever before. His work is summarized and divided up into periods. And a good many, embarrassed by these caesuras, say his texts are like toolboxes in which you can find something for the most widely varying of purposes. Yet others are indignant at such a casual attitude and write long, difficult commentaries, wanting, each in their own way, to convince us that Foucault's approach is right, or that it can be easily refuted. But, in spite of all these efforts and notwithstanding all these remarkably violent discussions, Foucault's work still lies before us, resistant and capricious, noncommittal where one expects firm argument, inquisitively questioning where one would have preferred a tactful silence, full of surprising turns and seductive in its doubts. So long as the aim is

* I am thinking here primarily of Sam IJsseling and Bernhard Waldenfels, who have tempted me by similar confessions, into reading Foucault *further*. Without this intellectual debt and the permanent challenge to sound out the full extent of it, these pages would perhaps never have been written.

1

only to repeat or refute it, it will elude us and continue to stand anxious watch over the secret of what is unthought within it.

What is the aim of the arguments presented here? To set up, using Foucault's text, a form of organized confusion and show that what organizes this confusion is a philosophical problematic. To sweep the dust from the pages in which Foucault formulates his critique of the human sciences and to make clear that this is where the decisions are taken which shape his work. To link these decisions to the question of the status of Foucault's critique, and to attempt an answer to that question which goes beyond the polarizations which all too often rob the current discussion of the problem of its charm. In short, what is intended is a philosophical reading of Foucault or, more precisely, a reading of Foucault as philosopher.

In a certain respect, this reading is but a long meditation on the quotation marks which one finds, time and again, in Foucault's works. We were initially amazed by these and put up defences against them and yet, before we became aware of it, this resistance became 'the point of incomprehension' which organized our reading.[1] In the second part of this Introduction, we look briefly at the risks and ambiguity of a critique which literally puts the scientificity of particular disciplines between quotation marks. The chapters which follow attempt to show that this danger is in no sense merely imaginary. A great number of the difficulties in *Histoire de la folie** (1), *The Order of Things* (2.1) and in *Discipline and Punish* (2.2) have their origins in Foucault's decision to contest the scientificity of the human 'sciences'. But the style of critique Foucault adopts here is not confined only to his dealings with the human sciences. Reading the three volumes of the history of sexuality (3.1), one notes that the quotation marks which were present in his early work return in one form or another and clearly shape, if not the analysis, then at least the conclusions drawn from it. Foucault's quotation marks are an exemplary expression of a model of critique which runs throughout his entire *oeuvre*.

At first sight, then, it would seem difficult to exaggerate the importance of these. Yet the Foucault debate (3.2) has taken them too seriously. Instead of seeing them as an obstacle which hobbles Foucault's problematic, they have been identified with that problematic. And this has doubtless arisen from the way in which

---

* Since there is no *complete* English translation of this work, we shall refer throughout to the French edition specified in the Bibliography.

Foucault has been read. So, at the beginning of the final chapter, we reflect on our way of reading Foucault and the concept of author with which we have implicitly been operating. Do 'Foucault''s quotation marks exhaust his problematic? Are they not rather an expression of the difficulties he has with 'his' problematic? In order to find an answer to these questions, we have no other solution than to move to (4.1) and fro (4.2) between these problems and that problematic in the hope that this manoeuvring will allow us to rescue Foucault's concept of order from his quotation marks in order ultimately to be able to link that concept with another type of critique (4.3). This linkage remains programmatic and we have ourselves in the end found it necessary to resort to quotation marks in order to refer to a project which we hope to be able to work out elsewhere: the possibilities of a critique of 'objectivism'.

2. The risks and ambiguity of Foucault's critique of science

Foucault is one of that small band of authors who can condense the entire meaning and force of their enterprise – and also all its difficulties and problems – into a single diacritical sign. In the same way as the inaudible 'a' in Derrida's *différance* – 'a mute mark ... a tacit monument'[2] – leaves the trace of a carefully pondered neographism in the margin of Saussure's texts, it seems that Foucault's 'gray, meticulous and patiently documentary' genealogies[3] have chosen to etch an unobtrusive sign on to the pages of our culture's great works in the humanities: 'our "scientific" knowledge of mental illness'.[4] Foucault's quotation marks sum up an entire programme. The critique of the claims of psychiatry and psychology to scientific status is, in later works, carried over to the human sciences as a whole.

Whereas Foucault is initially concerned to show up the unscientificity of the human sciences, in the methodological texts from the period of *Discipline and Punish* (1975), in which he once more casts into doubt the scientificity of such diverse disciplines as criminology, pedagogy, psychology and psychiatry by the use of quotation marks,[5] the emphasis shifts: 'it is really against the effects of the power of a discourse that is considered to be scientific that genealogy must wage its struggle'.[6] From this point on, a 'political economy of knowledge' analyses the claim to scientificity as an attempt to invest particular forms of knowledge – to the detriment

3

of others – with a surplus value: the value of scientificity. These reservations about 'theoretical sacralization' and 'scientific tabooing' seem to play their part when, in a discussion of Thomas Szasz's anti-psychiatry, Foucault describes the task of historical analysis as being to expose the unscientificity of science,[7] but immediately qualifies this with the remark that it is not the problem of what is scientific or unscientific which is essential but the understanding that the truth-effects of science are at the same time power-effects.[8]

We might ask to what extent this qualification may not be understood as an indirect, retrospective self-criticism or, rather, as a hesitation, which points to an underlying problem, a latent awareness of the perhaps unavoidable risks incurred by a programme which is, admittedly, very rich in material, but metatheoretically insecure. One cannot avoid wondering to what extent the shift of emphasis which occurs here is not directed in a particular, rather unexpected way against Foucault's own studies, when he writes:

> It is surely the following kinds of question that would need to be posed: What types of knowledge do you want to disqualify in the very instant of your demand: 'Is it a science'? Which speaking, discoursing subjects ... do you then want to 'diminish' when you say: 'I who conduct this discourse am conducting a scientific discourse, and I am a scientist'?[9]

For Foucault, both questions are variations on a single theme: what ultimately lies behind the concern of those who see it as primordial whether, for example, Marxism or psychoanalysis are scientific – indeed, behind all such endless discussions – is, ultimately, the patient hope and the silent longing that they may attach the index of scientificity to these disciplines.[10] And that index is by no means a neutral mark; it is a hallmark of quality linked to a system of qualification and disqualification. The scientificity of psychiatry disqualifies the patients' knowledge.[11]

It follows from this that the question whether a discipline has a scientific character ('is it a science?') must be treated with the greatest circumspection. And yet, it is precisely this question which is touched on in Foucault's critique of the human sciences' false claim to scientificity. But while the question of the scientificity of the human sciences is only posed by those sciences with a view to acquiring the status which would enable them to make capital of the accreditation which goes along with it, Foucault's programme runs in the opposite direction: his interest in querying the scientificity of

4

the human sciences ('are they sciences?') arises initially out of the observation that they lay claim to scientificity. Only the awareness of such a preceding 'I who am making these arguments am expressing myself scientifically' can prevent Foucault's reopening of the question 'Is it a science?' resulting in an unavoidable doubling of the discourse of the human sciences themselves. The entire radicalism, but also the entire risk, of Foucault's quotation marks ('science') is defined by the possibility and difficulty of maintaining the distance from the internal discourse of the human sciences and from science as the imaginary referent of this discourse. And Foucault is aware of this. He would be the last person to dispute that the criticism of the pretended scientificity of particular disciplines runs the risk of operating with a norm of scientificity which has the power-effects that he opposes. For this reason, he does not formulate his critique of the human sciences in terms of concepts like maturity or normality and thus avoids an ambiguity of the kind which arises, for example, with Kuhn's concept of pre-paradigmatic sciences.[12] Foucault's analysis does not have the hortative character which has often been accorded by the human sciences to Kuhn's paradigm theory. The human sciences are not disciplines which are at an immature stage and still have to cross the threshold of scientificity. They are structurally incapable of becoming sciences: 'It is useless, then, to say that the "human sciences" are false sciences [*fausses sciences*]; they are not sciences at all; the configuration that defines their positivity ... at the same time makes it impossible for them to be sciences.'[13]

But do these reservations deal fully with the difficulties posed by an immanent critique? Are they sufficient to avoid the danger of a critique-induced reinforcement of the norm of science? Doesn't a discourse directed chiefly against false claims to scientificity run the risk of introducing an unanalysed norm of scientificity or of taking over a particular model of that norm from the discourse under analysis? These problems go to the heart of Foucault's project. How can one criticize the false claims of psychiatry or psychology other than by oneself operating with an implicit norm of scientificity? How can one keep not just the norm but also conceptions concerning that norm, not just the ideal of scientificity, but also the scientific ideal of the disciplines under analysis, from pushing the analysing discourse and the metatheoretical instrumentarium of that discourse in an undesired direction, or even structuring it? Should one not 'first' analyse the concept of 'scientificity'?

5

It would be to misunderstand the meaning of this last question, which encapsulates all the preceding ones, to interpret it as a criticism of Foucault's actual research practice. 'First' here is directed not against the course which Foucault's researches follow *de facto*; it has, rather, a *de jure* status. As Derrida has already remarked with regard to a related question put to Foucault: 'it is true that once the question and the privileged difficulty are understood, to devote a preliminary work to them would have entailed the sterilization or paralysis of all further enquiry'.[14] The awareness Foucault perhaps had of this difficulty did not, in any case, lead him to accord it the character of a methodological or philosophical precondition. As a consequence, not only is the analysis of 'non-dubious' sciences methodically deferred on grounds of research strategy,[15] but also that of the concept of 'scientificity' itself. This deferral opens up a field of possibilities and difficulties within which Foucault's critique of the human sciences is able to unfold and ramify into other forms of critique. Yet that field is only opened up by accepting the risk to which the preceding questions have pointed. A risk which is, at the same time, a condition of possibility: the fact of running that risk does not exclude the possibility of success.

In order to avoid what is *in this sense* an unavoidable risk, or even merely to reduce that risk, it is perhaps not sufficient for the analysing discourse merely to call itself 'anti-science'.[16] Reversal is an old figure of thought, and one constantly beset by the danger that the traces of what it is directed against will remain attached to it. For the move which it announces to be successfully accomplished, a first step, in which thought is thrown off its familiar track, must be followed by a second which 'alters the configuration in such a way that the same elements return in a different way, i.e. in a certain sense do not return'.[17] The problems which are hinted at by the questions listed above are perhaps not insoluble and there is a chance that Foucault does hold a second step in reserve. But the framework sketched out here affords us some insight into the stubbornness of the resistance which awaits an undertaking which seeks to be more than a mere reversal.

From a Realism of Science to a Realism of Experience

In the second part of *Mental Illness and Psychology*,[1] and in *Histoire de la folie*, Foucault develops a critique of psychology and psychiatry. The distinction between these two disciplines clearly plays no systematic role in his analyses, which are directed precisely against the entire system which makes such a distinction possible. Foucault seeks to break the apparently obvious connection between psychiatry and the psychopathological. The connection with the pathological goes deeper than the division of the object domains into psychiatry and psychology suggests; in Foucault's opinion, it affects the very roots of psychology. Foucault's assertion that 'objective', 'positive' or 'scientific' psychology – the quotation marks are Foucault's – had its historical origin and basis in a pathological experience[2] is to be understood as a critique of a psychology which seeks to present itself as the psychology of the normal and, for that reason, is in danger of forgetting the context of its emergence – a context it shares with psychiatry: 'Man became a "psychologizable species" only when his relationship to madness made a psychology possible.'[3] This overlap in the genesis of psychology and psychiatry explains why Foucault can arrive at the conclusion, towards the end of *Histoire de la folie*, that that history of *madness* is simultaneously a history of what made possible the appearance of *psychology* as such.[4]

Foucault's use of quotation marks to refer to the objectivity, positivity and scientificity of psychology is a clear indication that he has some other object in mind than establishing the conditions of possibility of psychology. As will become clear in the following sections, he is more concerned in his analyses of psychology and psychiatry[5] with the impossibility of these disciplines than with their possibility. This peculiar procedure which – to put it in the form of a paradox – seeks to prove the impossibility of the phenomenon whose conditions of possibility are being discovered is a constant in Foucault's critique of the human sciences and much of his theoretical development can be understood by bearing in mind that, in spite of all difficulties, he always holds to it. One cannot overstress the importance of the two books on psychology and psychiatry in this development. Not only because almost all his later themes are already touched on there,[6] but also because the space in which his critique will be able to move is already more or less marked out. Yet it remains to be seen whether the ambivalence of the criticism (1.2) which is so characteristic of Foucault's early engagement with psychology (1.1), will disappear in his later works.

1.1. The engagement with psychology

Foucault's characterization of *Histoire de la folie* as a history of the conditions of emergence of psychology is a corrective to the image the naïve reader would have formed of his work: 'In our naïveté, we imagined perhaps that we had described a psychological type, the madman, over a hundred and fifty years of his history.'[7] Foucault projects on to the figure of the naïve reader, which constantly reappears from behind the unassuming first person plural so often employed in *Histoire de la folie*, the image he has of psychology. The naïveté he has in his sights can be attributed to a 'psychological sleep',[8] the sleep of a psychology into which Western man 'has put a little of his astonishment, much of his pride and most of his ability to forget'.[9] It may seem surprising that Foucault reintroduces this figure of a naïve reader right at the end of a work whose aim is to raise his readers from dogmatic slumber. One should perhaps not merely see this as a comment on the power of the tradition he is standing out against; it should also be related to the way he conducts his critique of psychology.

1. The critique of psychology's conception of history

Contrary to what one might have expected, Foucault's critical engagement with psychology remains, to some extent, in the background. His picture of psychology only takes shape gradually and indirectly, by way of scattered remarks on the image of the history of madness entertained by the naïve reader – and, above and beyond him, by psychology. These remarks set a basic tone which runs through the work, giving *Histoire de la folie* a deeper dimension – a tone that can easily be missed amid the wealth of historical material. Only if we pay attention to this basic tone does it become clear that *Histoire de la folie* is much more than a mere history of madness. It is, first and foremost, a counter-history – not so much a history casting doubt on the dominant interpretations of a particular aspect of our past,[10] as one contesting the way in which psychology constructs its own history.

The history of psychology – which is for Foucault, as we have already pointed out, enmeshed with the history of psychiatry – labours under a retrospective illusion,[11] which prevents it from seeing that its field of study is historically constituted. It starts out from the notion that what it characterizes with a calm, objective, scientific gaze[12] as mental illness (*maladie mentale*) in reality already existed[13] and was merely waiting to be discovered – 'that happy age in which madness was at last recognized and treated in accordance with a truth to which we had only too long remained blind'.[14] Psychology conceives its emergence literally as a discovery, as the exposure of an object which was already there before being discovered, not an object constituted by its discovery.

But this discovery, which is supposed to guarantee the scientificity of psychology, is at the same time relativized by that psychology. And rightly so: in order to avoid the positing of an object whose identity remains unassailed throughout history until the emergence of psychology becoming an unverifiable postulate, histories of psychology and psychiatry have recourse to the idea of an orthogenesis of knowledge, which develops from a vague group awareness of the special nature of certain social types to the positively scientific confirmation of these 'insights'.[15] 'All histories of psychiatry up to the present day have set out to show that the madman of the Middle Ages and the Renaissance was simply an *unrecognized* mentally ill patient, trapped within a tight network of religious and magical significations.'[16] Psychology, argues Foucault, is verified by a pre-scientific practice which, precisely because of its pre-scientific character, requires corroboration from psychology. Or, in other words, psychology must presuppose both the correctness and incorrectness of the practice that preceded it. It was a mistake to see the madman in terms of religious and magical categories, but right to characterize him as a madman. 'Social experience – an approximate form of knowledge – might be said to be of the same order as knowledge itself and already on the path to perfection.'[17] This idea of an object which is present but misinterpreted not only justifies the existence of psychology but also provides a particular interpretation of its possibility. Although a vague consciousness of the special nature of the object of psychology shows through in the misinterpretation – madman, insane or possessed individual[18] – the level of real knowledge is only attained with psychology. And a possible counter-argument against an epistemologically realist interpretation of psychological knowledge is – at least provisionally – invalidated. Everything seems to point to the fact that the object of psychology[19] is universally present and precedes psychology, rather than arising only in and through the constitution of that discipline: 'The object of knowledge precedes it [knowledge], since it is already this object that is being thought even before it is grasped rigorously by positive science. In its timeless solidity, it finds protection from history, enfolded in a truth which remains in semi-slumber until the wakeful positivity of thought breaks through.'[20]

Let us linger a moment on this reconstruction of the strategy which psychology is following here when it argues for the historical pre-existence of its object. This argument is important for psychology because it corroborates the possibility of a realist psychology:[21] if one really knew that the object with which one was confronted at the pre-scientific level in fact coincided with the object that is the concern of psychology, then this would render thoroughly plausible psychology's claim to possess knowledge of an independently existing object. This also explains the passionate intensity with which a kind of palaeopathology is carried on: 'a game which doctor–historians like to engage in: discovering the real illnesses concealed in the descriptions of the classics'.[22] For Foucault, however, this is an impossible game, in which what is really being sought always has to be assumed. The 'genuine illnesses' always have to be presupposed and the others rejected as misinterpretations. And, in order to find the 'real' illness behind the 'false' one, the 'classical descriptions' must first be rejected. As long as one cannot assume the viewpoint of a *pathotheoros*, to modify an expression of Merleau-Ponty's,[23] and one does not possess an 'apocalyptic objectivity',[24] such a procedure always amounts, in Foucault's view, to projecting present categories back on to the past: 'And in this way we lose sight of what clear awareness is in reality contained in this (at least as we see it) "misrecognition".'[25]

By this analysis, Foucault seeks to avoid the 'presentist'[26] implications on which the psychological reading of the history of madness depends. To an '*éclairage en aller*', which can only understand the past as an anticipation[27] of the present, he counterposes an '*éclairage en retour*', as an effect of which history retains that very resistance which makes it history.[28] For to be able to see the past only in the light of the present means, for Foucault, allowing historicity to be eclipsed by a crude idea of progress.[29] It means according value to the past only in so far as it already bears within itself the seeds of the present and striving to build a bridge between past and present, which, like the architecture in Borges's 'The Immortal', must appear bewildering since there is no gap to be bridged. As a good student of Nietzsche, Foucault suspects that the thesis of the misrecognized object which psychology employs to bend its history into shape conceals a 'metaphysical' move: 'In placing present needs at the origin, the metaphysician would convince us of an obscure purpose that seeks its realization at the moment it arises.'[30] In Foucault's view, the thesis of the misrecognized object relates to a search for an 'origin', i.e. for 'that which was already there'.[31] And the ambiguity in which psychology becomes entangled as a result of this thesis – a thesis which presupposes that the practices which preceded it were both correct and erroneous, that its insights were anticipated and yet that the failure to understand those insights occasioned delay – ultimately leads, in Foucault's view, to an incorrect appraisal of the historical constellation in which psychology arises, and also of the constellations which preceded it. The dual movement by which psychology builds its relationship to history on the basis of the thesis of the misrecognized object must therefore be resisted: 'As it is wrong to search for descent in an uninterrupted continuity, we should avoid thinking of emergence as the final term of an historical development.'[32] Psychology can only legitimate its own scientificity by reducing history to the overcoming of an inertia, which keeps an already originally present, but misrecognized object under the sway of a pre-scientific knowledge. It must constantly avert to an origin in which – and this is the meaning, for Foucault, of the palaeopathological game in which it so willingly engages – it seeks the guarantee of its scientificity. However, in order that the legitimacy and superiority of its own standpoint should not be brought into question, psychology can do no other than condemn that origin as

11

a cognition which remains attached to a misrecognition. The ambivalence of this attitude to the origin compels psychology to think its own historicity in such a wilful manner that one cannot help wondering whether the consciousness it seeks to have of its own historicity does not rather amount to a denial of the conditions in which one may speak of historical meaning or a consciousness of one's own historicity at all: 'Historical meaning presupposes an insuperable distance between epochs; it arises out of the forgetting of the original meaning of the past and is a meaning which could not in any way have been grasped in the original present time of the past.'[33] The charge contained in this happy paraphrase of Derrida's critique of Husserl's project of a complete reactivation of origins is, to all intents and purposes, the same one Foucault levels against psychology in this other context. For is it not the case that the *éclairage en aller*, with which psychology operates, not only overcomes the distance between epochs, but also sweeps away epochality and historicity? The meaning psychology is aiming for is, on its own view, one which could very well have been grasped in the original 'present time of the past' on which it casts its light: present *de jure* in the origin, but prevented in actuality from emerging. For psychology, the overcoming of the inertia of history corrects an error which could always have been avoided. It restores to what was in practice a false evaluation an elasticity which enables it now to recognize an object which was always already present. In Foucault's view, psychology deceives itself about the nature of this elasticity: it is merely the extension of the structures of our own epoch, and it overstrains them to such a point that not only the structures of other epochs, but even those of its own, become unrecognizable. It is against this distortion of history that Foucault throws his counter-history into the balance, a counter-history which does not have to confine itself to contesting facts and interpretations, but derives – or could have derived – its impetus from a reflection on what is understood by the term 'history'.

2. Foucault's counter-history: an *éclairage en retour*

Rather than 'writ[ing] a history of the past in terms of the present',[34] the 'history of the present', with which Foucault is already engaged in *Histoire de la folie* seeks an *éclairage en retour* which does not shed light on the past from the present, but, rather, illuminates the present from the past, 'by freeing the chronologies

12

and historical sequences of any "progress-based" perspective and restoring to the history of experience a development which owes nothing to the finality of *connaissance* or the orthogenesis of *savoir*'.[35] Instead of continuity and identity – basic concepts in the psychological reading of the history of madness – Foucault, thus offering what may be viewed as a genealogy *avant la lettre*,[36] deploys concepts like 'transformation',[37] 'restructuring',[38] 'modification',[39] 'simplification',[40] 'displacement',[41] 'recurrence',[42] and 'non-contemporaneity'.[43] And to a reduction of the historically polymorphic[44] experiences of madness to the monochrome model of 'mental illness', he counterposes an analysis which attempts to do justice to the differences between these experiences and takes every experience for what it is, as 'neither a progress nor a regression by comparison with another'.[45]

Starting out from these premises, Foucault arrives at a quite different assessment of the 'classical period' from that of psychology. This period – which begins with the 'Great Confinement' (1656) when, within a short time, one in every hundred inhabitants of Paris was interned,[46] and ends with the birth of the 'psychological gaze', when Pinel released the prisoners at Bicêtre from their chains (1794)[47] – is regarded by psychology merely as a transitional phase. It is seen as a time needed to complete the ascent, by a kind of orthogenesis of knowledge, from the level of an as yet indistinct social experience to that of a positive science.[48] It is psychology's conviction that beneath these confinements – in which, by the criteria of our perception, a whole string of extremely diverse individuals were locked up – there lay an obscure social finality which enabled society to eliminate elements which it regarded as heterogenous or harmful: 'Little by little, this initial perception would have been organized and would have formed itself, in the end, into a fully developed medical consciousness which would have formulated as a malady of nature what was still only recognized as relating to a malaise of society.'[49] But while confinement on the one hand laid the ground for the birth of psychology – 'almost all that was missing from the insane who were interned was the name of the mentally ill'[50] – it was still couched in a *chiaroscuro* which explains the ambivalence of the assessment made of it by psychology: 'The madman of the classical age, who is locked away with the sexually ill, the depraved, the libertines and the homosexuals, [has] lost the marks of his individuality.'[51] Foucault takes the view that, by this ambivalence, psychology betrays a distortion congenial to the retrospective gaze it casts over the history of madness.[52] This distortion allows psychology to interpret the mass character and absence of differentiation which characterize classical confinement as the inevitable consequence of an ignorance which will disappear only at the end of the process of the orthogenesis of knowledge.[53] What, in the eyes of psychology, is the effect of a lack of ability to differentiate is, for Foucault, an 'original and irreducible experience', a 'positive fact',[54] which contains within it the quintessence of the classical period: 'We have the impression that the madman was *misrecognized* in the truth of his psychological profile; but this only occurred to the extent that his deep affinity with all forms of unreason was *recognized*.'[55] The fact that, in the light of our categories,[56] such diverse types as sufferers from venereal disease, madmen or the Abbé Bargedé, who refused to see usury as a sin – considering it, rather, a matter of honour – are all reduced to a common denominator[57] within this experience of 'unreason' (*déraison*) means for Foucault that we are dealing with an experience which is *sui generis*: the experience of the classical age – an experience which is misrecognized by psychology because it remains unable to see in it anything other than a misrecognition. While, for psychology, the classical period is prevented, by lack of a capacity to differentiate, from recognizing an object which is already present (the 'thesis of the misrecognized object'), what emerges for Foucault in this incapacity to differentiate are the outlines of a different 'perceptual coherence',[58] the 'positive sense' of which is that it effortlessly brings together, 'against a different sky',[59] what is to our eyes an apparently heteroclite set of figures which seem to share only the fact of their confinement:

> 'The debauched', 'imbeciles', 'prodigals', the 'infirm', 'the deranged', 'libertines', 'ungrateful sons', 'spendthrift fathers', 'prostitutes' and the 'insane'. Between all these there is no hint of a distinction: they all bear the same abstract dishonour. The astonishment that sick people should have been locked up and madmen confused with criminals would only come later. We are, for the moment, in the presence of a uniform state of affairs.[60]

Foucault's emphasis on the peculiar nature of the classical experience seems to suggest that he is seeking to confront the continuity-based thinking of psychology with a discontinuity thesis. But in fact he takes the analysis in another direction:[61] by the rejection of the insane, which took the form of confinement, the

14

classical age carried out a 'moral revolution' which not only precedes the constitution of a scientific knowledge of madness, but makes it possible.[62] Pinel's act of liberation of the incarcerated was only possible on the basis of this 'preparatory work'. While this act has an emblematic character for psychology – it allows the breakthrough to positive science to coincide with the sensitivity of a humanization – Foucault compares the asylum Pinel dreams of with a 'juridical microcosm'[63] in which a substitution occurs for which the classical age laid the ground: Pinel replaces the material bonds by moral chains and thereby establishes the status of the doctor in the asylum as that of an agent of moral syntheses.[64] In Foucault's view, Pinel's contribution lies not in a humanistically motivated, positively scientific break with an ethical experience of madness by which the classical period had deprived itself of the opportunity of knowing, without prejudice, an always already present and self-identical object, but in the way he continues the 'moral revolution' of the classical period. While the ethical experience of madness in the classical period found its expression in confinement, which led to an obscure linking of madness with guilt,[65] Pinel's humanizing act by no means leads to the madman being spared that assimilation; he is, rather, subjected to it all the more intensely and even interiorizes it. Not only is the whole of the insane person's behaviour put under surveillance, not only are his mad ideas refuted and his errors ridiculed, he is made to supervise, refute and ridicule *himself*. It is he who must himself effect the moral syntheses which the doctor merely provides for him. Pinel's therapeutic techniques only achieve their ends when the juridical authority is interiorized by the subject being judged: 'The transgression is punished and its perpetrator confesses his guilt.'[66] In Pinel's asylum, in 'that world of a punishing morality'[67] treatments which, in the classical period, played both a physical and a psychological role – for example, baths and showers were meant both to refresh the minds and the muscle fibres of the patients – were accorded an exclusively repressive and guilt-inducing significance: 'With Pinel, the use of the shower becomes quite openly a juridical measure. The shower was the customary punishment meted out by the ordinary police tribunal which sat permanently at the asylum ... "One takes advantage of the circumstance of the bath, one reminds him of the transgression ... and suddenly releases a current of cold water on his head".'[68] Foucault, who is here, after his own fashion, writing a genealogy of morals, situates the emergence of psychology in this

15

arousal of feelings of guilt, which allows madness to slip into interiority: 'madness became a fact concerning essentially the human soul, its guilt and its freedom; it was now inscribed within the dimension of interiority; and by that fact, for the first time in the modern world, madness was to receive psychological status, structure, and signification'.[69]

Foucault's interpretation of Pinel's act is directed against psychology's self-understanding which sees this 'humanization' both as the index and also the condition of its scientificity. Behind this humanization which, in the opinion of psychology, was prevented – *de facto*, but not *de jure* – in the classical age by a moralizing misrecognition of madness, Foucault, for his part, uncovers a subtle moralizing which points to a continuity that runs deeper than the caesura in which psychology situates its breakthrough to scientificity. But Foucault not only sees an underlying continuity where psychology assumes that Pinel's act expresses a discontinuity, he also points to a discontinuity where psychology defends a continuity thesis. While, for psychology, the humanization which does not come about until Pinel's day is a belated realization of a possibility which might have been brought about earlier but was blocked, Foucault takes the quite different view that the classical experience is not reducible to something else: 'Thus there can be no question, in the seventeenth or eighteenth centuries, of treating madness "humanely", since it is rightfully inhuman, constituting as it were the reverse side of a choice which opens up for man the free use of his rational nature.'[70]

Foucault's analysis seems, then, to avert both to a continuity and a discontinuity. The contradiction one might suppose between these two perspectives points in reality to a tension which Foucault will later make a methodological principle of his 'genealogy'. Genealogy refers not only to a discontinuity which destroys the illusion of a linear development, but also to a deeper continuity which is the product of a sequence of transformations: 'the accidents, the minute deviations – or conversely, the complete reversals – the errors, the false appraisals, and the faulty calculations that gave birth to those things that continue to exist and have value for us'.[71] As opposed to the finalistic thinking which structures the psychological reading of the history of madness, Foucault speaks of interlocking transformations which are neither arbitrary nor determined. He does not trace the emergence of psychology back to an orthogenesis which is really nothing more than the actualization of an already present

16

possibility, but to a genealogy which, in *Histoire de la folie* and other texts from this period, takes on the peculiar character of a history of decline (*Verfallsgeschichte*): 'Man became a "psychologizable species" only ... when his relation to madness was defined by the external dimension of exclusion and punishment and by the internal dimension of moral assignation and guilt. In situating madness in relation to these two fundamental axes, early-nineteenth-century man made it possible to *grasp* madness and thus to initiate a general psychology.'[72]

The way Foucault sums up his argument here is less innocent than it perhaps appears. And although much seems to point to the fact that he is already in his first major work anticipating the later point of view of genealogy, we must none the less ask whether *Histoire de la folie* is not precisely led astray by this argument into a 'calligraphying' of the origin[73] – a calligraphying which can perhaps only be explained if it is related to the risk and ambiguity which threaten from within the inconspicuous gesture in which Foucault – for the first time here – employs quotation marks.

1.2. An anticipation of genealogy?

Within Foucault's discussion of psychology, which we have outlined, there emerged the project of a counter-history seeking to contest the way in which psychology construes its history. However, the status of this counter-history and of the attendant critique of psychology remained unclear. We now wish to show how this unclarity can be traced back to an ambivalence which is already bound up with the project of the history of madness – an ambivalence which, as we shall see, is already discernible in the title of the French original.

1. A genealogical suspicion

The need for a counter-history is motivated first of all by considerations which Foucault later systematized in the tenets of his 'genealogical method'. By counter-history, Foucault seems to mean a historical analysis which counterposes to the 'memory' of psychology or psychiatry a 'counter-memory'[74] which unmasks that memory as a forgetting. The way in which psychology or psychiatry remember their histories is based, in Foucault's view, on an inversion of the ends which one intuitively associates with historiography. Psychology/psychiatry writes the history of the conditions of its emergence not with the intention of remembering its origin, but in order to forget the shame of that origin (*pudenda origo*): 'What is called psychiatric practice is a certain moral tactic contemporary with the end of the eighteenth century, preserved in the rites of asylum life, and overlaid with the myths of positivism.'[75] Foucault sees this forgetting as a form of selective and idealizing memory which expresses itself in the way that psychology operates with the concepts of 'continuity' and 'discontinuity'. Psychology sees in the humanization which accompanies its emergence the expression of a discontinuity which is no more than the actualization of an always already present possibility. This humanization which, for psychology, is a precondition of its elevation to scientificity, makes possible an impartial gaze that breaks with the way of looking at the problem, clouded by religious, magic or moral categories,[76] which previously stood in the way of genuine knowledge. The thesis of the always already present, *de jure* knowable but in fact misrecognized object which operates here in the background both enables psychology to make a selective reading of history and necessitates that its origin be idealized:

> It was only by freeing itself from all that was capable of keeping it within the moral world of classicism that [the progressive recognition of madness as a pathological reality] was able to define its medical truth: this at least is the assumption made by every positivism tempted to retrace the course of its own development; as if the whole history of knowledge consisted in unearthing an objectivity, the fundamental structures of which gradually emerge.[77]

The thesis of the misrecognized object compels psychology to filter out everything specific to the periods which preceded it and, at the same time, to idealize the move by which, in its view, it makes its breakthrough to science. Psychology's claim to have achieved the first access to an object which was already present before its discovery can only retain its plausibility if psychology can link the disappearance of the mechanism which led to the false assessment of that object to its own emergence. For this reason, psychology can only interpret humanization as a break with the moralistic misunderstanding of madness during the classical period. Psychology cannot accept Foucault's interpretation of the act which founds it (a moralization), since, if it did, it would be forced to surrender its

18

explanation of how it possesses a historically privileged access to its object.

2. A critique of the scientific ideal of psychology

The significance of the 'misrecognized object' thesis for the selective and idealizing reading which psychology presents of the history of its emergence seems to suggest that Foucault's critique of this selectivity and idealization is directed primarily against the scientific ideal which psychology introduces with this thesis. Foucault's critique would then be directed not so much against the scientificity of psychology as against the manner in which it interprets its scientificity – an interpretation which makes the possibility of its scientificity depend on the 'unchanging persistence of a madness which comes fully armed already with its eternal psychological equipment'.[78] Hence the role which the 'recognize/misrecognize' opposition plays in its self-understanding: psychology establishes its scientificity by the discovery of an already existent, yet mis-recognized, object – a discovery which becomes possible as a result of a humanization which breaks with the conditions standing in the way of real knowledge of the object. For psychology, the ideal of scientificity is only attainable on the basis of the scientific ideal of epistemological realism. Foucault's critique of the historical pre-existence of the object could then be understood as a critique of the *possibility* of a realist self-understanding of psychology,[79] not as a critique of the possibility of psychology *in general*. He is opposed both to the universalizing strategy by which psychology seeks to reinforce the plausibility of an object independent of its constitution and also to the independence thesis itself. The object which psychology believes it 'discovered' not only arose historically, but is also dependent on that discovery in a way which excludes a realist interpretation. The object of psychology is not only co-original with the emergence of psychology, but it only comes into being in and by the constitution of that science. The mental patient is not independ-ent of the constitution of psychology, but is – as we have already shown above – the consequence of an interiorization of madness which cannot be separated from the emergence of psychology. The constitution of psychology depends on a transformation of the classical experience by which *a new experience* of madness arises: 'a new face: the very face in which the naïveté of our positivism believes it recognizes the nature of all madness'.[80]

19

Here Foucault's argumentation overreaches itself. His insistence on the mutual non-reducibility of classical and modern experience seems to open up a space in which more is at stake than a mere critique of the self-understanding of psychology. Foucault seems to develop a perspective in which it is not only the naïveté with which psychology thinks the authority of its scientificity that can be contested, but also the naïveté of a critique of science which confines itself merely to contesting the authority of science. The way Foucault grounds his critique of the *understanding* psychology has of its scientificity seems to render a critique of the *scientificity* of psychology, within the analytical framework in which Foucault is moving, if not impossible, then at least considerably more difficult. For, if it really should be the case that there is a 'new structure of experience'[81] which corresponds to the modern experience of madness – as indeed there was in the case of the classical experience of madness – then it is impossible to see how and why a discipline which arose contemporaneously with this new '*a priori*'[82] should forfeit its scientificity. To put it more precisely, if the object of psychology only arises in and by the constitution of that science, then this circumstance can only lead one to contest the scientificity of psychology if one adopts oneself the criterion by which psychology demarcates its scientificity. The idea that the object of psychology is dependent upon the constitution of that science can only be an argument for regarding psychology as unscientific if one somehow makes the scientific character of a discipline dependent on its objects being independently pre-given. Yet Foucault's arguments against psychology's self-understanding point, rather, away from this contention. He seems to oppose psychology not on the grounds that it has no independent object and cannot, therefore, be a science, but rather on the grounds that it falsely makes its scientificity dependent on the existence of an independent object and is thus seduced into a selective and idealizing reading of the history of its own emergence. Within the structure of this argument, the possibility of thinking the concept of 'scientificity' in a manner different from psychology remains open. To the extent that Foucault lays the ground for another interpretation of this concept, the intention of *Histoire de la folie* does not seem to be to contest the authority of science, but to create a standpoint which makes it possible to conceive that authority in a different way. And yet he does not seem content to confine himself to a critique of the interpretation psychology provides of its own scientificity.

20

3. Critique of the scientificity of psychology

Foucault combines the theme of a counter-history, from which a critique of the realist self-interpretation of psychology initially seemed to develop, with a curious kind of critique of positivism. By his own account, the positivistic forgetting in which psychology gradually loses itself, does not lead, as one might expect, to a crisis of psychology, but in fact covers up a crisis: 'a moral practice which is clear and transparent at the beginning but gradually forgotten as positivism imposed its myths of scientific objectivity; *a practice whose origins and meaning are forgotten, but which is still used and still present*'.[83] Psychology cannot, in Foucault's view, detach itself from the conditions of its emergence. Having arisen as a moral practice, it can only lay claim to being a science by forgetting the stigma of its conditions of emergence, a stigma which has never disappeared. The critique of the positivist myth of scientific objectivity is, for Foucault, simultaneously a critique of the myth of scientificity: 'our "scientific" knowledge of mental illness'.[84] Thus the crisis of psychology lies not so much in the forgetting of its conditions of emergence, as in those conditions themselves.[85] It has to do less with the process of forgetting in which psychology loses itself as a result of its positivist seduction than with the need for that seduction. Forgetting is the only possibility for psychology if it is to maintain an illusion of scientificity which it would lose if it remembered its conditions of emergence: 'If carried back to its roots, the psychology of madness would appear to be not the mastery of mental illness and hence the possibility of its disappearance, but the destruction of psychology itself.'[86] For Foucault, the conditions in which psychology arises are, at the same time, the conditions in which it also becomes eternally impossible. The impossibility of psychology rests, in his view, on an 'alienation' which prevents it from knowing what it believes it knows: 'What is called "mental illness" is simply *alienated madness*, alienated in the psychology that it has itself made possible.'[87] The psychological status which is conferred on madness at the birth of psychology depends not on the discovery of an object at last perceived with terminological exactitude ('mental illness'), but on a psychologization which is itself no more than the superficial effect of an underlying process of the moralization and culpabilization of madness.[88] In Foucault's view, this psychologization irrevocably vitiates the scientificity of psychology. Psychology is no more than an *a posteriori* legitimation of the practices which make it possible: 'What one discovers under the name of the "psychology" of madness is merely the result of the operations by which one has invested it.'[89]

The thinking which leads Foucault here to put (the scientificity of) psychology in quotation marks is not immediately easy to understand. One has the impression that, both for Foucault and for psychology, the possibility of a scientific psychology stands or falls with that of a scientific realism. From the fact that the object 'discovered' by psychology arises historically and is connected with the emergence of psychology itself, Foucault seems to conclude not only that one cannot assign to this discovery the value which psychology ascribes to it but also that it lies beyond the scope of genuine cognition. Psychology does not fulfil the conditions for such cognition because it does not detach itself from the practices which make it possible – its discoveries are '*only* the product of the procedures by which it was initiated'. Psychology and psychiatry, in Foucault's view, not only began as moral practices; they have also remained so: 'What is called psychiatric practice is a certain moral tactic ... overlaid with the myths of positivism.'[90] And yet we may ask whether the connection with a moral practice which, by Foucault's own analysis, leads to a new experience which cannot be reduced to anything else is sufficient not only to put in question a particular interpretation of the scientificity of psychology but its scientificity in general. Are not all discourses dependent on and connected with particular practices? What, then, is the special nature of this dependence which strips psychology of its scientific status? Can a discourse about madness – whatever status it may have – develop in any other than a 'broken' relation to its object? And is it not precisely the necessity of this 'break' which is enacted in the moral relationship of psychology to madness – a necessity which could have cast a different light on the sense of the 'alienation' in which mental illness comes into being?

Foucault was only to confront these questions in his later work. It is not by chance, but for theoretical reasons, that they remain in the background in *Histoire de la folie*. Foucault's critique of the scientificity of psychology seems, as it were, to deflect *Histoire de la folie* from the consequences and questions raised by his critique of psychology's self-interpretation of its scientificity. Thus the negative conclusions he draws from the assertion that psychology only discovers the product of the practices which make it possible seem now to fall back short of the idea that precisely in and by these practices there emerges a new, non-reducible experience of madness. Foucault seems to criticize psychology for its dependence on certain practices while, in another context, he uses that dependence to contest its claim that it is able to develop autonomously. While his critique of the thesis of a historically prior and independent object remaining identical over time seems to indicate that the dependence of the object on the constitution of psychology is to be understood positively, his critique of the scientificity of the discipline suggests the opposite. The assertion that the object of psychology arises only in and by its constitution is no longer intended here as a critique of the self-understanding of psychology, but as a reference to something which prevents psychology from being scientific: 'Psychology can never tell the truth about madness because it is madness that holds the truth of psychology.'[91]

What lies concealed beneath this paradoxical formulation is neither solely, nor even primarily a tension between two points of view – driving Foucault's engagement with psychology, in the one case, towards a critique of its scientific status, and in the other, by contrast, towards a critique of how it understands its scientificity – but rather an attempt to render this ambiguity unambiguous. Foucault here strikes up a theme which is to permit him to resolve at a metatheoretical level the tension between two at first sight irreconcilable aspects of his critique of psychology and provide a sure theoretical basis for the quotation marks by which he signals his doubts about the scientificity of psychology. The assertion that madness holds the truth of psychology is expressed here in a surprising turn of phrase: '*Madness*, in the unfolding of its historical reality, *makes possible*, at a particular moment, a knowledge of alienation in a style of positivity which defines it as mental illness.'[92] The syntactic position of madness here reflects a theoretical standpoint: for Foucault, madness is the (enfeebled) subject of a history which sub-jects and alienates. He does not develop this standpoint systematically in *Histoire de la folie*, but it is constantly presupposed: the idea that the 'emergence of the historical reality of madness' represents a degeneration or alienation provides a counterpoint in *Histoire de la folie* to a basically genealogical analysis which, as a result, is shifted towards the strange perspective of a history of decline. From the perspective of a genealogy which assumes the features of a history of decline, the historical transformations underlying 'the things that have value for us'[93] will now be called upon to testify that the value which things have for us is merely illusory and inauthentic. That at least is what is suggested by the vocabulary which Foucault repeatedly uses in this context: in the constitution of its historical reality, madness is at once 'disarmed',[94] 'invested',[95] 'confiscat[ed]',[96] 'mastered'[97] and 'deprived of its language'.[98] 'Madness is never manifested *on its own terms* and in its own language.'[99] For Foucault, the emergence of the historical reality of madness is, at the same time, a process of 'occultation',[100] in which an authentic experience of madness is eclipsed and deformed. Seen in this perspective, his historical analyses take on a quite different tone. He now connects the roots of the moral experience of madness, which was characteristic of the classical period and which returns in a modified form in the modern age, with an original catastrophe (*cette faute originelle*)[101] that puts an end to the tragic experience the Middle Ages and the Renaissance still had of madness: 'Up until the Renaissance, above and beyond the distinction between Good and Evil, the ethical world maintained its equilibrium within *a tragic unity*, which was that of destiny or providence and divine predilection. This unity would now disappear, *sundered* by the *crucial division* between reason and unreason. A *crisis* of the ethical world began . . .'[102] This image of an original Fall, which Foucault employs to interpret this crisis, plays a systematic role with regard to his intentions in *Histoire de la folie*. Having made it his aim to write a 'history of madness *itself*',[103] Foucault at the same time sees the actual course of the history of madness as a process in which the division between reason and unreason which occurs in the Renaissance causes madness to be alienated from itself,[104] to lose its language, and to recoil, behind the 'linguistic prison bars' (Celan) of reason, into a muteness broken only by a rare scream (Nietzsche, Artaud, Nerval, Roussel).[105] Within this framework, it seems inevitable that he postulate a 'primal alienation'.[106] Derrida has made a penetrating analysis of the resulting difficulties: 'The attempt to write the history of the decision, division, difference runs the risk of construing the division as an event or a structure subsequent to the unity of an original presence . . .'[107] The mythologeme of a primal alienation, a *faute originelle* not only suggests the possibility of a 'madness freed and disalienated, *restored* in some sense to its original language',[108] but also the possibility that madness could once have disposed of such a non-alienated liberty. With this suggestion, Foucault not only perhaps endorses the foundations of what Derrida would call 'a

24

metaphysics of presence', but also – and perhaps even in the same movement of thought – the foundations of psychology. The archeo-teleological model which underlies psychology's interpretation of history here acquires eschatological-critical undertones. But it is still, as will become clear, the same model.

4. The archeo-eschatological foundation of the critique of psychology

In the original preface to *Histoire de la folie*, which he later discarded, Foucault remarks that a history of the conditions of possibility of psychology flowed almost naturally from the perspective he adopted in that work.[109] And, in so far as the perspective was that of a history of madness itself, one might add that it was also almost natural to put that psychology in quotation marks: 'There is a very good reason why psychology can never master madness; it is because psychology became possible in our world only when madness had already been mastered and excluded from the drama.'[110] In Foucault's view, psychology's claim to be able to recognize an object independent of its own emergence runs up against an obstacle which plays a constitutive part in its emergence. The idea that madness was already occulted long before the emergence of psychology means, for him, that psychology always comes too late: it does not discover what madness is in its 'true nature' and cannot discover this. All that is left to it is 'the sedimentation of what the history of the West has made of it for the last three hundred years'.[111] We now also better understand the meaning of Foucault's remark that psychology 'only' discovers the results of the practices which made it possible. It is not simply that the object of psychology is not universally present, but co-original with and dependent on the emergence of psychology, as a critique of psychology's interpretation of its own scientificity might have shown. What is crucially important is that, historically, the object which psychology 'discovers' not only arose conjointly with this discovery, but that this discovery is also a concealment of the *real* object (*'la' folie*); it is based on a *de facto* alienation which is avoidable *de jure*: mental illness is alienated madness.[112]

The implication contained in the alienation concept, that a proper experience of madness must be possible – if not for our culture then at least in principle – means that we must perhaps understand Foucault's critique of psychology differently from what has been

25

suggested hitherto. If Foucault connects the pathologization of madness which is expressed in the concept of mental *illness* with a confiscation which had long been prepared in the history of our culture, but which was 'not in any way determined by the essence of madness itself',[113] then he surely does not mean by this merely to refute a realist self-understanding of psychology. His apparent objection to this self-understanding is not simply that this concept claims ultimately to pin down the essence of an always already present object, but that that essence cannot be pinned down in this concept because it eludes such confiscation. The concept of 'confiscation' seems not only to refer to an unwarranted absolutization which reduces the historically polymorphous experiences of madness to the monochrome model of mental illness, but also to the arbitrariness of a gesture which alienates madness from itself and keeps it within the bounds of a discourse, 'the neutrality of which is matched only by [its] capacity to forget'.[114] It is not, in this case, because madness – being only constituted in changing historical experiences[115] – could not be said to have an essence, that the concept of mental illness fails to grasp the essence of madness, but because psychology only emerges when madness is already alienated from its essence. And if Foucault points out that madness is 'never exhausted as a field of experience by the medical or paramedical knowledge that might be had of it',[116] then the meaning of this remark is more than just a critique of a crude privileging of a medical experience of madness. What we have here is not just a critique of a false generalization of a historical experience which reduces all other experiences to its model and thus misses their specificity, but a critique of the effective repression of a tragic experience of madness, the experience of a madness not yet alienated from itself, which the Renaissance had still known and which, for Foucault, has never disappeared but has merely been *covered over*: '*Beneath* the critical consciousness of madness and its philosophical or scientific, moral or medical forms a mute tragic consciousness *still* keeps vigil.'[117]

This thesis of a persisting tragic experience of madness, which flares up again like a rare meteor – an expiring flash of light which bursts open the night of reason – in Nerval or Artaud, Nietzsche or Roussel, is ultimately responsible for the genealogical perspective in *Histoire de la folie* acquiring the strange character of a history of decline. Or, more precisely, the character of a strange history of decline. For the problem lies not so much in this perspective of decline: Foucault may be right that the experience of madness was more diverse in earlier periods and that the modern period could only signal its own specificity by a reductive transformation (and even a repression) of these experiences into 'a strictly moral perception of madness'.[118] The problem is, however, that he does not confine himself to introducing a criterion of formal commensurability – problematic and arbitrary as this might be – but, by characterizing the tragic experience of madness as a more primal experience, goes on and postulates an absolute norm which is to be the standard of comparison. We may ask here, with Derrida, how Foucault knows that the tragic experience is the more primal: 'everything transpires as if Foucault *knew* what "madness" means. Everything transpires as if, in a continuous and underlying way, an assured and rigorous precomprehension of the concept of madness, or at least of its nominal definition, were possible and acquired.'[119] As a result of this situation, Foucault's discourse runs the risk of becoming a mirror image of that of psychology. Just like psychology, it seems Foucault too has to presuppose a privileged access to madness. While psychology sought to justify that access with scientific realism, Foucault appeals to a position which, with Macherey, we might term 'a realism of experience'.[120] This idea of the possibility of an original, 'authentic' experience of madness 'itself' leads in Foucault, no less than in psychology, to the idea that madness has been misconstrued. But, where psychology elaborates this idea by assuming a pre-existent but misrecognized object, which is only delivered up to the impartial gaze of psychology at the end of a process of orthogenesis of knowledge, in Foucault it is directed against psychology's claim to scientificity. And Foucault cannot avoid the quotation marks he puts around 'psychology' leading him – just as they lead psychology – to make the possibility of a scientific explanation of madness dependent on the existence of an object which is independent of its constitution. He does not merely confine himself to seeing mental illness as an object which only comes into being in and by the emergence of psychology, but simultaneously sees in that constitution the repression of a real, independent object. For this reason, in his view, the conditions of possibility of psychology are, at the same time, the conditions of its impossibility. The moment in which a scientific treatment of madness becomes possible at the same time delivers up the conditions in which it also becomes impossible.

This critique of the scientificity of psychology seems to be based on precisely the same elements which a genealogically-inspired critique of the scientific self-understanding of psychology had contested. Foucault's own version of the misrecognized object thesis seems, just like the psychological version, to be in pursuit of 'that which was already there'.[121] Psychology could only uphold this thesis by misunderstanding the specificity of the experiences which preceded it, and Foucault seems at times to be going down this same path: 'this madness, *so alien to* the experience that is contemporaneous with it'.[122] Just as, according to psychology, the solid kernel of madness can only be uncovered when one has broken down the outer shell of the religious and magical categories in which it is imprisoned – and into which it has come as a result of the idiosyncratic play of history – so also,[123] for Foucault, psychology is something which befalls madness, an unfortunate event, which can be traced back to an original catastrophe and continues to produce its effects in an inauthentic or an improper history – a history that has subjected its 'proper' subject. Arguing on these same lines, Macherey points out that the history of madness in Foucault's *Histoire de la folie* is not so much concerned with madness as history – a madness which is constituted in different historical experiences – as with a history which befalls 'madness', a history which alienates 'Western man' from madness, but which at the same time can also hold out the possibility for him 'that one day, perhaps, he will be able to be free of all psychology and be ready for the great tragic confrontation with madness'.[124]

The eschatological aspect which thus finds its way into the French title of the work seems to us not so much a consequence of a poetic exuberance, with which the work has occasionally been charged, as the expression of a train of thought which Foucault developed with great consistency, in the course of which what is in principle an ambivalent critique is rendered unambiguous and an initially genealogical perspective abandoned. The quotation marks Foucault puts around the discipline of 'psychology' must be regarded as the starting point of this train of thought, but also as its end-product. In a strange way, they constitute the secret axis around which Foucault's early reflections on madness revolve and it is they which re-emerge, in spite of all the 'turns' (*Kehren*) in his later work. In this regard, Foucault's further development is perhaps to be understood not so much as a succession of stages, which are concluded once he has passed through them, but rather as an incessant *reprise* – to use a word of which Merleau-Ponty was fond

– of a gesture which fascinated him from the outset and of the field of force in which that gesture is always situated. The question of the extent to which *Histoire de la folie* can be regarded as an anticipation of genealogy was thus raised not primarily from a concern with the chronology of Foucault's works but, rather, to reveal the metatheoretical openness of the space in which this simple, but very dangerous gesture was performed.

An open space, a field of force, a repeatable scene, Foucault would perhaps have recognized himself in these words: 'In short, I should like a book ... to be sufficiently uninhibited to present itself as discourse: as both battle and weapon; strategy and impact; struggle and trophy – or wound; as present circumstance and relic of the past; as irregular encounter and repeatable scene.'[125]

2

From an Archaeological to a Genealogical Critique of the Human Sciences

From as early as the first preface to *Histoire de la folie*, Foucault formulated the methodological ideal that it should be possible to write the history of madness in a language in which 'that distance by which modern man protects himself from madness is overcome'.[1] Although Foucault clearly thinks that the actual course of that history prevents it, perhaps for ever, from penetrating into the silence of a madness bereft of language, his own language none the less seeks to remain at least sufficiently neutral and open to permit an 'archaeology of this silence'. The theoretical basis which his early critique of the scientificity of psychology consequently acquired entailed an interweaving of archaeological and eschatological themes – precisely that interweaving which is manifest in the expression 'archaeology of an alienation'.[2] The search for an origin – even for one that is irretrievably lost – simultaneously meant the promise of a return – even if this is in actual fact impossible.[3] The 'archaeology of knowledge',[4] which unfolds in *Histoire de la folie* in the shadow of these two motifs, and which draws its critical impulse and its concepts from them, thus displays precisely the structure which, using the same term – 'archaeology' – Foucault rejects only a few years later: 'To analyze discursive facts ... is – quite apart from any geological metaphor, without assigning any origin and without the slightest gesturing towards the beginning of an *archè* – to engage in what one might call, drawing on the ludic rights of etymology, something like an *archaeology*.'[5] The archaeology of knowledge whose contours begin to emerge in the period following *Histoire de la folie* is an *an-archè-ology*.

Foucault's refusal to involve himself further in what Dreyfus and Rabinow have termed the search for secret ontological sources (madness 'itself'),[6] this break with an 'exegetic' or depth-hermeneutic perspective which was already heralded in the Preface to *The Birth of the Clinic* in the form of a latent self-critique,[7] this first 'turn', necessarily has effects on Foucault's critique of science. From this point on, Foucault can no longer adopt the strategy which still permitted him to cast doubt in *Histoire de la folie* on the scientificity of psychology. He can no longer assert that the epistemological realism on which psychology staked its claim to scientificity is ultimately impossible because the constitution of that very psychology only confirms the disappearance of an authentic experience of madness 'itself'. And if he can no longer counterpose a 'realism of experience' to 'scientific realism', then the critique of the scientificity of psychology or a similar discipline would have to be replaced, at best, by a critique of the interpretation it gives of its own scientificity. In this case, Foucault would no longer have to pit the one realism against the other and could thus avoid the risk of his argument being surreptitiously contaminated by the categories of the discourse under analysis. The question would then no longer be whether the epistemological realism of psychology were well-founded, but whether one might legitimately interpret scientificity within the framework of such a realism. Or, rather, the problem would be the following: why does a discipline like psychology present itself in these terms and even go so far as to appropriate a history for itself at the cost of a retrospective illusion which misconstrues the discipline's own historicity and the specificity of the periods which preceded it? The question Foucault faces is, then, whether it is more than accidental that these themes (realism, historical universality of the object, orthogenesis as archeo-teleology)[8] form part of the internal discourse on the scientificity of a human-sciences discipline like psychology. If he were able to explain what was the decisive motive for psychology (or the human sciences *tout court*) to develop – on more than merely random grounds – precisely this particular self-understanding as a science, then he might possess the means to shield a potential *critique* of that self-understanding from the charge of arbitrariness.

After *Histoire de la folie*, Foucault thus finds himself faced with the problem of whether the human sciences possess some specific characteristic which can explain why the interpretation they offer of their scientificity is more than merely random. Both *The Order of Things* (2.1) and *Discipline and Punish* (2.2) seek a solution to this problem of the specificity of the human sciences. But, on each

31

occasion, Foucault's quotation marks (human 'sciences') seem to suggest that he obstinately clings to the idea that the discourse which the human sciences conduct about themselves serves to conceal their lack of scientificity.

2.1. An archaeological defence of the specificity of the human sciences?

1. The stakes

By contrast with *Histoire de la folie*, Foucault's remarks on the human sciences (or psychology) in *The Order of Things* (1966) are not inconspicuously scattered throughout the text. They are to be found at the end of the book, and the title of the chapter in which they figure ('The Human Sciences') indicates that the essential purport of this work – subtitled 'An Archaeology of the Human Sciences' – is to be found there. Yet the connection with the preceding parts of the book is not so direct as might be expected: the way Foucault makes connections and draws, in his treatment of the human sciences, on arguments derived from the formal framework of the earlier analyses of the classical and modern periods is counter-intuitive.[9] But it is precisely this peculiarity which made *The Order of Things* – a work which virtually elevates the counter-intuitive into a methodological principle – an archaeology of the human sciences.

Foucault's defence of the specificity of the human sciences is structured in a remarkable way. It unfolds within the framework of an argument which amounts to saying that all the 'wearisome discussions' on whether the human sciences should be accorded the title of sciences and the conditions which have to be met for this to be the case necessarily remain 'vain and idle',[10] but, at the same time, the argument itself seeks to make a particularly obdurate contribution to this debate. Foucault's contribution is, at any event, just as ambivalent as this foundational problematic itself: he wishes to render superfluous the discussions which have accompanied the human sciences since their inception. The goal of his defence of the specificity of the human sciences is not, however, to prepare a critique of the interpretation they have given of their own scientificity, but, rather, to criticize them because of this special status. For Foucault, the need to recognize their special status only follows from the need to deny them the status of sciences.[11] It should come as no surprise that the difficulties which were already latent in the early parts of *The Order of Things* and which later motivated Foucault to write *Discipline and Punish* start to crystallize at this point, since this 'reaction' was endemic in the structure of this project itself.

Foucault does not regard the scientific disciplines (political economy, biology, philology) which he brings together under the title 'the new empiricities' (labour, life, language) at the beginning of his discussion of the modern period, as belonging to the human sciences.[12] What is more, the human sciences, which only later emerge into the field of knowledge, represent the greatest danger to which not merely these empirical disciplines but also the deductive sciences and philosophical reflection are permanently exposed. So long as these disciplines remain within their own domain, they can avoid the risk of their arguments becoming lost in the *'impurity'* (*impureté*) of the discourse of the human sciences. But even the smallest infringement of boundaries gives rise to those conflations of levels of argument known as the dangers of 'psychologism' or 'sociologism',[13] dangers which always arise when the problem of the relationship between thought and formalization, which is posed at the frontier between mathematics and philosophy, is not correctly formulated or when, in a regional ontology of the objects of biology, economics or linguistics, the modes of being of life, labour and language are incorrectly analysed. However, the danger of 'anthropologism' is not restricted solely to the relations between philosophy and mathematics or between philosophy and the empirical sciences (biology, political economy, the sciences of language), but also threatens, for example, all attempts to determine the realm of the mathematicizable in linguistics, biology or economics. Whenever a discipline such as philosophy, mathematics or one of the empirical sciences oversteps its bounds and seeks a connection with one of the other disciplines in this series, it runs the risk that the connection will only be made at the expense of anthropologization. In all these cases, the epistemological contamination which, in Foucault's view, occurs here, gives rise to a dangerous anthropological supplement[14] which is parasitic upon the philosophical, empirical or deductive-scientific plane of argument, overwhelms it and leaves it unrecognizable. '"Anthropologization" is the great internal threat to knowledge in our day.'[15]

Foucault's statement that anthropologization is an internal danger which threatens knowledge from the inside must be taken literally. In his view, the human sciences constitute 'a cloud' in the three-dimensional field of knowledge which is formed by the dimensions of philosophy, mathematics and the empirical sciences and the at first sight erratic movements of the shadows which are cast by this cloud on to the intermediary planes can be predicted, using the archaeological apparatus he brings to bear, with an exactitude no meteorology can match.[16] As a consequence of this spatial localization of the human sciences, they not only represent a permanent threat to the interzonal traffic between the axes, but they are also constantly under threat of losing their own specificity. The whole difficulty of epistemological figures like psychology (or sociology and the cultural sciences), the precarious and uncertain nature of their scientific status, lies in the vagueness of the relations they maintain with the disciplines which delimit the empty space in which they are 'included' and whose dimensions and intermediary planes remain out of bounds to them. In this paradoxical co-occurrence of an inclusion and an exclusion, Foucault sees the grounds for the 'essential instability' which has always characterized the human sciences, as is shown up clearly in the various discussions of their foundations.[17] Against all expectations – and this marks the originality of his approach, as it also shows its limitations – he seeks an explanation for this instability not in the 'extreme density of their object', nor yet in the 'inerasable transcendence of this man they [the human sciences] speak of',[18] but in the peculiar nature of their position in the complex epistemological configuration of knowledge, in that 'trihedron' which stakes out the field of modern knowledge. It is clear that Foucault's attempt to find in the specificity of the human sciences an argument for their instability (and, as we shall see, also for their unscientificity) can only succeed if he can call on a formal criterion of demarcation which necessarily prevents the collapse of the painstakingly constructed trihedron.[19] He must avoid the trihedron being flattened out into a two-dimensional space by one of its dimensions bending inward and bringing the whole construction – which is also that of *The Order of Things* – down with it.

The second and third paragraphs of the chapter Foucault devotes to the human sciences focus on the problem of their specificity, a line of inquiry the significance and motivation of which must be clear from the preceding remarks. We have reason to take a look at his presentation of the argument here. In the section on 'the three planes of knowledge' (the English translation somewhat misleadingly speaks of three 'faces'), various important decisions have already been taken: the dimensions of this trihedron have already been designated and the unstable position of the human sciences has already been related to their peculiar place within these co-ordinates (inclusion/exclusion). It is clear that the success of this procedure depends, at least in part, on the 'logic of contamination' (anthro-[pologization as dangerous supplement) which asserts itself here. The identification of the (planes between the) axes presupposes that one is in a position to justify this 'logic of the supplement' (Derrida): $\wedge$ one must be able to prove that – and why – the anthropologization in which a discipline 'loses' itself constitutes an inessential component of its discourse. If, for example, one detects a tendency to anthropologism in economics at the very moment when it begins to mathematicize itself, one must be able to show that this impure and contaminating discourse constitutes a real but avoidable danger, which only accompanies mathematicization and possibly hinders it, but is in no sense necessary to make its occurrence possible.[20] For this reason, Foucault must not only specify the special status of the human sciences but at the same time take into account in this the de-specifying tendency of anthropologization which may affect other disciplines. The formal criterion he seeks must also allow him to draw a dividing line between the proper kernel and the anthropological supplement in those disciplines, other than the human sciences, which have been contaminated by them.

It would perhaps be an exaggeration to assert that, if not all, then at least the most important, decisions are already taken before Foucault can introduce his criterion of demarcation. But the remarks on the trihedron of knowledge define very clearly the demands Foucault must make of his own argument. It all depends, then, whether the arguments which Foucault can muster further to justify the prior introduction of the trihedron of knowledge are not, for their part, dependent on the very introduction of that trihedron.

2. The specificity of the human sciences

Foucault accepted the self-imposed limitation of determining the possibility of the human sciences without recourse to a reflection on their object. His aim was to discover what were the conditions under which man is – or, more precisely, was – able to appear as a possible object of science. He sought out these conditions in a reflection on the relationships between those disciplines which are already constituted and are normally counted among the sciences of man and the dimensions or axes of the 'trihedron of knowledge'. He wanted to show that there is no alternative for the human sciences but to enter into these relationships, but that, precisely by so doing, they enter upon a state of instability which immediately and irrevocably deprives them of their scientificity. These relationships with the axes of knowledge constitute the only element in which the human sciences could develop and yet, at the same time, imply that the project of the human sciences is doomed from the outset. Precisely as in *Histoire de la folie*, Foucault sets out to discover conditions of possibility which indicate the impossibility of what they are supposed to make possible. Relating the human sciences to the dimensions of knowledge necessarily provides an insight into the conditions of their impossibility.

Foucault here leaves the dimension of mathematics out of account: the project of mathematicization also appears in other disciplines (economics, biology) and thus the particular character-istics of the human sciences are not, in any sense, to be found in that project.[21] Of the two remaining dimensions, that of the empirical sciences plays a privileged role. And not by chance, since the human sciences – i.e. the disciplines which have the human being as their object, in so far as that being is an empirical datum – are directed towards it as a living, speaking and producing being.[22] But unlike biology, the sciences of language and economics which confine themselves to the study of life, language and work – the life which is also that of the human being, the language and production which make of him a speaking and producing being – the human sciences direct their attention to the being which can produce a *representa-tion* of life for itself (and hence has a psychology), the being which can *represent to itself* both its needs and the society in which the process of satisfying those needs is enacted (and hence becomes a sociological phenomenon) and, lastly, the being which can express itself in language and lose itself in an unsurveyable mass of verbal traces and which is at any point capable of breathing life into the 'dead letter' of its literature and its myths, because it is the being which in its speech can *represent* the meaning of words which are always threatening to slip from its grasp. The object of the human sciences is the human being who can represent to itself the life it shares with all that is organic, and the economy and the language which set it apart. The object of psychology is no more the intracortical connections between the different centres of linguistic integration (auditive, visual, motor) than phonetic mutations, semantic shifts or the affinities between language groups are part of the study of literature or myth. One may only speak of human sciences when the mechanisms which the empirical sciences can isolate are no longer questioned 'in terms of what they are but in terms of what they cease to be when the space of representation is opened up'.[23]

Yet the human sciences cannot simply take up residence without further ado in the space of representation. The fact that there is something like a space of representation for the human sciences is only possible by virtue of their relation to the dimension of the empirical sciences. The human sciences only gain a purchase on their object by allowing themselves to be guided by models which they take from the empirical sciences.[24] What we have in these models are not concepts transposed into the human sciences from another sphere of knowledge in order that they may more easily represent certain processes to themselves (as, for example, with organicistic metaphor in nineteenth-century sociology – Spencer *et al.*), nor empirical categories of a relatively broad generality. These models are what make it possible in general for man to emerge as an object of knowledge. They are categories in a sense reminiscent of Kant: 'they make it possible to create groups of phenomena as so many "objects" for a possible branch of knowledge; they ensure their connection in the empirical sphere [*empiricité*], but they offer them to experience already linked together.'[25] The field in which the human sciences are able to operate first emerges on the basis of categorical models taken from the empirical sciences. Thus the man of psychology only 'appears against' the background of biology when psychology has introduced, with the categories of norm and function, a basically biological model. On the basis of considerations on the similar role economics plays for sociology and the science of language for the study of literature and myth, Foucault comes to the conclusion that the entire field of knowledge in the human sciences can be delimited by three pairs of concepts: function/norm, conflict/rule (sociology) and signification/system.[26]

The entire field of the human sciences, the space of representation within which they are able to operate, rests upon categorical schemata taken over from other disciplines. The fact that this field can appear, and that something can appear within it, is only possible as a consequence of having borrowed constituent models from the empirical sciences. Thus, for example, according to Foucault, economics studies needs 'an objective process in labour and production', but it is not a human science.[27] Only the sociological conception of man as the being which represents its society and the process of the social satisfaction of needs to itself, can be counted among the human sciences. For sociology, man is projected on to the 'surface of the economy' as a being which has needs and desires and hence interests which bring him into an intersubjective constellation which is constantly threatened by *conflict* with the other who is inscribed in his basic needs as a primal datum. But *homo sociologicus* is also that being who wishes to evade his conflicts and seeks a lasting solution to them in *rules* which both tame violence and yet also bind him to the violence of a conflict which keeps flaring up.[28] For Foucault, the concepts of conflict and rule function like categories. The concepts of 'conflict' and, analogously, 'function' and 'signification', enable need, interest or desire – even if they are not present as such to the naïve consciousness that is subject to their effects – to be admitted into the order of representation and hence to 'appear' as possible objects for the human sciences. In a similar way, the concept of 'rule' enables the human sciences to form a positive and empirical conception of the finitude with which man was confronted in a new way at the beginning of the modern period,[29] a finitude which caused him to free himself, with the whole of his philosophical art, from the dogmatic sleep of 'classical' metaphysics but which ultimately seduced him into the thoroughly anthropological philosophy which sought the reason for this finitude in the being of man himself. Like the concepts of 'system' and 'norm', that of rule refers to something which eludes naïve consciousness but can, none the less, 'appear' as an object of knowledge in the human sciences: it refers to an 'unthought' which 'not only prescribes [the] rules [for organizing the violence of conflict], but renders [it] possible upon the basis of a rule' (the law which is inscribed in desire, but which also institutes it); it refers to something which lies at the origin of every 'signification' and prevents that signification from being entirely present to itself, and, lastly, it refers to the way in which a function provides itself with its own conditions of possibility and the frontiers within which it is effective.[30]

With these unmistakable allusions to the figures which Foucault had recognized in self-anthropologizing modern philosophy,[31] the human sciences are related, almost in passing, to the remaining dimension of the trihedron of knowledge. But the distinction which both separates the human sciences from modern philosophy and keeps them in a state of 'dangerous familiarity' with it[32] is, for Foucault, cause to insist on the *specificity* of their instability. In Foucault's view, the human sciences embody within the structure of their 'scientificity' an instability which philosophy has set 'in [the] interiority or at least in [the] profound kinship of a being who owes his finitude only to himself'.[33] Philosophy puts instability into the being of man himself, a being which must be able to ground everything which refers him to his finitude. While this philosophical 'analysis of finitude' sees in man a peculiar 'dual being' which is both empirical and transcendental, which knows itself to be surrounded, as *cogito*, by an unthought that it has constantly to render transparent and, lastly, knows itself to be borne by an origin with which it can never coincide and which it is always trying to recover, the human sciences seek to present this finitude with the aid of the categories of 'norm', 'rule' and 'system' in a 'positive and empirical' form. While the corresponding concepts 'function', 'conflict' and 'signification' still referred to the way 'life', 'need' and 'language' could be presented in what was *possibly* not a form accessible to the naïve consciousness, the mode of representation congruent with the concepts 'norm', 'rule' and 'system' is *in principle* only accessible to a reflexive knowledge, namely that of the human sciences.[34] The categories of the human sciences bring with them a 'dissociation ... of consciousness and representation': functions, conflicts and significations which make 'life', 'need' and 'language' representable *may be* unconscious; norms, rules and systems which empirically represent human finitude *are* unconscious. As a result of this dissociation, the problem of the unconscious is inscribed in the heart of the human sciences. It is as a consequence of the categorial models which cause a human-sciences object to 'appear' projected on the surface of the empirical sciences that the project of these disciplines is always concerned with a demystification of naïve consciousness: 'the problem of the unconscious ... is a problem that is ultimately coextensive with their very existence'.[35] As a result, in Foucault's view, the human sciences run up against a problem here which they cannot solve: it is coextensive with their own existence because it is given in their categorial conditions of possibility. The problem of demystification, with which the human sciences burden themselves, always comes to grief on a need for self-demystification which is given in the concepts with which it operates. These concepts determine how life, need and language or human finitude can be represented, i.e. how they can be admitted into the order of representation which is the order of the human sciences. Life, need and language are only conceivable for the human sciences in the (representational) form of functions, conflicts and significations, just as finitude can only be empirically grasped in the (representational) forms of norm, rule and system. The object of the human sciences only becomes comprehensible in and through these concepts. For sociology, for example, operating at the level of representation – i.e. at the sociological level – needs and interests can only be studied *as* rules and conflicts, and this is so *because* rules and conflicts play a categorial role in that discipline. Thus, argues Foucault, the human sciences are forced to proceed constantly 'from that which is given to representation to that which renders representation possible, but which is still representation'.[36] With this paradoxical formula, Foucault is seeking to point up a paradox which infuses the human sciences with a kind of 'transcendental mobility'.[37] The object of the human sciences coincides with their own conditions of possibility. And the demystification of their object is always a laying bare of the conditions under which that object can appear for them: 'the human sciences, when dealing with what is representation (in either conscious or unconscious form), find themselves treating as their object what is in fact their condition of possibility'.[38] The human sciences only find their object in the space of representation (which does not coincide with the realm of consciousness), but this object confronts them again and again with their own categorial conditions of possibility. The discourse of the human sciences on representation is, at the same time, a discourse on what makes representation possible. The epistemological basic structure of the human sciences has a peculiar, *empirical-transcendental* form.

For Foucault, this argument has nothing less than the status of an 'archaeological' explanation of the tendency of the human sciences to seek constantly to put themselves in question, and of the fact 'that, *unlike other sciences*, they seek not so much to generalize themselves or make themselves more precise as to be constantly demystifying themselves'.[39] Yet he connects this instability, which seems to be characteristic of the human sciences, and the 'quasi-transcendental' mobility which he discovered behind it, not with the specific features of their scientificity, but with a specificity which means that they are not sciences at all, but 'constitute . . . side by side with the sciences and on the same archaeological ground, *other* configurations of knowledge'.[40] The constant impression of haziness, inexactitude and imprecision left by 'almost all' the human sciences is for Foucault merely a 'surface effect' of the specific position they occupy in the field of knowledge.[41] The human sciences have no special place within the realm of the sciences but occupy a position which separates them off from that realm. In *The Order of Things*, Foucault does not question the effect of the human sciences' interpretation of their own scientificity, but the fact of their understanding themselves as sciences or orienting themselves towards an ideal of scientificity which, in view of their position in the field of modern knowledge, must remain a pious wish: 'the configuration that defines their positivity ... makes it impossible for them to be sciences'.[42]

3. The 'neutrality' of archaeology

The (an-)archaeology of knowledge which is systematically developed in *The Order of Things* had set itself the task of establishing the epistemological position of the human sciences and showing how the configuration characterizing them 'is radically different from that of the sciences *in the strict sense*'.[43] This determination of the singularity of the human sciences which establishes their position outside the domain of scientificity, without regarding them as 'illusions' or 'ideologies', is meant to prevent the 'futility' or 'injustice' of these non-scientific forms of knowledge being 'confronted' 'historically' or 'critically' with other forms of knowledge which may be termed scientific in the strict sense.[44] Such a declaration of intent does not, however, absolve us in any way of asking to what extent Foucault's assessment of the position of the human sciences is not itself the product of the procedure he adopted, which confines itself to a purely *formal* characterization of these disciplines.

Foucault's decision to derive the specificity of the human sciences from the form of their epistemic configuration was meant to put him in a position to defend the counter-intuitive standpoint that it is not 'man' who tempts them on to a specific and complex terrain of investigation, but the general constellation of the modern *epistemè*, which finds expression in the trihedron of knowledge[45] and which enables them, in accordance with their specific position, to constitute man as object. Foucault neither sought the conditions of possibility of the human sciences in 'man', nor looked to man's complexity for the reasons why the human sciences have such a difficult task, but wanted to show that what makes the human sciences possible can at the same time explain the appearance of man as a possible object of knowledge. The only definition which can, in Foucault's view, be given of the human sciences is a formal one: 'We shall say, therefore, that a "human science" exists not wherever man is in question, but wherever there is analysis – within the dimension proper to the unconscious – of norms, rules, and signifying totalities which unveil to consciousness the conditions of its forms and contents.'[46] The long detour which Foucault made in order to arrive at this formal definition seems to provide *a posteriori* grounds for the intuition which underlay the construction of the trihedron of knowledge: the idea that the only site the human sciences can occupy within this trihedron, from which they are, strictly speaking, excluded,[47] is an impossible one which condemns them to an 'essential instability'. Foucault now relates this instability to the formal characteristic of the human sciences which consists in their finding themselves in a position of 'duplication' with regard to the empirical sciences. As we have seen, the consequence of this 'ana- or hypo-epistemological position' is that their object coincides with their conditions of possibility and, hence, a kind of transcendental torsion occurs which finds expression in incessant attempts at (self)-unmasking.[48]

The archaeological serenity with which Foucault separates off the human sciences must not, however, cause us to forget his critical intentions: he wants, at least, to contest the human sciences' right to pursue an ideal of scientificity which in principle lies beyond their scope. Great as the contrast may be with the pathos Foucault had put into contesting the scientificity of psychology in *Histoire de la folie*, beneath the archaeological neutrality of *The Order of Things* a similar problem lies concealed. Foucault can only dispute the scientific ideal of the human sciences by basing his arguments, in an unclear but by no means negligible way, on a specific conception of what constitutes the scientificity of a science, though one which is nowhere further explicated: the difference between the position of the human and the other sciences, and the ensuing instability, is for Foucault an argument – the only argument – which leads to the direct conclusion that they are unscientific in character.[49] While *Histoire de la folie* took over the scientific ideal (realism) from the discipline under analysis and tried to develop a more or less immanent critique, the critical intention of *The Order of Things* seems to introduce an external criterion. Not only would Foucault seem compelled to identify the scientificity of the disciplines which belong to the empirical dimension of the trihedron (economics, biology, the sciences of language) with scientificity *tout court*, but, in so doing, he is also operating with an unexplicated scientific ideal.[50] As a result, *The Order of Things* also remains in thrall to an unanalysed concept of science which – as in the earlier engagement with psychology, but even more dangerously and with scarcely calculable consequences – prevents Foucault from finding the force, in an analysis of the specificity of the human sciences, to rethink the concept of 'science' and the authority of that science.

This omission which, in spite of (or because of?) its (an)archaeo-logical approach, connects *The Order of Things* with *Histoire de la folie*, not only points up the difficulties attaching to a *formal* definition of the specificity of the human sciences, but also takes its revenge in the determination of their formal *specificity*. The problem with Foucault's ambiguous, archaeological 'defence' of the human sciences lies not only in his establishing its poles of reference as model sciences and models of scientificity, but also in the choice of those poles and, hence, of the dimensions of the trihedron. With the concept of 'anthropologism', Foucault introduced a pattern of argument which renders this choice unverifiable at an important point: in so far as a similarity arises, on the basis of an 'anthro-pologization', between the human sciences and a discipline which forms one of the dimensions of the trihedron, that similarity is secondary and inauthentic – a false appearance, which can only come about as a result of a perversion of that discipline. The whole difficulty with this 'logic of the supplement' (Derrida) is the following: in his determination of the specificity of the human sciences as primary bearers of the 'anthropological danger', Fou-cault has to start out from 'pure', 'de-anthropologized' disciplines and, moreover, only by so doing does he possess a criterion which permits him to determine where and when one may speak of anthropologization. It is a consequence of his formal definition of sociology, psychology etc[51] that the definition of sociologism, psychologism and anthropologism must remain entirely formal, and all this in a way which is dangerously close either to a stipulative definition or a *petitio principii*. In the first case, the domain of the human sciences is restricted arbitrarily to sociology, psychology and the cultural sciences, which is rather to evade the problem of demarcation than to resolve it. In the second case, a solution to the problem has already to be assumed, since the determination of the specificity of the human sciences – and hence of the indices which point to anthropologization – is based on the existence of disciplines which, though susceptible of anthropologization, would have to be known already in their de-anthropologized versions. Foucault is forced to operate with a prior understanding of anthropologization which would have to *precede* a formal definition of its concept, but which at the same time, by the logic of his argument, can only be the *product* of that definition.

Foucault's treatment of economics gives few grounds for believing that this circularity might be that of a 'virtuous' epistemic-hermeneutic circle. By contrast with the human sciences, economics does not, in his view, move within the space of representation. Its strength lies in the fact that it does not involve itself with human beings: it uses the representations (interest, the search for profit, saving, need), which become the object of sociology, only to the extent that these are necessary to economic functioning which, indeed, presupposes human activity.[52] But does this not mean that economics takes its basic concepts, as Foucault himself suggested earlier,[53] from a psychology of needs, and does this not in turn mean that the trihedron of knowledge is put at risk? Is there not concealed, beneath the empty shells formed by what in economic jargon are called the 'arguments' of saving or consumption functions, an embarrassment with regard to the basic concepts of economics? And does this not mean that the danger of 'anthropologism' cannot be regarded as a second-order accident since it is always already contained in the basic concepts of that discipline and is, indeed, what makes possible the project of a 'pure economics'? This emphasis on the significance of the 'impure' discourse which, at least in its initial phase, accompanied the mathematicization of economics,[54] is not intended to extend Foucault's critique of the claim to scientificity of the human sciences to include economics. The point is, rather, to provide a different evaluation of the status of that 'impure' discourse from that offered by Foucault himself. The impurity of economics was perhaps not so much an obstacle to its scientificity – which the movement towards a 'pure economics' had to overcome[55] – as what in fact enabled it to be scientific. The anthropological supplement – and, with it, the relation to the human sciences – would seem not so much a perversion of an already present discourse as, rather, an originary 'supplement' which retrospectively brings into being precisely that to which it is supposed to be added.[56] Foucault may be right to see the specific feature of this discipline as lying in the '*tendency* towards a pure economics', but it would seem less obvious to regard this tendency as constituting an argument for differentiating economics from the human sciences. He himself provides an argument, rather, for seeing the anthropologization of economics as an internal characteristic, and not one ascribed to it later: the representations with which economics works are matrices which are always already predisposed to anthropologization. For Foucault too, anthropologization could have had the status of an '*originary* supplement' (Derrida). Seen in its own terms – independently of the (compulsion to fit into the) systematic context within which it emerges – Foucault's presentation of economics seems not incompatible with the idea that the basic concepts of economics contain an 'anthropologization' because, in their interrelations with one another, they articulate the elements of an anthropology which may, in the development of economic theory, have been filled out differently, but in each case presuppose this originary and impure 'supplement' which made them possible.

If we relate these difficulties – the model character of the empirical sciences, the peculiar circularity of the anthropologism argument and its 'application' to a concrete discipline – to the trihedron of knowledge, then it becomes apparent that the construct we are dealing with here is not only idiosyncratic, but also rickety. The presence of an economics which, in its basic concepts, bears within itself, if not an actual anthropologization, then none the less an ever-present possibility of anthropologization – and this within the central dimension of the empirical sciences on which Foucault's argument largely rests – threatens to erode this pillar of the trihedron. It all depends, then, whether the remaining structure is sufficiently reinforced to remain immune to this attack and keep the pyramid upright.[57] Moreover, it would seem to be arbitrary to charge the human sciences with borrowing concepts and models without investigating whether and to what extent economics, for example, has not always – or at least from a particular moment in its development – taken its basic concepts from psychology (or a proto-psychology), and thus whether the distribution between the dimensions of the trihedron and the space they delimit does not have to be revised.

These problems which threaten the symmetry of Foucault's

arguments are perhaps less important for his later development than another, more profound one that is linked with them and, in an unexpected way, connects the formal approach of this argumentation with the anthropologism question. Foucault sees anthropologization only as a threat to the pre-established scientificity of a number of model disciplines. He neither investigates the content of this anthropologizing discourse nor the consequences for the concept of scientificity which ensue from the fact that certain disciplines are accompanied by such a discourse. As a result of his faith in the anthropologization idea, which suggests that the impurity of this discourse *threatens* the self-sufficiency of pure scientificity, he forfeits the theoretical means to problematize that self-sufficiency. Foucault thereby misses the opportunity to pose in all its rigour, on what was for him an unexpected terrain, the question which remained open in *Histoire de la folie* and which, since the 'archaeological' corrective in *The Birth of the Clinic*, had become all the more urgent. Paradoxically, it is not on the terrain of the human sciences that *The Order of Things* confronts the question of the significance of the interpretation of their scientificity which certain disciplines provide in an internal discourse; it confronts that question, rather, in the anthropologism which (in Foucault's view) threatens the non-human-science disciplines. The fact that this question, from which Foucault could have distilled a motivation for his critique of the human sciences, is not posed (and cannot even be posed within the formal framework of *The Order of Things*) allows the meaning and status of that critique to remain unclear. The enigma of *The Order of Things* – this hazy glow which, as in Matisse's painting, swatches the round dance that celebrates the end of Man in a red which may herald either a new dawn or the onset of a long night – is for Foucault also the enigma of the human sciences: 'Western culture has constituted, under the name of man, a being who, by one and the same interplay of reasons, must be a positive domain of *knowledge* and cannot be an object of *science*.'[58]

Armed with the experience of an archè-ology of psychology, but also disarmed by the an-archèological corrective which culminated in *The Order of Things*, Foucault will, in *Discipline and Punish*, inflect this enigma into a genealogical critique of the human sciences – a critique that does not, however, draw a line under a problem at last resolved but becomes entangled in a new and complex field of problems which is grafted on to the old one and in a certain sense repeats it.

2.2. A genealogical critique of the human sciences

1. The stakes

More than any other work in the series of major historical studies Foucault produced, *Discipline and Punish* (1975) has the appearance of a late synthesis. The subtitle ('The Birth of the Prison') indicates that he is going back beyond *The Order of Things* to a theme which connected the studies of madness (of 1961 and 1962) to *The Birth of the Clinic* (French original, 1963).[59] After the asylum and the clinic, the investigation of the 'Birth of the Prison' offered Foucault an opportunity to rethink the history of these modern institutions and articulate the results arrived at earlier within a new theoretical framework.[60] Yet it would be wrong to relate the originality of *Discipline and Punish* and the issues raised in this book solely to this problematic. In contrast to the expectations which the subtitle creates, Foucault's subject here is not simply the birth of the prison, but also the birth of the human sciences.

It is not from any lack of systematicity that Foucault brings together in one work what are, at first sight, two such disparate themes. The incorporation of the human sciences into the 'chapter from the history of penal thought' which Foucault is attempting to write in *Discipline and Punish*[61] follows from the complexity of the problematic under consideration – 'how man, the soul, the normal or abnormal individual have come to duplicate crime as objects of penal intervention; and in what way a specific mode of subjectivizing subjection was able to give birth to man as an object of knowledge for a discourse with a "scientific" status'.[62] With this dual line of inquiry, Foucault wishes to avoid relating the development of penal law to the history of the human sciences in a superficial way, in which they would be seen as running in parallel. He is seeking after a common genealogical moment which can explain both the humanization of the penal phenomenon and the project of the 'human sciences'.[63]

The intention of writing a genealogy of the human sciences brings *Discipline and Punish* closer, in a sense, to *Histoire de la folie* than to *The Order of Things*. In spite of the strategic intention common to all three works – to contest the scientificity of the human sciences – there are tactical differences between them. Unlike the approach in *The Order of Things* but running parallel, to a certain extent, with *Histoire de la folie*, the arguments for the unscientificity of those sciences no longer relate to their position within a complex epistemic configuration like the trihedron of knowledge, but to the contexts of their emergence. The problem of the human sciences no longer – or no longer mainly – lies in their epistemological, but in their genealogical, dependency: 'The archaeology of the human sciences has to be established through studying the mechanisms of power which have invested human bodies, acts and forms of behaviour.'[64] Strictly speaking, the effects of these mechanisms of power can no longer be regarded as so many corresponding alienations. At least since the *Archaeology of Knowledge*, it had been Foucault's aim finally to jettison the naturalistic assumption that 'under power with its acts of violence and its artifice, we should be able to rediscover the things themselves in their primitive vivacity'.[65] The same restriction which made possible the an-archaeological project of *The Order of Things* was now to enable *Discipline and Punish* to revive the intentions of the preceding works without becoming embroiled once again in the difficulties of an archèological or an-archaeological critique of the human sciences. The investigation of prisons not only offered him the opportunity to devise another type of critique, it also provided him with a motive for elucidating the necessity of such a critique.

2. The necessity of a genealogy of the human sciences

Anyone inquiring into the origin of the prison system today is confronted with a long tradition in which prison has been regarded as a self-evident penal measure.[66] But that such an inquiry has now become possible points, in Foucault's view, to the fact that the historical obviousness of the prison system has begun to crumble. *Discipline and Punish* seems to have wished to hasten this process in that it problematizes the development which prisons have undergone since the beginning of the nineteenth century. The development of prison into the preferred modern penal technique did not occur by chance, just as it is not by chance that the 'power to punish' has been able to base itself in recent times on a 'scientifico-juridical complex'.[67] In Foucault's eyes, these two movements are related. Admittedly, they do not have the historical obviousness frequently ascribed to them, but that does not mean they are arbitrary. They form the object of a genealogy and at the same time show why a genealogical study of the emergence of prison cannot avoid the question of the emergence of the human sciences.

The fascination exerted on Foucault's early work by the human sciences problematic has not lost any of its force in *Discipline and Punish*. But the contrast between this genealogical problematic and the archaeological approach pursued in earlier work is striking. If the need for an (an-)archaeological specification of the human sciences in *The Order of Things* was still motivated by the permanent threat which these represented for the scientificity of other disciplines, the motive for an investigation of the conditions of emergence of those sciences in *Discipline and Punish* no longer lies in their epistemologically dangerous position, but in the context of their application. Foucault no longer wishes to protect the scientificity of certain disciplines from the human sciences but to show how the latter's claim to scientificity provides a historically improbable institution like the prison with an opportunity to defend against its own failure.

The objections levelled against the prison system are familiar: it does not reduce criminality, it promotes recidivism, it encourages the formation of a criminal subculture, it promotes delinquent behaviour by the monotonous existence imposed upon the inmates and the stigma which attaches to an ex-convict and, lastly, it can force those members of the family who are left behind, despite their good intentions, into a criminal career.[68] This is not a new critique. Since its origins, there have been endless polemics on the subject of prison. Reform proposals are as old as the prison system itself. Right up to our own day, its history has been the history of the reforms of the prison system. These two historical developments overlap to such a degree that one might ask whether the mechanisms apparently intended to correct the prison system do not 'form part of its very functioning'.[69] Foucault even goes so far as to see the failure of prison, which has so often been remarked upon, as its real success. This would mean that prison was the most extraordinary of institutions, its success being determined by the extent to which it deviated from its goals and was untrue to its initial programme. However this may be, the failure of prison contrasts oddly with the ease with which, though it was a (relatively) new[70] penal technique, it quickly came to be regarded as a self-evident one. And the situation seems even odder when one takes into account that the criticisms formulated since the emergence of the prison at the beginning of the last century are in fact older than the institution itself. The counter-productive effect of prison was already one of the arguments of the enlightened penal reformers of the late eighteenth century for restricting its role to that of a special measure for particular offences.[71] Yet it was precisely prison – and not the whole arsenal of picturesque punishments the reformers dreamed of – which became established as a general punitive technique. Instead of allowing the nature of the punishment to flow from the nature of the offence, a 'grey, uniform penalty' was introduced, which immediately met with resistance: '[I]f I have betrayed my country, I go to prison; if I have killed my father, I go to prison ... One might as well see a physician who has the same remedy for all ills.'[72]

The real reason for this successful 'colonization of the penalty by the prison'[73] lies not, however, in the at first sight striking difference between the monotony of the prison sentence and the extremely differentiated sanctions envisaged by the reformers. Prison could be used to give concrete institutionalized form to an important point in the penal reformers' programme: the length and modalities of a term of imprisonment give such scope for differentiation that the punishment can be fitted perfectly to the individual misdeeds. Prison might even be seen as providing the better solution to the problem of imposing a special penalty tailored to the individual case, in which a correspondence between the crime, the lawbreaker and the penal sanction is to be expressed as precisely as possible. But the point at which prison in a sense fulfils the reform programme is also the point at which it offends against the spirit of the reforms.

The reason why it breaks with that spirit is not to be found in any theoretical difference regarding the grounds for punishment, but at the level of its concrete, 'technical' execution. For the penal reformers, the aim of punishment was not to make reparation for the crime committed, but to prevent a possible repetition – either by recidivism or imitation. There were semio-technical grounds for the extreme differentiation of penal techniques they advocated: every enforcement of a penalty was to evoke a page from the great 'Linnaeus of crimes and punishments'.[74] The 'hundreds of tiny theatres of punishment'[75] together formed 'a Garden of the Laws',[76] of which not only the actors involved were aware, but also the general public. Whoever had placed himself beyond the social pale could be rehabilitated as a legal subject by his punishment turning his offence into a signified which evoked the penalty (signifier) laid down in the code. The corrective effect of the punishment on the lawbreaker had a general social function which was to disappear entirely from the competing prison-based model. Missing from this closed 'total institution' is not just the public

50

character of the execution of the penalty, but the whole semio-technical apparatus of the reformers: 'Exercises, not signs: time-tables, compulsory movements, regular activities, solitary meditation, work in common, silence, application, respect, good habits.'[77] The effect of this new penal technology lies not in a 'juridical redefinition' of the person who has broken the social pact but in the production of an 'obedient individual'. Not a reactivation of the code but a training (*dressage*). For Foucault, prison is a – if not indeed *the* – disciplinary institution.

The disciplinary apparatus which came into force with the prison, in a move running counter to the principles of penal reform, not only enjoys extensive administrative autonomy, but carries this claim to autonomy to extremes, in that it has sought, from its very inception, to usurp the position of judicial power. A perfectly individualized punishment was now not so much the expression of a correlation between the transgression, the transgressor and the sentence, but was to be assessed on the basis of the prisoner himself. If the prison wishes to correct the individual entrusted to it, it must have scope to modulate the punishment. In the end, the decision as to the length of the penalty must lie with the institution charged with administering it. The point of intervention for a perfectly individualized penalty is not, as the reformers had it, the juridical subject, responsible for his offence, but the punished individual himself. Neither the action of the lawbreaker, nor the circumstances of his act were to provide the criteria for the extent of the punishment, but the penalty itself as it takes place in actual fact. Judgment is to be based not on the offender, but on the interned individual, who conforms to the mechanisms of control within the walls of the prison or, alternatively, resists them, thereby proving it would be premature to release him, irrespective of the sentence of the courts.[78] Beneath this claim to 'punitive sovereignty', Foucault sees nothing less than a 'Declaration of Carceral Independence', which is a consequence of the 'penal logic' that characterized the prison from its inception.[79]

One can see from the endlessly recurring criticisms of the prison system that the meaning of this penal technique extends beyond the mere deprivation of liberty. More is expected of the prison than that it take certain persons out of social circulation, that it confine itself to taking them into its 'protective custody' and imposing on them a regime of socially dead time. The time the prisoner spends in prison is not an abstract measure of the seriousness of his offence, but a time the rhythm and intensity of which is determined by a disciplinary process that is to transform him into a socially (and not just juridically) 'rehabilitated' individual.[80] The solitude of his confinement, the perpetual confrontation with a hierarchy, the compulsory labour carried out in silence are to give him a new 'habitus'[81] which breaks with his criminal past and affords him a right to a free future. From its beginnings, prison filled up the dead time of incarceration with the intensity of a disciplinary procedure. Prison time is a time directed to an end. What is important is not the punctual event of the criminal act, but the duration of the process in which an individual is (trans)formed. Prison does not simply confine itself to locking up the culprit; it is a 'reformatory'.[82] This 'corrective supplement' is, in Foucault's view, something specific to it.[83] A specificity which means not only that, on the basis of its own logic, it necessarily comes into conflict with a traditional separation of powers, but also that it was able, in spite of this conflict, to attain the status of privileged penal technique. Curiously, the attractiveness of prison for the penal law arises precisely at the point where it threatens to depart from the principles of codification and demands a punitive autonomy for itself. Foucault attempts to explain this strange state of affairs by the legitimation pressure clearly exerted on the modern 'power to punish'. Modern judicial power is characterized, argues Foucault, by a sense of shame in punishing.[84] The aim of punishment no longer lies in the physical suffering which had to compensate for a real or symbolic assault on the ruler, embodied in the law.[85] It has become, to a certain extent, 'non-corporal'.[86] Punishment no longer fulfils its purpose by the pain it inflicts on the body, but by its therapeutic effects on the 'soul' of the criminal. The modern power to punish can, it seems, only acquire legitimation by being more than a power to punish – a situation which, in Foucault's opinion, enables us to explain the presence of psychiatrists, psychologists and criminologists in the courtroom. This extension of judicial power to a 'scientifico-judicial complex' not only fits in with the penal logic of the prison, it finds in that logic the conditions of its possibility.

The prison is, admittedly, more than a mere 'house of detention', but it is also more than a rather strict reform institution. Or, more exactly, it can only develop into a great reformatory because it is, at the same time, a 'permanent observatory'.[87] The reform of the inmates is only possible within an apparatus able to base itself on a kind of 'clinical knowledge about ... convicts'.[88] Only such knowledge puts the prison in a position to recast the punitive sanction as a successful penitentiary intervention. The knowledge it ceaselessly gathers about the inmates therefore relates not so much to the criminal offence and the circumstances surrounding it, but is rather concerned to discover the 'biographical dimension' behind the offence.[89] The prison is interested not in the lawbreaker, but in the delinquent: 'The penitentiary technique bears not on the relation between author and crime, but on the criminal's affinity with his crime.'[90] The whole way the 'little soul of the criminal' has 'come to duplicate crime' as 'an object of penal intervention'[91] has its basis in this interest on the part of the prison in the biography of the delinquent. The 'scientific' label[92] which attaches to a criminologically-oriented psychiatry and, beyond it, to the whole discourse of the human sciences by which the same interest in the genesis of abnormality came later to be justified in the administration of justice[93] ought not to allow the history of the emergence of this modern curiosity to be forgotten. Delinquency is the 'product' of the prison, just as, in a certain sense, the prison is the product of delinquency: 'in fabricating delinquency, it [the prison] gave to criminal justice a unitary field of objects, authenticated by the "sciences" . . . It is understandable that justice should have adopted so easily a prison that was not the offspring of its own thoughts. Justice certainly owed the prison this recognition.'[94]

As always with Foucault, the quotation marks in the preceding quotation are not innocent. They indicate that the investigation of the origin of the prison is not just historically, *but also philosophically important*. Foucault does not just seek to explain the historical success of the prison in quasi-functionalist fashion by the fact that it offered judicial power the opportunity to determine the meaning of the penal sanction extra-juridically (not a punishment, but a therapy) and to feel reinforced, as a result of this alloreferentiality, by a 'scientific' legitimation. He does not simply see prison's discovery of delinquency as the condition of possibility of a juridical alloreferentiality, behind which the modern power to punish can hide its shame, but wants to call into question the basis of that alloreferentiality itself: 'how could psychology, psychiatry and criminology today legitimate [*justifier*] justice, since their history reveals a single political technology at work at the point where they were all formed'.[95]

It is clear that, given these considerations, Foucault could not avoid a genealogical study of the human sciences. The argument that the prison *made possible* the modern 'scientifico-judicial' complex is an insufficient basis on which to ground a critique of this historically successful alliance. It can at best explain why the power of the penal law was able to derive support from the results of the human sciences, but no conclusions can be drawn at the level of legitimation from merely establishing the fact of this alloreferential legitimation strategy. It is understandable that Foucault, for whom such factual observations were clearly insufficient, should see the context of application of the human sciences as a motive for research into the context of their emergence. One can understand why a genealogy of the human sciences is necessary. But one also perhaps sees the difficulties of an undertaking which seeks to uncover not just the context of the emergence of the human sciences, but also, at the same time, the conditions of their (im)possibility.

3. A *genealogical* critique of the human sciences?

(i) *Genealogy, a philosophical problem*

The above analysis of the basic structure of *Discipline and Punish* has shown how, on the basis of an at first sight purely historical investigation, Foucault came up against a problematic which exceeds the framework of purely historical inquiry. That the question of the genealogy of the human sciences also has consequences at a philosophical level is already clear from the idiosyncratic, but very characteristic manoeuvre by which this genealogical concern is introduced: within the framework of Foucault's analysis, it is almost self-evident that a genealogy of the human sciences also functions as a critique of these disciplines.[96] In so far as the genealogical elucidation of the conditions of emergence – of the human sciences, for example – seems to stake a claim to be able simultaneously to reveal the conditions of their possibility and impossibility, the question of the status of genealogy shifts into the background or is given an indirect (and perhaps over-hasty) answer. One of the problems of the analyses in *Discipline and Punish* concerns precisely this transition from conditions of emergence to conditions of possibility and impossibility, and we shall have to ask – particularly in relation to this latter step – whether it is not carried out on the basis of a residual, non-genealogical problematic. And incidentally, this problem of whether genealogy *as such* implies genealogical critique arises not only in the case of the genealogical investigation of the human sciences, but also in that of the long analysis of disciplinary mechanisms which branches off from the historical researches into prisons and develops into a more or less self-contained section of the book.[97] The privileging of the problematic of the human sciences, where the problem of the status of a genealogy arises in a form familiar to us, will, however, enable us to recognize the role of Foucault's quotation marks in other domains too. Moreover, the kernel of the theoretical problematic which provides the background to what are, at first sight, the diverse studies of material grouped together in *Discipline and Punish* can only be closely analysed when those studies are no longer seen as prompting a genealogical investigation of the human sciences, but as the consequence of such an investigation.[98] That the author of *The Order of Things* wished to write a 'history of punitive reason' reflects not just a diversity of interest, but also a continuity: the question of the birth of the prison not only leads to the understanding that a genealogy of the human sciences is necessary, but is infused from the outset with such an understanding, which in fact constitutes its real motive. Foucault did not see the genealogy of the prison as a prelude to a genealogy of the human sciences that was to be developed independently, but as a self-contained contribution to such a genealogy. It is in the interplay of these two genealogies that the problem of *Discipline and Punish* lies.

It will be remembered that Foucault's explanation of the improbable historical success of the prison is that there was a congruence between penal logic and the logic of the 'scientifico-judicial complex'. The alloreferential dependency of the administration of justice on the human sciences is not, however, the ultimate explanation of this success. Its particular conditions of possibility are to be found in the development of prison into an apparatus of knowledge which, through the figure of the delinquent – on which psychiatry, criminal anthropology, psychology and criminology obtained a firm hold[99] – opened the way to 'a whole field of recent objects, a whole new regime of truth and a mass of roles hitherto unknown in the exercise of criminal justice'.[100] Foucault is not only trying here to correct the impression that the scientifico-judicial complex plays the role of an independent variable in his analysis, he is not only attempting to allude to the interdependence between the success of the prison and the successful penetration of the human sciences into the courtroom, but to bring out another, much more fundamental interdependence: between the history of the emergence of the prison and the genealogy of the human sciences. Or rather, since the expression 'interdependence' perhaps says too much or not enough, what is in question is how the suggested connection between these two '*Entstehungsgeschichten*' should be understood. Foucault is, however, cautious enough to exclude a naïve reduction of the one to the other: 'I am not saying that the human sciences emerged from the prison. But, if they have been able to be formed and to produce so many profound changes in the episteme, it is because they have been conveyed by a specific and new modality of power.'[101] Foucault is, without doubt, aware of the danger that the problem of the relationship between power and knowledge, which is alluded to here, can all too easily be oversimplified and sloganized – knowledge is (simply) power etc.[102] He therefore seeks a solution by employing a hyphen: 'The carceral network constituted one of the armatures of this *power-knowledge* that has made the human sciences historically possible.'[103] It is clear that nothing would be gained by this hyphen, and that a problem would be concealed rather than solved, if the two terms brought together here were merely being juxtaposed. The whole radicalism of the 'power-knowledge' concept and its entire right to exist must depend on the extent to which the meaning of the two terms – power and knowledge – is successfully displaced in and by the hyphen.[104]

Whether this displacement is possible and desirable constitutes the true core of the problematic to which the analyses in *Discipline and Punish* owe their theoretical significance. At the same time, however, as we shall seek to demonstrate, these analyses are characterized by a hesitation which sets in train a kind of counter-movement, through which they risk falling short of the exigencies of Foucault's problematic. The more he strives to give impetus to the terms of the 'power-knowledge' complex, the greater his efforts to formulate his problematic precisely, the more difficult it becomes to follow him in his critique of the human sciences. So long as we remain within the framework of a historical investigation of the prison, the motive for a critique of the unscientificity of the human sciences seems unproblematic. As soon as we leave or extend that framework, however, and look to the underlying philosophical problematic, we run into the difficulty of reconciling Foucault's genealogical concern with the intention of his critique of the human sciences. The genealogist's act of putting terms in quotation marks is by no means self-explanatory. It is not at all evident whether it is his problematic that is expressed in these quotation marks or, rather, the problem he is having with his problematic.[105] We shall have to return to this question when we have shown how the overall structure of *Discipline and Punish* is determined by a balancing act between two movements: the one which seeks to formulate a type of critique which is hindered or rendered less plausible by the problematic treated in the work; the other which seeks to articulate a problematic which cannot but cause us to doubt the meaning and possibility of a certain critique of the human sciences.

(ii) *What is at stake in the power-knowledge concept*

What is surprising about the connection Foucault makes between 'power' and 'knowledge' pertains not so much to the interrelation itself as to the consequences he draws from it. The hyphen placed here between two concepts which have, within a long philosophical tradition, almost always been understood as antonyms, by no means expresses a theoretical scepticism with regard to the attainability of any particular knowledge-ideal or of an ideal of knowledge in general. On the contrary, with the power-knowledge concept, Foucault wishes to 'abandon a whole tradition that allows us to imagine that knowledge can exist only where the power relations are suspended and that knowledge can develop only outside its injunctions, its demands and its interests'.[106] To use the connection between power and knowledge as an argument against the actual possibility of 'real' knowing, of achieving 'genuine' knowledge or 'authentic' science would mean sharing a particular conception of knowledge with the tradition and conserving that conception in the unhappy consciousness of a melancholy science, or overturning it with a joyful cynicism and thus, involuntarily, confirming its validity. Foucault would seem to want to do neither of these things, and he is apparently aware that the whole meaning and radicalism of his hyphen, its very claim to existence, depend on the extent to which he manages to dispense with the conceptual baggage associated with the traditional knowledge-ideal. The power-knowledge concept neither indicates scepticism with regard to the possibility of (genuine) knowledge, nor a critique of actual knowledge (on the grounds, for example, that, because of its link with power, it is not real knowledge), but refers, rather, to a constitutive condition of knowledge and science in general: 'there is *no* power relation without the *correlative* constitution of a field of knowledge, nor any knowledge that does not presuppose and constitute *at the same time* power relations'.[107] In so far as, in adopting this position, which makes the direct, reciprocal intrication of knowledge and power explicit, Foucault has in mind more than a fact-based argument, he cannot avoid rethinking the meaning of the concepts 'knowledge' and 'power'. And, whatever he may mean by the idea that 'power produces knowledge',[108] it is clear that this must lead to a revision of our conceptions both of knowledge and of power. Whatever may be the consequences of enduring such a double ignorance, it is clear in any case and *a priori* that those consequences do not allow us to formulate a critique of knowledge, science or even the human sciences, based only on the argument that a particular form of knowledge or science is bound up with power. If the connection between knowledge and power really points to a constitutive aspect of knowledge, if it is really attempting to express a condition of the possibility of knowledge and science in general, then the critique of the human sciences cannot consist in accusing those sciences of a *liaison dangereuse* with power. And yet this is precisely what happens in Foucault. Or, more precisely, this is what *also* happens, for we are dealing here with a movement which develops alongside his problematic – or against it.

Foucault's critique of the human sciences' claim to scientificity only becomes clear if one takes this second movement into consideration. By this, I do not mean that this counter-movement is developed in some second phase, such that it might be separated from a first phase in which the power-knowledge relationship is articulated. It is more of the order of an inert force, which brakes or deflects this attempt at articulation or, perhaps more accurately, marks or signs it. The interplay of these two movements determines the totality of Foucault's subsequent analyses of the power-knowledge concept and one of its consequences is that, on closer inspection, two different types of analysis become apparent. The problem lies not so much in this differentiation itself as in the fact that it causes Foucault's analysis to abandon the logic of the power-knowledge concept: the hyphen between 'power' and 'knowledge' leads to a differentiation which ultimately turns against the conjoining of these two terms.

(iii) *First attempt at differentiation (*autre pouvoir, autre savoir*)*

At a first level, the need for this differentiation seems connected with the logic of the 'power-knowledge' concept. The combining of two, at first sight unrelated, terms under what sounds like a general concept – 'power-knowledge' – runs the risk of being conceived as an attempt to conceptualize the constitutive link between 'power' and 'knowledge' in general. Foucault sought to avoid such a misunderstanding, which would render any form of typology impossible, by dropping the French definite article (not *le pouvoir*, but *pouvoir*): the hyphen does, admittedly, indicate a relationship which no knowledge can escape, but this does not prevent *specific* forms of knowledge being attached to specific forms of power.[109] Moreover, Foucault seems to want to derive the specificity of a particular form of knowledge from the link with a particular form of power. Hence the 'another power, another knowledge' adage, which is advanced in explanation of the difference between the natural and the human sciences.[110] The *differentia specifica* of the human sciences seems to lie not in their object but in their genealogy:

> These sciences, which have so delighted our 'humanity' for over a century, have their *technical matrix* in the petty, malicious minutiae of the disciplines and their investigations. These investigations are perhaps to psychology, psychiatry, pedagogy, criminology, and so many other strange sciences, what the terrible power of investigation was to the calm knowledge of the animals, the plants or the earth.[111]

It is clear that little is gained from such 'genealogical' assertions, which would seem to relate to the differing contexts of emergence of the natural and human sciences, so long as the 'technical matrix' concept is not clarified. For what do we really learn when we read that 'in Greece, mathematics were born from techniques of measurement', that 'the sciences of nature, *in any case*, were born, to some extent, at the end of the Middle Ages, from the practices of investigation', or that 'the great empirical knowledge ... had its operating model *no doubt* in the Inquisition'?[112] What can it mean to know that measurement (*la mesure*), and investigation (*l'enquête*) and examination (*l'examen*) are, respectively, 'matrices' for mathematics and physics, for the empirical and natural sciences and for what 'is called the human sciences'?[113] Even if such a knowledge were to provide insight into the context of emergence of these various disciplines, it would still be an open question whether that were sufficient to ground – or even give a plausible account of – the particular natures of, and specific differences between, these disciplines. Is it significant for the 'internal meaning' of geometry or the natural or human sciences to know that they stand in an as yet unelucidated connection with forms of 'power-knowledge' such as measurement, investigation and examination?[114] Does not such knowledge belong solely at the level of the external (pre-)history of a science? Can such knowledge regarding the 'soil' on which a particular mode of cognition grew up and the 'model'[115] which gave it its orientation ever represent anything more than an account of the external conditions which made that form of knowledge possible?

If one wishes properly to evaluate the complexity of the problematic which forms the backdrop to Foucault's differentiation between human and natural science, one ought to be aware of the role of the preceding questions. They are too general to be direct expressions of one of the various theoretical perspectives by which they might be oriented to formulate a critique of genealogy.[116] On the other hand, they are sufficiently general to prevent the answer to the problem they pose itself being a genealogical one: any further specification of the type of power with which one of the disciplines seems linked could only lead to a more insistent return of these same questions.[117] They relate, in fact, to the status of genealogy itself. They force genealogy to provide clear answers regarding the kind of 'analyses of descent [*Herkunft*]'[118] it conducts, and the status of the insights we might expect to derive from such analyses. Or, to put it another way, to give some sense of the uncommonly difficult range of problems with which a *reading* of Foucault is confronted, they compel genealogy to conceive its own text as an 'answer' to a 'question' which it ought to have posed, but perhaps, for some reason, could not. Even Foucault's explicit methodological thoughts on the status of genealogy offer no grounds to suppose that his text might escape being that 'paradox of *an answer which does not correspond to any question posed*' (Althusser):[119] '... truth or being do not lie at the root of what we know and what we are, but the exteriority of accidents. *This is undoubtedly why every origin of morality from the moment it stops being pious – and* Herkunft *can never be – has value as a critique.*'[120]

This passage would seem to be more a symptom of the problematic perceptible here than an adequate articulation of it: for why, 'the moment it stops being pious', does 'every origin of morality' (or science) imply 'critique'? How is this critique different from base curiosity and the desire to belittle all that is lofty[121] which can apparently reconcile the historian, from whom the genealogist seems to distinguish himself, with his archival existence? Where does the passion come from with which Foucault played off the *pudenda origo* against the human sciences: 'the birth of the sciences of man? It is probably to be found in these "ignoble" archives, where the modern play of coercion over bodies, gestures and behaviour has its beginnings.'[122]

The idea that the 'forms of power-knowledge ... are means to exercise power and at the same time rules which establish knowledge'[123] could only be regarded as the answer to all the preceding questions if this idea were at the same time to imply that the investigation of the conditions of emergence of, for example, the human sciences, has other effects, structurally, than the uncovering of their context of application. If Foucault wanted to be able to defend himself against the objection that he was seeking, with functionalist arguments (the context of application), to found a critique which could not be founded in such a way,[124] he would need to show that the conditions of emergence ('technical matrix') of a particular discipline are more than just incidentally connected to the internal structure of that discipline. The 'answer' *Discipline and Punish* gives to this problem is an astounding one:

> On the threshold of the classical age, Bacon, lawyer and statesman, tried to develop a methodology of investigation [*enquête*] for the empirical sciences. What Great Observer will produce the methodology of examination [*examen*] for the human sciences? *Unless, of course, such a thing is not possible.* For, although it is true that, in becoming a technique for the empirical sciences, the investigation has detached itself from the inquisitorial procedure, in which it was historically rooted, the examination has remained extremely close to the disciplinary power that shaped it. It has always been and still is an intrinsic element of the disciplines.[125]

The tenor of this critique can no longer surprise us: it is not the self-understanding of the human sciences, but their claim to scientificity which is at issue. What is surprising is that, in order to safeguard the continuity of his critique of the human sciences, Foucault seems prepared – or is compelled – to put the entire scope of the power-knowledge concept at risk. The connection between human-science 'knowledge' and the disciplinary 'power' with which the human sciences are linked by their 'technical matrix' acquires a critical force here. The idea which established the connection between 'power' and 'knowledge' – that, 'far from preventing knowledge, power produces it'[126] – is evidently to be made to give way to the idea that genuine knowledge or genuine science only becomes possible when that link is broken: 'The great investigation that gave rise to the sciences of nature has become *detached* from its politico-juridical model; the examination, on the other hand, is *still* caught up in disciplinary technology.'[127] The natural sciences seem to possess a kind of independence from the politico-juridical model which made them possible, an independence which the human sciences have not yet achieved and, in Foucault's view, cannot. It is impossible to develop such a thing as a body of human-science knowledge without forming a link with a disciplinary power that would vitiate the scientificity of that knowledge: 'Knowable man (soul, individuality, consciousness, conduct, whatever it is called) is the object-effect of this analytical investment, of this domination-observation.'[128] The hyphens which occur in this passage are once again an example of the problems confronting Foucault's analysis: either one sees power as an obstacle to knowledge – an idea which he rejects – and takes the link between 'observing' and 'dominating' as indicating a form of improper knowledge – or (with Foucault) one ascribes a constitutive significance to the connection between knowledge and power and refrains from a critique based on the fact of that link. It would seem to be impossible to rescue both the quotation marks and the hyphens. That the passages cited none the less attempt to do this points to an inconsistency which is systematic.

One cannot escape this inconsistency by dissolving power-knowledge into a tripolar power-knowledge-science relationship. Quite apart from the fact that the *science/savoir* (science/knowledge) distinction would no longer seem to play the same role in *Discipline and Punish* as in *The Archaeology of Knowledge*,[129] allowing it to remain in that role would only displace the problem: one would then have either to defend the possibility of a discontinuity between the domains of knowledge and science – an idea which would be directed entirely against the sense that this distinction seemed to have for Foucault[130] – or consider science as a form of knowledge which takes on a specific profile within the domains of knowledge, in which case one runs up against the problem which motivated Foucault's transition from an archaeological to a genealogical critique: namely, that archaeology seemed compelled to privilege a particular model of scientificity in order to be able to reject as unscientific the way in which the human sciences were able to take their place within these domains of knowledge.[131]

Little would seem to be gained, then, by such attempts to soften the contradiction between the quotation marks and the hyphen. They could at best lead to the problematic of *Discipline and Punish* becoming embroiled in a debate on a stipulative definition of scientificity and thus abandoning the terrain of genealogy. This would be to forget that neither the reason for the distinction Foucault draws between the natural and human sciences, nor his arguments against the scientificity of the latter, are archaeological. His evaluation of the human sciences is no longer simply an effect of the fact that he is operating with an implicit norm of scientificity. Nor, indeed, does it follow from a distinction regarding the object of these disciplines, but supposes, as will be clear from what follows, a distinction in respect of the relation they enjoy to their object. *This* distinction should really have led to a differentiation of the power-knowledge concept. The fact that it disappears beneath the generality of this concept seems to be, on the one hand, a consequence of the systematically equivocal nature of the concept of power in *Discipline and Punish* and, on the other, the cause of the one-sided attempt – which connects with Foucault's critique of the scientificity of the human sciences – to render the concept of power unambiguous.

(iv) *Second attempt at differentiation (external link between power and knowledge)*

The consequences Foucault would like to attach to the distinction between the human and the natural sciences do not seem compatible with the way he seeks to justify this differentiation. Even if we leave out of account the objections which can be levelled against a genealogical grounding of this difference in terms of the 'another power, another knowledge' phrase, this adage still does not seem sufficient to undermine the scientificity of the human sciences. Such a critique of the human sciences would only seem possible if one were to give up what is at stake in the 'power-knowledge' concept.[132] Yet Foucault does not seem at all prepared to do this. And he would seem equally unprepared to revise the style of his critique of the human sciences in such a way as to escape the 'dilemma' of combining a particular type of critique with an incompatible conceptual apparatus. It is perhaps for this reason that a *second* attempt at differentiation cuts across the power-knowledge concept: in this case, it is no longer the connection with a particular form of power (the 'investigation' or the 'examination') which is decisive, but the various meanings that must be attributed to such a connection. The critique of the human sciences is then no longer based on the fact that they are linked to a particular type of power, but that this type of power gives that link a specific character not present, for example, in the natural sciences. The nature of the hyphen between power and knowledge could be said to be a different one, then, for each of these two groups of disciplines. And the difference is even so great that the concepts of power and knowledge could be said to have a different meaning – effectively (in the case of power) or possibly (in that of knowledge) – in each case.

A first kind of connection between power and knowledge seems to be motivated by the fact that power affords knowledge access to its object. One finds this model in the passages where Foucault is investigating the conditions for 'epistemological "thaws"'[133] in particular disciplines. The case of medicine is exemplary here: 'The "well-disciplined" hospital became the physical counterpart of the medical "discipline"; this discipline could now abandon its textual character and take its references not so much from the tradition of author-authorities as from a domain of objects perpetually offered for examination.'[134] In order for the hospital to develop into 'a medically useful space',[135] it must first be 'disciplined' and reorganized from an apparatus designed to assist into one designed to examine:[136] the transformation of the internal hierarchy (rise of the physician, decline of the religious personnel); individualization of bodies, illnesses, symptoms; registers, controls, isolation cells, identification and localization. The hospital is made intelligible like a table (*tableau*): 'It was a question of organizing the multiple, of providing oneself with an instrument to cover it and to master it; it was a question of imposing upon it an "order".'[137] For Foucault, such an order is not a consequence of clinical medicine, but what makes it possible. On the one hand, as the expression or terrain of a '"cellular" power'[138] operating 'microphysically', this is an 'anti-nomadic technique';[139] on the other, it is also what makes possible a 'science of the individual' and thus solves a problem which goes back to Aristotle:[140] 'the entry of the individual (and no longer the species) into the field of knowledge'.[141]

More important than the details of Foucault's description of this link between power and knowledge is the question of its status. In this model, power appears as a kind of efficient cause (*causa efficiens*) by which knowledge can attain an object which is, in principle, already present. That the hospital – and, subsequently, also the school and the workshop[142] – make possible an epistemo-logical thawing of particular disciplines (not just medicine, but also child psychology),[143] on the basis of a 'refinement of power relations' that expresses itself in an internal disciplining, would seem to be explained, in this model, by a kind of *'searchlight theory' of power*.[144] The object of knowledge becomes knowable because a light is fixed on it and illumines it: examination establishes 'a visibility ... over individuals'.[145]

Although Foucault's remarks on medicine bring this discipline into relation with the 'technical matrix' which will make the human sciences (im)possible ('examination'), we would seem to be forced back here, rather, on a parallel with the genealogy of the natural sciences: both forms of knowledge or of science[146] would seem to owe the access to their object to a particular form of power. Naturally, one might ask, once again, whether such insights are sufficient to motivate the introduction of the new concept of 'power-knowledge'. In reality, the link suggested by this model is an external one. This 'cratology of knowledge', if I may be permitted the term, seems to have no more succeeded in displacing the meaning of the concept of knowledge or of science than did the sociology of knowledge in altering the meaning of the concept of knowledge. This shift of meaning would seem to be possible only on the basis of a second 'model' which introduces another concept of power.

As with all the preceding differentiations, this second model is also in danger of disappearing beneath the generality of the power-knowledge concept. The surface structure of Foucault's text seems to summon up all possible resources to cause the need for a differentiation, which imposes itself at the level of the deep structure, to be forgotten.[147] In this regard, the passage on the human and natural sciences has the status of a lapsus. A lapsus one must insist upon and defend against the rest of Foucault's text, if one wishes to avoid being dazzled – or, rather, benumbed – by the apparent polish and solidity of that text. The whole of the difference between genealogy and archaeology stands revealed in this lapsus. To protect it against the remainder of 'Foucault' 's text, not to allow it to harmonize with the seamless train of thought, means ultimately to attempt to rescue genealogy from a threatened loss of identity. A loss of identity, since Foucault's remarks on medicine (and, subse-quently, on the natural sciences) repeat almost word for word a programme already formulated in *The Archaeology of Knowledge*:

'[The point is to show] how medical discourse as a practice concerned with a particular field of objects ... is articulated on practices that are *external* to it, and which are not themselves of a discursive order.'[148]

Such power practices stand in an external relation to knowledge. They make possible a particular relationship between knowledge and an external referent, but they are not what makes the referent itself possible. This power deprives individuals of their anonymity, puts them in another light, provides them with a number or a label, documents their lives and forms the basis of a 'new describability'[149] – 'these small techniques of notation, of registration, of constituting files, of arranging facts in columns and tables that are so familiar to us now, were of decisive importance in the epistemological "thaw" of the sciences of the individual'.[150] It is a power that is voyeuristic and intrusive, it counts the beds and gives itself access to what had long been forbidden spaces.[151] It lays bare an intimacy, which from this point on becomes an object of knowledge, surprises individuals in their sleep, observes and presents them.[152] It is a power that is pro-ductive (from *producere*, to bring forward), but not productive: 'In fact, power produces; it produces reality; it produces domains of objects and rituals of truth.'[153] *Discipline and Punish* is on the trail of another conception of power. A conception which, as will become clear, threatens to render the relationship between (an)archaeology and genealogy distinctly more complicated and, at any rate, no longer permits the juxtaposing of the two disciplines merely on the basis of the same external connection that prevailed in the first power-knowledge model. A second model obtrudes itself, a model in which the hyphen seems to eat away at the meanings of the two terms conjoined. But this model is already weighted down with the structure of Foucault's quotation marks. Foucault's attempt to make the genealogy of the prison bear fruit for the genealogy of the human sciences is at stake here in its entirety. And yet, precisely this 'common history of power relations and object relations'[154] runs the risk of lapsing back to pregenealogical conceptions.

(v) *Third attempt at differentiation (internal connection between power and knowledge)*

As we have already shown, the prison is, for Foucault, a kind of 'permanent observatory'. It functions like 'an apparatus of knowledge' keeping a constant watch on the behaviour of the inmates in order to be able to know and combat the potential dangers lurking within their conduct.[155] The kind of control exerted here is '*a la fois connaissance et pouvoir*' – '*both* knowledge and power'.[156] This control confronts the individual with a normality he must match up to and, at the same time, registers his deviations from this axis of normality. In Foucault's view, the prison introduces a new type of power: a power which disciplines and normalizes, but which is, by that same token, also compelled to observe the individuals it seeks to form: 'the elaboration [*aménagement*] of a power-knowledge over individuals'.[157] Power-knowledge: one has control over the person one observes; one sees 'without being seen'[158] and one can only see what one sees in this way because one is oneself not seen. One can only observe because one controls, and one controls all the more and gains the more power as one observes and acquires knowledge. This is doubtless one of the meanings Foucault ascribes to the words '*à la fois*' (both) when he writes 'both knowledge and power'. But, given the foregoing analysis of the power-knowledge concept, it must also be clear that this cannot be the basic meaning. If this were the case, then the genealogy of the human sciences could only be linked to the prison in an external way: power would direct its light on individuals and thereby gain knowledge,[159] and, on the basis of this knowledge, it would open up a field of objects or data about objects (record cards, registers, biographies, statistics) for the human sciences.[160] We recognize our first model again here. A model on the basis of which, strictly speaking, it is not possible to think the *commonality* of these two histories – that of 'power relations' (the prison) and that of 'object relations' (the human sciences). Foucault can only hold to this thesis by basing himself on another concept of power which is built up around another network of metaphors: 'production', 'technology', 'manufacture' *fabrication*).

He seems to want to take these – industrial – metaphors very literally. The individual is now no longer that which is taken unawares by the light of power and which loses its anonymity when entered in a register. It is a product, 'a *reality* fabricated by this specific technology of power that I have called "discipline"'.[161] The registering, observing, labelling, and rendering (re-)cognizable, the disciplining and normalizing does not leave what it relates to unaffected. Rather, it calls into being a reality which did not previously exist, as though the light of power is not only something which illuminates, but rather an element or milieu in which something flourishes: 'a *new object* was being formed'.[162] But this light metaphor is perhaps too peaceable; it ascribes too ethereal a character to power and leaves out of the account the enormous power of invention by which disciplinary techniques fabricate useful individuals.[163] It takes an unconscionable amount of time and energy and requires a great deal of organization and a particular kind of architecture to turn an inmate into a delinquent, and, for Foucault, this means someone with a 'soul', 'the little soul of the criminal, which the ... apparatus of punishment fabricated'.[164] He is clear and apodictic here: that soul is a 'produced ... reality',[165] the 'correlative of a technique of power'.[166] More importantly, it represents 'the reference of a certain type of knowledge, the machinery by which the power relations give rise to a possible corpus of knowledge, and knowledge extends [*reconduit*] and reinforces the effects of this power'.[167]

If Foucault is right to see in the 'soul' a kind of link between power and knowledge, then not only would the – at first sight – curious programme of linking the genealogy of the human sciences with that of the prison be made more acceptable, but the 'power-knowledge' concept could itself gain by it. The ground for this connection would then no longer lie in the fact that power affords knowledge *access* to a domain of objects (first model), but in the fact that it itself 'produces' this object domain. The link would no longer be 'external' but 'internal': 'The processes of objectification originate in the very tactics of power and of the arrangement of its exercise,'[168] writes Foucault, and his entire analysis of the prison would seem to be directed towards demonstrating this point of view. Hence the insistence with which he defends the idea that the delinquent is a *product* of the prison. The shifting of the judge's attention on to the 'person' behind the offender, the desire to cure rather than to punish – this juridico-anthropological turn within penal functioning[169] – is an effect of the penal logic of the prison and not, for example, the result of a need, which already existed before, to be able to provide better grounds for the sentence in relation to the question of guilt: 'It is as a convict, as a point of application for punitive mechanisms, that the offender is constituted himself as the object of possible knowledge.'[170] The motivating force for the movement by which the delinquent becomes an 'individual to know' (*individu à connaître*)[171] originates in the prison. This movement is not the effect of the discovery of the delinquent by human-scientific rationality.[172] It is, rather, that this movement makes that rationality possible by creating a possible 'field' for it. The fact that, with the figure of the delinquent, the prison calls into being 'a whole horizon of possible knowledge',[173] that it is a place 'where ... the power to punish ... silently organizes a field of objectivity'[174] means for Foucault that power is linked with or doubled by (se double de) an 'object relation',[175] a field of possible knowledge. Knowledge or the possibility of knowledge seems to be generated in – or by – these practices of power.

So far as this analysis of delinquency is concerned, it can at any rate be said that Foucault takes great pains not to think the connection between knowledge and power in the sense of a mere juxtaposition. And yet there is much that remains unclear here: if one must speak of an internal connection, why should one then deny that the human sciences emerged from the prison?[176] What can it mean to say that they did not emerge from there, but none the less were 'conveyed by a specific and new modality of power' which was able to develop in exemplary form in the prison system?[177] That power is a vehicle of knowledge or is laden with knowledge would seem on the one hand to mean for Foucault that it contributes to a climate within which certain forms of knowledge could arise: 'the fact ... that, from a particular point onwards, the behaviour of human beings became a problem to be analysed and solved is linked ... to power mechanisms. Which, at a particular moment in time ... cut out [découpé] this object – society, man etc – and presented it as a problem to be solved.'[178] The concept of découpage[179] – cutting or carving out (!) – points, at the same time, however, to the violence associated with the conditions of possibility of the human sciences. The mechanisms of power not only give rise to a possible problematization of a particular object, but bring that object itself into being. The human sciences only possess a referent – man, the soul, the individual, the delinquent – because and in so far as that referent is a product or fabrication of power, incorporated in 'a technological ensemble that forms and cuts out the object to which it applies its instruments'.[180] Power and knowledge are linked internally: they are linked by the referent.

(vi) *Falling back to pre-genealogical conceptions?*

The understanding that the referent of knowledge or of particular forms of knowledge is not pre-given, but presupposes a genealogy, would seem to be capable of salvaging the 'power-knowledge' concept, but not in such a way as to satisfy Foucault. It is perhaps possible on the basis of this understanding to formulate a genealogical critique of the self-understanding of a particular knowledge. It is even conceivable that such a genealogy of the referent can be employed to explain the non-contingent link between particular forms of knowledge and their contexts of application.[181] It is quite inadmissible, however, to make use of this understanding to underpin a (non-trivial)[182] critique of the scientificity of the human sciences. Asserting that power is productive and produces reality (or referentiality) or postulating the need for another concept of power could perhaps compel us to break with a particular illusion, which might be inherent in knowledge or some forms of knowledge. But even if the meaning of knowledge were thereby shifted, even if we were thereby forced to rethink the whole relationship between knowledge (or science) and ideology,[183] this would still not put us in a position to provide a critique of the scientificity of particular disciplines. Genealogy would seem not to make such a critique easier but more difficult. Everything points to the price for such a critique inevitably being a lapsing back to pre-genealogical conceptions. Hence the importance of Foucault's quotation marks. They are much more than the expression of a stipulative definition of scientificity: they reveal the fragility of its entire conceptual armoury.

In reality, the difficulties Foucault finds himself confronted with in his critique of the scientificity of the human sciences originate in the shift of meaning the concept of power undergoes – and must undergo – in the course of his analysis, in order to rescue the power-knowledge concept. The break with the traditional idea that power 'excludes', 'represses', 'censors', 'abstracts', 'masks', 'conceals'[184] leads to such a thoroughgoing change in the meaning of the concept of power that there emerges, beneath the empirical phenomena of power, a constitutive dimension which threatens to make a critique of the pure actuality of power or the factual link between power and knowledge impossible. The understanding that this connection is constitutive, that no knowledge can escape it, that power is productive and not repressive, could lead one to think that it can only be bought at the price of the 'systematic ambiguity' of this power concept.[185] Foucault's concept of power would then, as it were, be caught up in the 'irritating dual role' of an empirical-transcendental analysis: 'empirical' in so far as it involves power relations which have to do with the conditions of emergence and context of application of knowledge; 'transcendental' because it

figures at the same time in an 'analysis of power technologies' ...
'which are meant to explain how scientific discourse about man is
possible at all', and, consequently, relates to power relations as
conditions of the constitution of knowledge.[186] This much is clear:
if Foucault wanted to avoid the collapse of his entire programme, he
would have to further nuance his concept of power and differentiate
between the two levels of analysis. He would have to ask, for
example, under what conditions 'power' can be productive and
whether the productivity of 'power' does not render a 'repression'
necessary. Were it to be based on this conception of a 'necessary
repression', such a concept of power would have broken with all the
usual connotations of the empirical category of power and the entire
problem would consist in connecting the two levels back together.
But it would also enable us better to understand the workings of
empirical phenomena of power and to clarify the conditions under
which a 'critique of power' (Honneth) can be carried out. Foucault's
quotation marks prevent him from taking this path. They lead to a
levelling of the concept of power, a systematic reduction which has
led to Foucault forcing together '[i]n his basic concept of power ...
the idealist idea of transcendental synthesis with the presupposi-
tions of an empiricist ontology'.[187] Deleuze sums up this difficulty
in the formula 'Power "produces reality" before it represses'[188] –
this 'before' bespeaking a logical relation, which names a problem
rather than solving it: power is *at the same time* productive and
repressive.

Paradoxically, Foucault's critique of the human sciences brings
the repressive aspect of power to the fore. This leads him into the
very danger he was trying to avoid: if power (also) represses, then
there is an instance which is repressed and, in that repression, its
originarity is infringed.[189] For Foucault, this instance is the body.
It is clear from many of his statements here that this plays the same
systematic role as, earlier, the concept of 'madness itself'. He
speaks, for example, repeatedly of a 'revolt' or a 'resistance' of the
body and regards discipline as a procedure for reducing the
'political force' of the body.[190] And the body is said to be 'directly
involved in a political field'; hence it necessarily becomes the object
of a 'political economy', a 'political technology' or 'anatomy'.[191]
This understanding that bodies have a history, which derives from
Nietzsche's genealogy of morals,[192] forces us, in Foucault's view,
into a 'microphysics of power, whose field of validity is situated
in a sense between these great functionings [the apparatuses and

the institutions] and the *bodies themselves* with their materiality and their forces'.[193]

These expressions are sufficiently misleading to embarrass an author who wished to forsake any 'depth-hermeneutic perspective'.[194] They are, however, indispensable *if he is to hold to his critique of the human sciences*. That critique presupposes that the idea of the productivity of power be so qualified as to lose its meaning: *if* power is ultimately repressive, if it 'train[s]' bodies and 'forces' them 'to carry out tasks', 'submit[s]' them and 'reduce[s]' them,[195] then what it brings into being is only apparently an autonomous 'reality'.[196] One cannot, then, in any sense understand what it might mean to say that 'through this technique of subjection a *new object* was being formed',[197] *unless* one were prepared to regard that subjection as necessary and inevitable. Yet *Foucault's quotation marks* forbid him that outlet. They stand around the referent of knowledge itself: 'The man described for us ... is already in himself the effect of a subjection much more profound than himself. A "soul" inhabits him and brings him to existence ... the soul is the prison of the body.'[198]

The human sciences do not seem to be sciences at all because they do not possess any 'genuine' referent or, more precisely, because their referent only comes into being through a subjection of the body: 'a "soul" to be known and a subjection to be maintained'.[199] This subjection is unavoidable if the human sciences are to be able to emerge and if, by their existence, they keep that subjection in being. It is unavoidable *de facto* but not necessary *de jure* – it is illegitimate: 'de-individualization'[200] must occur and, for that reason, it is necessary to call into doubt the scientificity of these 'sciences of the individual'.[201] Quotation marks must be put around them.

Everything points to these quotation marks being responsible for the fact that genealogy in *Discipline and Punish*, as earlier in *Histoire de la folie*, only ever remains a project for the future. And here too, as in the critique of psychology, the critique of the scientificity of the human sciences would seem to be based, in the last instance, on the idea of an original harm inflicted: not until the body is subjected to compulsion can we speak of the human being (*l'homme*).[202] In espousing such conceptions, Foucault runs the risk of becoming a proponent of precisely that 'metaphysics of origins' against which he was seeking to arm himself with his claim to be engaged in genealogy.[203] It would be going too far, however, to assert that *Discipline and Punish* really only covers the same set of issues which lay at the heart of *Histoire de la folie*. Thus, for example, Foucault presents his analysis of discipline as a genealogy of a *specific* set of techniques applied to the body.[204] That the critique he sought to underpin with this genealogy ultimately led not to these techniques *in their specificity* being called into question, but the application of techniques as such, and that it was not the particular way the body is subjected but the fact of its subjection that was adduced (and had to be adduced) as an argument against the human sciences, would all seem more to be opposed to the problematic of *Discipline and Punish* than to follow from it. All of this would seem rather to distort than to express that problematic. The implications of this analysis are clear: *if one does not wish to distort Foucault's problematic, one must break with the kind of critique of which his quotation marks are symptomatic.*

Before we attempt, in a last move, to protect the project of a critique of objectivism from these quotation marks, we should first, more or less summarizing the argument so far, look into their exemplary status in – and influence on – the Foucault debate. As soon as it becomes clear that Foucault's later work on sexuality and the discussion to which it gave rise also stand under the sign of these quotation marks, the question of the author can no longer be avoided. What is important here is not so much to ask 'What is an author?'[205] as to ask *where* he is, where he locates himself in a work which escapes – and must escape – his grasp if it wishes to retain its significance with regard to the questions it has posed or, more precisely, the questions which it allows to be posed.

The Exemplary Status of Foucault's Quotation Marks

A history of madness, an investigation of the order of things, a genealogy of the prison: there is, at first sight, no connection between these three works. Only the signature of an author, who had always dreamed of being able to write from a position of perfect anonymity,[1] seems able to supply a non-arbitrary connection between books which, without that author's name, might perhaps have ended up in quite different libraries. Perhaps Foucault is right: '*Le nom est une facilité.*'[2] Without that name as guarantee, there would be no periodizations. His texts would have been taken for what they are: a small hand-grenade lobbed into the camp of psychiatry, a rather obtuse study for specialists in the classical period which gets carried away towards the end in a prophetic vision of the end of man; a document arising out of discussions on prison reform. There is no reason, then, to do violence by reading anything into them, no compelling grounds to read the texts as a whole or as a development – as a *train* of thought – except the apparently irrelevant fact that they were written by the same 'individual'. And that this is known. And importance is attached to it.

This may well be true. It indicates to what extent our reading is dependent on the identification of texts.[3] And one can understand someone mourning this lost anonymity. It reminds us how much our reading itself has become a text-identifying mechanism.[4] But one may, none the less, ask whether it would simply take the author's name being left out to restore this anonymity in its original state. Reading Foucault suggests, rather, the opposite: what makes the texts recognizable and lends them unity is not so much the name of the author, printed in capitals on the cover, as the inconspicuous, little signature which is characteristic of his work and defines it to such a degree that, without these quotation marks, it might be the work of another. There is, without any doubt, a unity and continuity between Foucault's studies of madness, the *epistemè* and the prison: this is the repeatedly renewed problematization of the scientificity of the human sciences. Were it not for this 'will to critique' and the specific form of that critique, the difficulties would not have arisen which ultimately kept Foucault, in *Histoire de la folie*, from a definitive turn away from the scientific ideal of psychology. And, similarly, the need would not have arisen for the (an-)archaeology of *The Order of Things* to base itself on an ideal of scientificity borrowed from the empirical sciences. Were it not for his quotation marks, we should not have had the contradictions produced by the power-knowledge concept – contradictions in which this concept in its turn became so entangled.

And yet, are we not doing Foucault an injustice when we tie down his work, which is so diverse in its subject-matter, to the theme of the human sciences? Did not the analysis of *Discipline and Punish* already clearly show that a subject like discipline would have to be treated separately if one does not want to miss what is at stake in such a 'microphysics of power'? Was it not precisely due to our fixation on the theme of the human sciences that we were led to believe that, in spite of all his genealogical intentions, Foucault's quotation marks caused *Discipline and Punish* to run aground on a metaphysics of origins (*les corps eux-mêmes*)? Would not all these hesitant analyses and endless deconstructions lose their purpose if one were for once to take the title literally and resist the temptation to pursue once again, in the studies on sexuality, which represent the next step in Foucault's thinking, the question of the function of the notorious quotation marks? Quotation marks which may perhaps have played a part in shaping Foucault's development up to *Discipline and Punish* but which, in his more mature thinking on power – thinking which only occasionally concerned itself with the problematic of science – would have disappeared once and for all.[5] Foucault had, it seems, only to leave the field of the human sciences and write a history of sexuality (3.1) to clarify definitively the status of his critique (3.2).

3.1. A history without quotation marks?

1. The stakes: the break with the repression hypothesis

In the first part of *The History of Sexuality*, Foucault has not just a theoretical but also a political motive for deepening his conception of the productivity of power. What is at issue here is not simply the historico-theoretical problem of whether 'prohibition, censorship, and denial [*dénégation*] [are] truly the forms through which power is exercised', but also the political suspicion that the critique of the repression of sexuality 'is ... part of the same historical network as the thing it denounces ... by calling it "repression"'.[6] To believe that power is only effective in a repressive mode, to believe that it represses sexuality, and that this repression can be combated by speaking uninhibitedly about what was (and had to be) for so long discreetly kept silent might not only, in Foucault's view, rest on a misunderstanding of the nature of (modern) power, but might even strengthen that power in its essential mechanisms.[7] The 'naturalistic' hypothesis of a *sexe sauvage*,[8] of a relentless drive resisting a power that does all it can to repress it, is not only theoretically unattractive, but also politically dangerous.[9] It contributes in fact to allowing the real power mechanisms to remain hidden. If one wishes to understand these, one must abandon the traditional theories of power which underpin such 'repression hypotheses'.[10] The critique of power must be freed from all relics of a philosophy of origins. One must write a genealogy of sexuality which is 'historical and critical',[11] but which none the less differs from the way the critique is shaped in the earlier works. One must write a history without quotation marks.

Foucault does not take on the repression hypothesis on its own terrain.[12] It seems the shift of perspective he effects is able to free him from the task of an attempt at refutation in the strict sense: 'The question I would like to pose is not, Why are we repressed? but rather, Why do we say, with so much passion ... that we are repressed?'[13] Our sexuality would not so much seem to be repressed as, rather, to seduce us into an unstoppable drive to confess. The belief in a sexuality condemned to silence would seem to be constantly spurring us to speak about it; it provokes us to ignore the prohibition on speaking and to talk at length and with a conspicuous sense of detail about our own silence. The theme of repressed sexuality is, in Foucault's view, only 'a way of giving shape to the requirement to speak about the matter, a fable that is indispensable to the endlessly proliferating economy of the discourse on sex'.[14] That economy maintains itself by presenting sexuality as that which, above all else, is kept silent. Every attempt to bring out into the open what is kept unsaid seems necessarily self-defeating – not because it is unsuccessful, but because it is too successful. The secret seems not so much to be what cannot and must not be spoken, as what is constantly, repeatedly being spoken. The secret of this secret would seem to be that everyone speaks about it and yet firmly believes it to be inexpressible.[15] The secret is the *simulacrum*[16] which enables power to unfold its effects: instead of limiting discussion of sex, it produces a discourse which spins off and ramifies in all directions, and which gradually acquires the form of a '*scientia sexualis*'. A science which would perhaps not be conceivable without the repression hypothesis and which, none the less, by the mere fact of its existence, disproves that hypothesis. There is no less discussion of sexuality, but it is different, and conducted from other discursive perspectives and through other agencies: 'there is not one but many silences'.[17] But there is speech, and that speech feeds on the hope that at its as yet very distant end, when, at the last gasp, there is no longer any veil to conceal the secret, a truth will come to light which will not leave the pain and effort of its 'will to knowledge' unrewarded.

In order to 'define the strategies of power that are immanent in this will to knowledge',[18] Foucault had to leave the terrain of the repression hypothesis. In order to understand why, in a society like ours, there is so much talk about sex and how it came to be believed that our truth has to be sought in sexuality, one must stop comparing the effects of power with those of a gigantic apparatus of repression. Sexuality has not always been embroiled in a grim struggle with a power which apparently could never totally subdue it. It is a more recent phenomenon, and one *produced*[19] by a power which has found in the 'will to knowledge' an instrument which makes its operations acceptable, but also an 'effect' which situates them in a broader field: the régime of 'power-knowledge-pleasure', which has set the discourse on human sexuality in train and continues to keep it in being.[20]

2. The 'production' of sexuality

It was a consequence, and also a presupposition, of Foucault's critique of the repression hypothesis that one cease to look for an allegedly repressed substrate.[21] The question whether sexuality/sex is repressed[22] seems to have to cede its place to a formulation which appears initially to function as a kind of research indicator: the repression of sexuality is to be read off from the silence on that subject. That it is not spoken about would indicate that one is dealing with a forbidden area, something whose existence is being denied by the maintenance of silence about it.[23] This shift from an analysis of repressed sexuality to an analysis of a possibly censored discourse on sexuality, which is, at first sight, motivated by considerations of research *technique* is, in fact, rather an expression of a research *strategy* which is to allow Foucault to leave the terrain of the repression hypothesis even before he has set foot upon it. An investigation of sexuality, operating with a vocabulary cast in terms of drives or energetics, is supplanted by a decision to conceive its history as a history of the discourse on sexuality: 'The history of sexuality ... must first be written from the viewpoint of a history of discourses.'[24]

This shift to the level of a discursive analysis is not always clear. Thus Foucault suggests at times that the repression hypothesis is wrong while elsewhere he stresses that he does not wish to refute it.[25] However, this 'confusion' cannot always be put down to an inadequate specification of the level of analysis. The wrongness of the repression hypothesis is not always due to the fact that Foucault 'refutes' it on a terrain which is not its own or, more exactly, lures it on to a terrain where it cannot be thoroughly refuted. Several times in the course of his analysis, Foucault ventures upon the terrain of the repression hypothesis itself. In order to be able to spend time upon that terrain, however, he first had to leave it. In order to know what sexuality is in reality and whether it is repressed, he had first to analyse the discourse on sexuality. Or, more precisely, for this is where he differs from the repression hypothesis, he had to analyse sexuality as discourse, i.e. as something which comes into being in and through discourse and does not precede it. While, from the point of view of the repression hypothesis, censorship maintains a silence about a pre-given something which already has an identity, the 'discursive explosion' which takes the place of a particular kind of silence and perhaps has its condition of possibility in that silence[26] is not for Foucault the event by which the long concealed truth of sexuality stands revealed, but the historical incision which first shapes and produces sexuality by bringing it into relation with truth. Hence, it is not unimportant to operate first on the level of a discourse 'on' sexuality. For it is at this level that what one believes to be repressed is in fact produced.

(i) Sexuality as discourse

There is no *single* discourse on 'sexuality'. What is called sexuality can be traced back to a sudden increase in discourses which, over the course of the eighteenth century, directed their attention from the most varied quarters and within diverse institutional contexts to a number of 'timeless gestures',[27] ancient secrets and almost involuntary caresses beneath which, suddenly, a disturbed nature came to be suspected. The difference between the sexes has always, admittedly, had something of a mystery about it, and the relationship with one's own sex has certainly never been unproblematic. Perhaps the 'deadly secrets'[28] which influence the rhythm of fertility or are directed against its effect are as old as mating itself or as onanism, a *touchant-touché*, as yet without intentionality, except perhaps for that of an awakening sexuality.[29] What was new and not self-evident, however, was that, within the space of a few years, the body of the woman was hystericalized and sodomy or hermaphroditism related to the structure of the perverse personality. It was new that demography and politics concerned themselves with 'spontaneous' birth control and that the sexuality of children became a problem of public policy, capable of determining the future of the species. Masturbating children, Malthusian parents, perverts and hysterical mothers:[30] a whole new population stepped forth from the shadows, a population whose existence had previously not been suspected and which would perhaps have remained forever unknown were it not for the insights of medicine, psychiatry and psychology, pedagogy, political criticism, penal justice and demography. Or at least it appears so. The glow from all these various *foyers* 'from which discourse emanated'[31] was supposed merely to make visible what had too long remained hidden. We would at last know what had been going on in the dark. We would at last grasp the deeper meaning of all these strange noises – the cries and whispers which had long been familiar but never regarded as serious, since little attention had been paid to them.

So long as one thinks in these terms, one has not left the terrain of the repression hypothesis. One would still be compelled to refute it. One would have to point out, for example, that sexuality is not repressed, at least not in the sense that it cannot be spoken about. And, with this argument, one would become entangled in the 'ambiguity' of repression-thinking: medical discourse was, admittedly, able to express itself on homosexuality or masturbation, but this does not alter the fact that 'spontaneous' talk of sexuality was cleaned up at more or less the same time: expressions were deleted, the vocabulary recast, popular fantasy reined in.[32] One would find oneself compelled to compare the one silence with the other and come to see, ultimately, that there is no possible comparison between them: something always remains in the dark, no *foyer* of discourse is powerful enough to cast light on its own areas of shade. One can understand why Foucault might wish to leave the field of the repression hypothesis behind: not just because it is unverifiable at the discursive level (one silence gives way to another), but also because it prevents us from understanding what happens when speech occurs and a discourse forms.

In order to distinguish his own position from the repression hypothesis, Foucault wishes to defend a kind of 'historical nominalism'.[33] Homosexuality, for example, is not a timeless experience which has only been correctly conceptualized in recent times.[34] Even less is it the name by which only recently a different, more profound experience has been misunderstood. It only becomes comprehensible in terms of a discourse carried on about it at a particular point in time. It does not precede that discourse, *nor, however, is it an effect of that discourse*. The light of this discourse is not a neutral source, illuminating something which was already present in the semi-darkness. Rather, it allows something to 'solidify',[35] it organizes a *materia prima*, which could also be organized differently, has been organized differently. It reorganizes shadows and gives them an unpredictable form. Or, to put it yet another way, since the expressions employed so far still suggest too strongly a pre-given distribution of light and shade and are still based too much on the idea of an external source of light: in some way or another – and Foucault wishes to understand in what way – something like a chemical reaction takes place, things which have long been 'solidified' become fluid again and take on another form, shadows reorganize themselves or are compelled by the glow from this process to conform to other laws of light and darkness. Without this solidification process there would be nothing to see, but the fact that something is seen is not a result of the arbitrariness of this process: homosexuality no more exists than does madness, 'but, for all that, it is not nothing'.[36]

These light metaphors may seem exaggerated, but Foucault faces an immense problem here. On the one hand, he wishes to deny the transhistorical reality of phenomena like homosexuality or madness; on the other, however, he wants also to leave them sufficient objective reality that they remain, none the less, in need of explanation. (Homo)sexuality does not precede its discourse and yet it is also not a discursive illusion. In the first case one would fall back into a realism which, after *Histoire de la folie*, Foucault sought to combat with all the resources at his disposal; in the second case, one would be promulgating a kind of discursive idealism which, instead of according too little weight to discourse, would go to the opposite extreme.[37] It makes no sense either to have the object precede the discourse or to have it dissolve into that discourse. One must think their co-originarity and understand how they are 'co-constituted'.[38]

Thus Foucault sees himself confronted in the first volume of *The History of Sexuality* (French title: *La Volonté de savoir*) with the same problem he sought to resolve in *Discipline and Punish* by means of the power-knowledge concept. It will be remembered that the transition there from an external to an internal relation between power and knowledge risked stripping the concept of power of all its usual connotations: the empirical phenomenon whose mechanisms Foucault wanted to investigate seemed to possess a kind of quasi-transcendental capacity to create a field of empiricity. In order to rescue its empirical-critical connotation (and his critique of science), Foucault had to make recourse to the solution of *Histoire de la folie*: the process (of solidification) which connects power and knowledge or makes up their internal articulation, ultimately does violence to the 'matter' to which it relates, a violence which is to be avoided and therefore condemned. *La Volonté de savoir* takes a different course: the effect of power lies not in doing violence to an as yet intact, virginal 'matter', but in seducing it. Foucault discovers subjectivity – a 'matter' which can be seduced. In order to understand what is going on in the discourse on sexuality, he directs his attention to mechanisms of subjectivization: procedures which enable 'something to recognize itself as subject'.

(ii) *Power and pleasure: a subjectivizing subjection?*

Discipline and Punish saw in the disciplining of bodies a process which brings individuality/subjectivity into being in many different kinds of ways. Whether that subjectivity is a primary one, a historically subjective cluster of amorphous vital forces, or a secondary one, which normalizes an already existent subjectivity, is not important here. Foucault's analysis was confronted with the problem that power produces a form of subjectivity which cannot, admittedly, be an illusion, but which also would not seem to fit with the intuitions that normally accompany the concept of subjectivity. The term 'subjectivizing subjection' (*assujetissement*), which was introduced in the course of these analyses, was the name given to this embarrassment: the emphasis can be placed either on the first part of this term or on the second, where it reminds us that we are still dealing with a product of power of which we must rid ourselves. *La Volonté de savoir* goes a step further: here again, '*assujetissement*' means something like 'subjectivizing subjection' (and not subjectivization *tout court*),[39] but the first part of this expression seems almost to dominate the second: admittedly, subjectivization is imposed, but it is also accepted. The play of power becomes more subtle: it is connected with pleasure, as Foucault suggests with a hyphen.[40]

Foucault sees this connection between power and pleasure as being represented *par excellence* in confession, a procedure which is indeed much older than the modern *dispositif* of sexuality, and yet defines its essential properties.[41] The fact that homosexuality, in contrast to sodomy, forms part of this *dispositif* connects with this relationship to confession. Unlike sodomy, it is not the name for a transgression by a juridical subject, but a *narrative* about 'a past, a case history and a childhood . . . a character of life, a form of life'.[42] It is characteristic of the investigation of homosexuality that it does not confine itself to establishing that a transgression has taken place, but also wants an explanation of that act. Like the delinquent, the homosexual must also say who he is. He must not only confess his guilt, he must recognize *himself* in it. He becomes a 'personage', a bearer of a particular biography: one whose essential characteristics lie in a kind of 'interior androgyny', in an 'hermaphrodism of the soul'.[43] His sexuality explains his person in its totality. This is why it must be spoken. And since, to a large extent, it lies beyond the scope of external observation, it requires a first-person discourse. A discourse which tells everything and leaves nothing out, not even the most intimate thoughts. At the beginning of the nineteenth century the homosexual, together with many other representatives of what Foucault terms 'peripheral sexualities', became a '*confessing animal*'.[44] He thus situated himself (or was situated) within a Christian monastic tradition of confession: 'an indefinite objectivization of the self by the self' – but an objectivization which was subjectivizing in its effects.[45]

That this objectivization of the self can be subjectivizing in its effects is not perhaps so amazing if one considers the status of verbalization in psychoanalysis. Here too we find first-person discourse which constructs all kinds of identifications and breaks up others, and in this way expresses its desire and thereby becomes the 'subject' of that desire. Foucault's perspective is, however, different from the psychoanalytic in that, for him, verbalization in the confession would not seem to result in one becoming the subject of one's desire by assuming it in the first person. He would seem rather to take the view that, in this process, something which precedes desire has a form pressed upon it which it cannot have *de jure*. Power seems to make use of the procedure of confession to impose a form on a kind of original, diffuse and as yet unencoded pleasure: 'so many pressing questions *singularized* the pleasures felt by the one who had to reply. They were *fixed* by a gaze, *isolated* and *animated* by the attention they received.'[46] The confession is not an innocent procedure. It enables power to function as a 'siren', which attracts ('*attire*') and 'draws out' ('*extrait*') the 'peculiarities' ('*étrangetés*') over which it keeps watch.[47] Hence the effect of power is not to be conceived as exclusion or repression. It does not set boundaries for sexuality, but rather 'multipl[ies]' it by 'includ[ing]' many 'singular sexualities' in individual bodies and, as a result, it possesses a mechanism of classification.[48] All these endless lists of perversions (exhibitionists, fetishists, zoophiles, zooerasts, auto-monosexualists, mixoscopophiles, dyspareunist women and many others),[49] all these distinctions of sexuality by different ages, by types of relation between the partners (doctor–patient, teacher–student ...), by place (prison, school ...) are, for Foucault, the 'correlate of exact procedures of power' which are all more or less mirror images of the confessional or can be derived from it: 'These polymorphous conducts were actually extracted from people's bodies and from their pleasures; or rather, they were solidified in them; they were drawn out, revealed, isolated, intensified, incorporated, by multifarious power devices.'[50] It is as a consequence of the process of solidification associated with confession that particular 'things' ('timeless gestures') become meaningful, and also that they come at that same time – and not before – to be conceived of as autonomous elements.

Solidify, isolate, fix, draw out: it is the aim of these expressions to underscore the productivity of power. The discovery of the perversions is not, for example, to be interpreted as a sudden shift of attention to things long tolerated which are now condemned in the interest of promoting a privileged model-sexuality. They are, for Foucault, 'really extracted from people's bodies and from their pleasures'.[51] Or, to adopt a formulation reminiscent of *Discipline and Punish*, from the undifferentiated muddle of bodily behaviours and delights, power 'cuts' out particular segments and names them. But these segments only come into being through this cutting and only acquire their internal character from it: they do not exist before they are isolated, but their being isolated is, rather, a condition of their existence.

We are already familiar with the problems to which such an interpretation of the effects of power can lead: what is produced by power seems to acquire, by a kind of process of e-mergence, an autonomy or a character of reality which emancipates the product from its point of descent (*Herkunft*). These are products of power, but if they are not to be illusions and genuinely to constitute a reality, then they are also more than merely this. Although the overall analysis pointed in this direction, in *Discipline and Punish* Foucault had ultimately denied such an emergent quality.[52] Yet in *La Volonté de savoir*, he would seem to be making an attempt to explain it.

That the violent 'cutting' or 'carving out' (*découpage*) which is produced by the appearance of power might, in the end, give rise to something which escapes the influence of that power (in our context, the confessional subject of one of the many sexualities) is only strange if one sees all the activity as lying only on one side of the process and views that activity as a demiurgic act shaping an indifferent material. For Foucault, power may perhaps have a demiurgic effect, but 'power' (le *pouvoir*) itself is no demiurge. Here, Foucault is once again seeking to be 'nominalistic'.[53] One cannot really speak of 'power' (le *pouvoir*) without further qualification. Power is not localized somewhere, in the hands of a particular person like a piece of transferable property. It is a relation, the name of a connection or a strategic relationship between two relata which provoke one another and allow themselves to be provoked. If confession were based merely on compulsion, it would be unsuitable as a procedure of power. Anyone who confesses is also seduced into doing so and his confession in turn seduces the person listening: 'The power that lets itself be invaded by the pleasure it is pursuing; *and opposite it, power asserting itself in the pleasure of showing off, scandalizing or resisting.*'[54] But if, as is asserted in this quotation, power is not located exclusively on the one side, if its effects are rather to be found in a reciprocal 'seduction', a charm or an excitation, if it caresses bodies 'with its eyes, intensifying areas, electrifying surfaces',[55] then must not the modern *dispositif* of sexuality be regarded as a grandiose legacy of the nineteenth century, binding together 'parents and children, adults and adolescents, educators and students, doctors and patients, and the psychiatrist with his hysteric and his perverts' in 'perpetual spirals of power and pleasure'?[56] Why continue to speak here of subjectivizing *subjection*? Who or what is really being subjected? And if a subjection is taking place, is it not happening in an improper sense? As a consequence of allowing oneself to be seduced? Can one allow oneself to be seduced and yet still feel subjected, particularly when the effect of this is that one recognizes oneself as the subject of a particular sexuality? What objection can there really be to the 'will to know' (*la volonté de savoir*); why must one 'refuse to be identified by and with the aid of a particular form of sexuality'?[57] Why should we really oppose the *dispositif* of sexuality?

We are not arguing that Foucault did not ask these questions or that they had, by some incomprehensible myopia, escaped his attention. They are, to the contrary, present in more than one place in the first part of his studies on sexuality – if not as questions explicitly posed, then at least as a kind of unease which keeps the analysis moving forward. But the answers which these questions prompted are not always satisfying. Thus Foucault points out that the enormous dissemination or distribution of procedures of meaning-generation in the course of the eighteenth century is not an isolated phenomenon which could simply be explained as increasing curiosity or a new mentality. That these procedures were deployed outside the sphere of Christian spirituality is attributed to the fact that they were functionally useful to the development of particular power-mechanisms to which the discourse on sex had become essential.[58] Certainly, this political, economic and technical 'administration' of sexuality is a clear sign of the connection between the *dispositif* of sexuality and empirical power interests, and recent discussions of organ transplants give us every reason to take very seriously what Foucault has termed 'bio-power'. The problems with which this development confronts us are, without any doubt, enormous. They indicate how natural the move to a totally 'administered world' could become.[59] But the current relevance of these analyses cannot be allowed to prevent us from examining more closely the arguments on which they are based. It might well be that our will to know is not just historically unique and far from natural, but also dangerous. It is quite possible that a consequence of this whole compulsion to confess and the will to discover the truth in ourselves (in that part of us which remains most hidden) may be that the process in which we become subjects of our desire simultaneously subjects us. But the means which Foucault deploys to corroborate this supposition are, at many points, incompatible with his other analyses. Thus, for all his arguing against the repression hypothesis, this does not, in the end, prevent him from merely displacing that hypothesis himself, as, for example, when he writes:[60] 'The rallying point for the counterattack against the deployment of sexuality ought not to be sex-desire, but bodies and pleasures.'[61]

To be sure, Foucault wanted to write a 'history of bodies' and not a 'history of mentalities' investigating changing conceptions about the body.[62] But all the trouble he took to show how this 'sexual body' was 'touched' (*frôlé*) by power and, as a result, took on other forms, how it solidified in 'regional' sexualities and 'anchored' and 'incorporated' these[63] – all this stressing of the productivity of power which bases itself on the body and its pleasures does not seem able to prevent him from calling in the end on the same 'bodies and pleasures' to provide support for the resistance to that power. The bodies which so easily allowed themselves to be worked upon, which so readily assumed the form of polymorphous sexualities, are, at the same time, supposed to possess a greater originarity which enables them to escape the spirals of power and pleasure and repulse all these products of power. Curiously, the history of bodies becomes here again something which happens to them. To prevent the history of sexuality from becoming another 'history "of ...", in the sense of a study of the transformations of an objective content',[64] the history of the body is again cast, against Foucault's own intention, in terms of the same model of a history of decline deployed in *Histoire de la folie*. This is all the more surprising since, in *La Volonté de savoir*, Foucault saw the 'initiative' for this decline lying partly with bodies themselves. For this reason, the history of decline is not based, as it is in *Histoire de la folie*, on a catastrophe descending, in this case, upon a pure, inviolate corporeality. The possibility of decline lies in the origin itself. Unlike 'madness itself', the body allows itself to be seduced.

But what does this mean? Who or what is the agency in the body to which the pleasure of seduction can be ascribed? Who is really the subject of confession?[65] Who is the bearer of the will to know? One finds no answer to these questions in *La Volonté de savoir*. They require a 'turn' which, rather than resolve these questions, turns its back on them.

3. Subjectivization – a 'turn'?

The analyses of the first part of the history of sexuality run up against what we can now see as a characteristic difficulty: everything which made the assumption of an emergent subjectivity plausible seemed, at the same time, to render a critique of that subjectivity impossible. One must either accept that confession entails a power-relation in which the play of seducing and being seduced brings a specific subjectivity into being or one must see in seduction a kind of corruption by which one of the relata is affected, in which case one is faced with the problem of having to reject this corruption without being able to explain its possibility. Either one accepts the 'susceptibility to corruption' and the possibility of seduction (*plaisir-pouvoir*) and, consequently, forfeits the means of resisting its results, or one holds firm to this resistance, regards seduction as a kind of original evil and forfeits the means to think it. It is clear that neither of these possibilities can satisfy Foucault, the former because it would mean all commitment would disappear from the analyses, the latter because it would rescue the commitment at the cost of the analysis.

The next two parts of *The History of Sexuality*, which did not appear until eight years later, give an impression of wishing to avoid this alternative. They no longer employ the concept of power and would thus seem to have removed the cause of the first difficulty. At the same time, they avoid emotive references to 'bodies and pleasures', thereby creating the impression that they wish finally to leave behind the figures of thought of a metaphysics of origins. Foucault now conceives subjectivity not as a product of power, but as a result of techniques of subjectivization which may indeed have connections with techniques of power but are essentially distinct from them. And instead of appealing to the possibility of 'a different economy of bodies and pleasures'[66] which is to succeed our own, he directs his attention to other such economies preceding ours with the aim of being able to ground this possibility rather than having to presuppose it.

As in volume one of the *History*, this change of perspective also leads to a changed theory being associated with a different perception of the field of research. These two movements are interconnected. The shift of emphasis from the problematic of subjectivizing subjection (*assujetissement*) to that of subjectiviza-tion (*subjectivation*) allows Foucault to outline another 'grid for deciphering history' and the renewed contact with the historical material forces him to give precedence to the analyses of sub-jectivization over those of subjectivizing subjection.

(i) *A genealogy of the ethics of sexuality*

It would be wrong to see in this focusing on the process of subjectivization merely a return to the philosophy of subjectivity. Foucault leaves us in no doubt that this is not his intention. He wishes to investigate the historical constitution of the subject and to use such a genealogy in order to break with the traditional 'philosophy of the subject'.[67] Hence the accent on the 'historicity of the subject', which, in Foucault's view, deprives it of its sovereignty and its 'constitutive character'.[68] In Foucault's view, the subject has a history and it has more than *one* history.[69] Not only is there no 'universal subject form, which one can find everywhere',[70] but there are many ways to experience oneself as a subject and many corresponding subject forms. The subject, notes Foucault with evident satisfaction, is a 'historical and cultural reality' and, as a consequence, subject to change.[71]

These arguments are not by any means new. Foucault had already drawn this lesson in *The Order of Things* from the collapse of a theory of (scientific) knowledge grounded in the philosophy of consciousness and had distanced himself, in his study of the historically variable structures of knowledge, from the idea of a meaning-endowing subject which could explain neither the formative mechanisms of signification nor the structures of systems of meaning. What is new, however, is that, in *The Use of Pleasure* and *The Care of the Self*, Foucault believes he has found arguments which enable him to transpose this critique of the subject to the level of 'practical subjectivity'.[72] The subject does not (or does not exclusively?) experience itself as a moral subject; *it* constitutes *itself* – one sees the difficulty here – as this particular subject of morality. And this is not something which occurs in relation to morality in general, but the process of ethical subjectivization itself determines the material to which this moral experience can be related – a material which is, moreover, as will become clear, itself historically variable.

Whatever else one may think of Foucault's motivation for writing a 'history of the subject',[73] it is clear for the moment that this decision necessarily brought about a clear shift of emphasis within the context of the history of sexuality. In order to understand how the modern individual can experience himself as subject of a 'sexuality', Foucault no longer analyses the processes of power which lead to the 'production' of sexuality, but the 'forms and modalities of the relation to self [*rapport à soi*] by which the individual constitutes and recognizes himself *qua* subject'.[74] The history of sexuality is recast as a 'genealogy of the ethics' of the sexual.[75]

Here Foucault's attention is not directed in the first instance to the moral prescriptions to which sexuality has been subjected, but to the fact that that behaviour came up for ethical 'problematization'. He evinced astonishment that this required an 'exercise of self upon self by which one tries to work out, to transform oneself and to attain a certain mode of being'.[76] Without such an 'exercise of self upon self', one does not become a 'subject of desire' and a subject of sexuality in the modern sense of the word.[77] Other forms of *askesis*, which have led to other *forms of subjectivity* or have been practised for other *reasons*, are conceivable and actually exist.[78] And one is not simply dealing with the same sexual behaviour when one sees in homosexuality the structure of a specific desire or when, like the Greeks, one problematizes erotic relations between men only because they put one of the partners in a subordinate position.[79] In both cases, the *material* to which morality is applied not only has a distinct significance, but also a distinct form. The way it is problematized – with the concepts of desire or those of activity and passivity – in-forms that material in different ways. One recognizes Foucault's *nominalism* here: there were erotic relations between men in Greece, but there was no 'homosexuality'. Homosexuality is not a *universal*, but it is, none the less, something – namely, the result of a problematization, i.e. of a process, which 'doesn't mean representation of a pre-existing object, nor the creation by discourse of an object that doesn't exist'.[80]

One can see how Foucault is keeping here to the theoretical intentions of *La Volonté de savoir* – with the distinctions mentioned above between the what, why, how and wherefore of ethical self-experience – but is none the less fitting them into a different context. The aim is still to understand sexuality (in the modern sense) as a historical 'experience',[81] but this experience is now primarily regarded as a way of behaving towards oneself, as 'the subject's experience of himself'[82] – a formulation which occurs repeatedly and indicates that Foucault is concerned more with gaining insight into the nature of this experience of self than with casting doubt on its authenticity. This is the difference between an analysis which embarks directly on the problematic of subjectivizing subjection and one which seeks first to understand subjectivization before the themes of power and domination are introduced. This is an important shift: instead of stressing the connection between power, knowledge and subjectivity and pushing the whole burden of explanation on to the hyphens between these terms (power-knowledge-pleasure), the texts from Foucault's later period tend increasingly to distinguish between these dimensions and understand them in their internal functioning first, before relating them one to another.[83] And this shift of emphasis certainly has its effects: where *La Volonté de savoir* got into difficulty in its attempt to put the idea of 'subjectivization' alongside that of 'subjection', the late works not only encounter difficulties when it comes to explaining how particular ways of experiencing oneself as a subject lead to a subjectivization *stricto sensu*, but also when they have to elucidate how specific forms of subjectivization can, none the less, result in subjection.

(ii) *The beginnings of the hermeneutics of the self*

This connection between subjectivization and subjection would doubtless have occupied a central place in the unpublished fourth part of *The History of Sexuality*, which was to have formed a kind of transition between the studies of Greece and Rome, one the one hand, and *La Volonté de savoir* on the other. Foucault wanted this analysis of the 'confessions of the flesh'[84] to provide an insight into the process which had led individuals endlessly to analyse and interpret their desire in the hope of gaining insight into the truth of their being. He hoped to show how this Christian 'hermeneutics of desire'[85] made possible the modern 'will to knowledge' and hence in a certain sense anticipated a way of behaving towards oneself which should no longer be regarded as worthy of saving.[86] Whatever surprises the as yet unpublished manuscript of the fourth part may hold in store, it is clear that the significance of the specificity of Christianity cannot chiefly be a question of historiographical completeness. It is theoretical and critical. Theoretical, because Foucault wanted to investigate there to what extent the concepts mobilized in *The Use of Pleasure* (volume 2) and *The Care of the Self* (volume 3) are able to resolve the difficulties of the first volume, without necessitating his abandoning the project of writing a history of sexuality. And critical, since not only the unity, but also the political commitment with which the history was written is at stake. The burden of proof is great: Foucault would have to succeed in demonstrating that involved in the Christian 'hermeneutics of the self' there is not just a subjectivization *stricto sensu*, but also a subjection.[87]

Without the earlier studies on pre-Christian ethics, he would perhaps never have succeeded in formulating the problem of Christianity in these terms. He might have been able to justify his interest in Christian confessional techniques on the grounds of the part they play in 'putting' sex 'into discourse' (*'mise en discours' du sexe*)[88] or he might perhaps have felt compelled to move back on to the terrain of the repression hypothesis and look for the specific nature of Christianity in an intensification of the moral code. He would perhaps have dropped this hypothesis and taken the view that 'so-called Christian morality is nothing more than a piece of pagan ethics inserted into Christianity'[89] and that there are few differences between the two at the level of the content of the moral code.[90] But he would never have been able to distinguish between morality and ethics. He would never have seen that, alongside the moral codes and forms of behaviour, an ethical relation of the individual to himself was also in play and that the specificity of Christianity had to be located on this terrain. It is not the content of the codes that is important here, nor the extent to which the behaviour of moral subjects accords with them, but subjectivity itself and the nature of the relation to the code, a relation which plays a role in the constitution of subjectivity.

Foucault is by no means, of course, trying to argue that no changes at all occurred in moral codes with the coming of Christianity. He even points out that the Christian Middle Ages saw a progressive codification of moral experience.[91] But this intensification of the attentiveness with which the Christian pastoral regulated everything – positions, frequency, permitted and forbidden acts and even the state of mind of the two partners[92] – is quite a late development, and one which does not lend itself to a proper assessment of what is peculiar to early Christianity. The history of *ethics* is 'more decisive'[93] than that of the codes here. Indeed, one might say that the success of the later codification can only be understood in the light of the changes which Christianity brought about in the realm of the ethical relation to the self.

The idea that sexual activity poses a danger and thus must be restricted may well be found in fourth-century B.C. Greece, yet it surely does not have the significance there which it is later accorded in Hellenism or Christianity. The same goes for the ideal of chastity which is pursued in relations between men or for the eschewing of extra-marital intercourse.[94] There is a major difference between regarding marital fidelity as being motivated by the status of the husband, as in classical Greece, or, on the basis of considerations concerning the nature of the bond between the two partners, by the universal form of that bond and the mutual obligations ensuing from it, as in the Roman continuation of Hellenism.[95] And the fidelity which testifies to the self-control the *polis* expected of figures of authority is, strictly speaking, not the same as the fidelity which confines the sexual bond to marriage, on the grounds that only in that way can it regain a part of the innocence it had lost as a consequence of the Fall.[96] The various ways in which sexual activity is constituted as a moral problem in classical Greece, the Rome of the first centuries A.D. or in Christianity are widely divergent, in spite of the fact that the things which are permitted or forbidden, recommended or disapproved of, seem largely to be identical.[97] Christianity, for example, is no less troubled by sexual behaviour than ancient Greece, but it does not see in it the threat that arises from a confusion of forces which are difficult to control (*ontology*). Similarly, the Christian moral individual does not have the 'aesthetic-political choice' (*deontology*)[98] to control these forces in order to give his existence 'the most graceful and accomplished form'.[99] He does not strive for self-mastery (*teleology*), nor does he regard the various domains in which he can come into contact with pleasure as so many challenges to develop a technique of living (*techné tou biou*) which is appropriate to the framework within which it must perform its role (dietetics, *oikonomia*, *askesis* in erotism). In all these fields, the Christian tradition sees itself confronted with the same power of the flesh, a power which pervades all these domains homogeneously and hence requires a single strategy rather than many and varied arts of living. The moral subjectivization of Christianity is not constructed, in classical Greek fashion, around 'the use of pleasures', but is developed out of a 'hermeneutics of the self' – a long torment in which one must forsake the flesh without being released from one's body.[100]

All these shifts in the way Christian ethics redefines the subject's relation to his/her sexual activity constitute, for Foucault, an internally coherent whole, but the main emphasis here is unquestionably on the change in ethical substance and in the techniques of the self. It is as a consequence of the intrinsic nature of the sexual act, of the stigma which connects it to the Fall, that it is only permitted for the purpose of reproduction and that the attempt is made to uncouple it from pleasure, rather than regard it as an activity which requires a certain measure of self-control (ontology).[101] It is as a result of the definition of the sexual act as an evil, which falls under the power of an Other, who keeps the movement of desire in being with all the ruses at his disposal, that desire is no longer something to which one gives form in an 'aesthetics of existence', but something one resists in order to eradicate it (teleology). Hence the significance of the constant self-observation, the perpetual disciplining of the stirrings of desire and the need to 'confess' to these. The verbalization of desire is the only possible way of escaping it and discriminating between the true path and the false promptings of the Other, who rules over the flesh.[102] And it is understandable that one must not simply be left to one's own devices in this unequal struggle, that Christian *askesis* calls for unconditional subjection to the spiritual guide and that this person must be able to draw on a new and ever more precise codification of sexual behaviour which informs him which practices are permitted and subjects the realm of the flesh to the divine law (deontology).[103]

What makes Christianity so interesting for Foucault is precisely this combination of subjectivization and subjection which is expressed in the combination of a contemplative 'technology of the self' with absolute obedience to the word of the spiritual guide and to the law of a personal God. Among the later Stoics, the deontological driving force towards ethical subjectivization shifted from the free choice – provided by aesthetic and political factors – to make one's life into a 'work of art' to the obligations one has to oneself as a rational being.[104] And the examination of conscience and confession in the form of conversation with a master were common forms in the late Hellenistic and Roman philosophies.[105] But these practices did not result in an individualization of the confessing subject. The point was not to reveal a long-concealed inner truth, but to call into memory the truth of a forgotten rule of life. The conversation with the master was not intended to extend one's knowledge, but to convert knowledge one already had into a good life.[106] The examination of conscience had not yet acquired the typically Christian form of self-observation. It was not yet the aim of confession to disclose a secret reality within the individual. The constituting of thoughts as a field of subjective data requiring analysis and interpretation is a typically Christian invention.[107] The constant vigilance needed to disarm the power of the Other within oneself and the resultant perpetual suspicion of oneself are elements which belong to a Christian hermeneutics of the self.[108] They place the subject in a relation to him/herself which, though it will change over time, none the less already contains all the basic aspects of the modern experience of self.

With the determination of the historical singularity of this hermeneutics of the self, Foucault came a step nearer to answering the question 'how it comes about that, at a particular point in time, sexual behaviour becomes an object not just of practical, but also of theoretical, endeavours'.[109] It now becomes clear that the problem of *La Volonté de savoir* has Christian roots. In order for modern man to be able to recognize himself as a 'subject of sexuality' and to seek after his truth in his sexual behaviour, he had first to constitute himself as a 'subject of desire'.[110] Sexuality had to be uncoupled from the social relations with which it was inextricably interwoven in the pre-Christian traditions.[111] The paradigm of the moral problematization of sexuality had to shift from penetration to erection.[112] Sexual desire is no longer conceived as something which has to be controlled, but as something which must be eradicated – a shift which, as we have seen, is effected in the Christian monastic traditions and is given shape in the changed function of the examination of conscience. To keep in check the slightest stirrings of thought, the minutest images and associations which constantly threaten to disturb the purity of contemplation, is a long way from calling into memory rules of action and considering whether one wishes to allow one's life to be directed by them.[113] Such an examination of self is not directed to self-control but the renunciation of (a part of) oneself. The aim is, by a continual diagnosis, to distinguish inner truth from the false illusions which distort it beyond recognition. Sexuality, subjectivity and truth are thus referred back to an interiority which is the product of a specifically Christian ethical self-transformation of the individual. Generalizing the effects of this 'epistemological seduction'[114] to the broad mass of the population was to give the Christian pastoral a great deal of trouble. And when it finally succeeded in breaking down the ossification of the code by which it had managed up to that point, and in diverting attention from the detail of the act to 'the stirrings – so difficult to perceive and formulate – of desire',[115] it had, at the end of the eighteenth century, to give way to other discourses which release confession from the problematic of sin and the flesh and shift its subjectivizing effect on to the terrain of the many peripheral sexualities which modern man was ceaselessly to investigate in the hope that they would impart to him something of his truth. The Christian problematic of the flesh gives way to the problematic of sexuality. A sexuality which will call forth confessions that are no less *individualizing*, but will also have no less *homogenizing* effects. Like the flesh, sexuality refers to 'a single entity' and makes it possible for 'diverse phenomena to be grouped together, despite the apparently loose connections between them, as if they were of the same nature, derived from the same origin, or brought the same type of causal mechanisms into play: behaviours, but also sensations, images, desires, instincts, passions'.[116] In this way, Christian subjectivization lays the ground for precisely those effects (individualization, homogenization) which provided grounds, in *La Volonté de savoir*, to speak of a subjectivizing *subjection*.

(iii) *Subjectivization and subjection*

With the discovery and dissemination of confession as a technique of subjectivization, Christianity built a bridge to modernity. The unity of Foucault's history of sexuality would seem to have been rescued by this fact. The mutation of that history into a 'genealogy of ethics' did not necessarily imply that the way the problem was formulated several years before in the first volume of *The History of Sexuality* had to be given up. But Foucault not only wished to treat of the anything but evident relationship between sexuality and truth, he also seemed to believe that the Christian and modern 'hermeneutic of the self' went astray when it implemented this relationship in the manner that is so characteristic of it. The self, says Foucault, is '*nothing more* than the correlate of technology built into our history'[117] and he apparently wants to suggest that it is, therefore, *less* than the Christian and modern technologies of the self make it out to be. He gives the impression that he wishes to hold that tradition responsible for the disappearance of the old idea of an 'aesthetics of existence' and, for example, for the fact that recent liberation movements have only been able to base themselves on an ethics 'founded on so-called scientific knowledge of what the self is, what desire is, what the unconscious is, and so on'.[118] Foucault wishes to release ethics from any form of legality and he believes that, to do this, he must break the hold of religious, scientific or metaphysical authority on the self. The self is not something pre-given; it has to be made. We must again, as in classical Greece, but without nostalgia, seek to make 'everyone's life ... a work of art'[119] and, in order to do this, we must first contest 'the appropriation of morality by the theory of the subject' which began 'with Christianity'.[120]

These diagnoses may be interesting in themselves. But, whatever one may think of them, and however much one may welcome Foucault's commitment or reject it, the question remains whether and under what conditions the theoretical instrumentarium of *The History of Sexuality* provides Foucault with the means convincingly to ground the 'political'[121] consequences he associates with it. In what sense can one really speak of a Christian theory *of the subject*, which one must resist in the name of an 'aesthetics of existence'? And can one do this without exposing the programme once again to the treacherous effect of quotation marks? Is it possible, after the 'turn' effected by *The Use of Pleasure* and *The Care of the Self*, both to think something like subjectivization and at the same time to take into account the possibility of subjection?

Foucault seems to have his doubts. He knows that the revision of his conceptualization prevents him from having further recourse to quotation marks as a figure of argumentation. It ought no longer to be possible, for example, to put subjectivization in quotation marks, as was done in *Discipline and Punish* (the 'soul') or to base one's position on 'bodies and pleasures' and to seek a way out of one's difficulties by recourse to a metaphysics of origins. The concept of 'problematization' which stands in the centre of the late studies[122] would seem to exclude this possibility. This can be used to point out differences in ethical substance, but it does not allow us to conclude that any particular matter is more originary, so far as ethical self-constitution is concerned. What Christianity problematized as 'the flesh' is not the same thing as modern sexuality, but it is also no less originary than what classical and Hellenistic Greece meant by *aphrodisia*.[123] The flesh will be 'brought down to the level of the organism'[124] and the doctors, therapists, psychiatrists, pedagogues and psychologists of the nineteenth century will, with striking unanimity, seek something more – and other – than mere 'bodies, organs, somatic localizations, functions, anatomo-physiological systems, sensations, and pleasures'.[125] But it is not clear why we should resist the 'fact' that these elements are connected in the concept of 'sex' and appeal instead to 'bodies and pleasures'.[126] Is the unity being sought here in any sense more fictitious[127] than that which the Greeks sought to create between act, desire and pleasure in the concept of *aphrodisia*?[128] Whatever role the 'intrinsic properties'[129] of sex and its own 'laws' may have played in the break with these classical associations and in whatever way these may have been a cause of the disappearance of pleasure, of the loss of meaning of the act and of the concentration of our attention on 'desire' as 'the structure characteristic of the human condition',[130] it remains unclear to what extent this should count against 'sexuality' as ethical substance. The instrumentarium of the subjectivization 'theory', which was developed after volume one of *The History of Sexuality*, can only lead, at best, to the conclusion that, in the modern conception of sexuality, there is virtually no room to take pleasure into account and that, as a result of this, a theoretical counterpart to the moral devaluation of pleasure developed by Christianity comes to the fore.[131] And it can at best indicate that the same central role is attributed to desire in the determination of ethical substance in Christianity and in modernity, but that this has different practical consequences at the level of ends (modern desire must be liberated, Christian desire must be eradicated).[132] But the disappearance of pleasure, the neutralization of action, the dominance acquired by desire is precisely what will make possible the distinction between the 'matter' to which the various epochs refer the process of subjectivization, and Foucault can really do no more than point to this distinction and lay bare a historicity which modernity would perhaps have preferred to keep hidden. He does not have the means at his disposal to exploit this distinction in any other way against modernity or to find an argument in the 'theoretical devaluation' of pleasure[133] which would make modern subjectivization into a subjection. If he wants to rescue the unity of his history of sexuality, everything seems to point to Foucault having to abandon his political commitment. For the function of confession which still led, in *La Volonté de savoir*, to a subjectivizing *subjection* must also be revised. The Christian and modern forms of confession are now techniques of *askesis* which, like other techniques, make a practical subjectivization *possible*. What could be subjected by this subjectivization? One is perhaps inclined to say: the individual. But, in that case, either one would have to assert against the Foucault of volumes two and three that subjectivization entails no experience of oneself as *practical-ethical subject*, but leads only to a non-ethical compliance with obligations, or to see this 'subjection' as a necessary condition of the existence of something like a practical subjectivity[134] and one then forfeits all grounds for contesting it.

All this would seem to mean that Foucault ends up once again with an intuition which could be said to have already virtually been established in the first volume of *The History of Sexuality*: (practical) subjectivization is something which is imposed, but also accepted. The subsequent studies on sexuality do not develop this conclusion any further: in *The Use of Pleasure* and *The Care of the Self* Foucault in fact always presupposes the distinction between a constituting and a constituted subjectivity,[135] and his determination of the process of subjectivization says a great deal about the forms which the latter can assume, but nothing about the former. Foucault postulates subjectivization, but he does not explain it. For that reason, the questions which remain open in *La Volonté de savoir* have in no way disappeared. But the later works turn away from the problematic of the quotation marks without consciously breaking with them. They replace a theory of subjection which cannot explain subjectivization by a 'theory' which postulates the existence of subjectivization and presupposes the actuality of subjection, without being able to think its possibility. They thus open the way for an empiricism and descriptivism of power which has rendered Foucault's genealogy so vulnerable in a debate which does not really match up to the level of his problematic.

3.2. Can genealogy be critical? Lines of force of the Foucault debate

The difficulties in which Foucault finds himself with his history of sexuality both before and after the turn *seem* to indicate that those who, with Habermas, believe his commitment requires 'the introduction of normative notions of some kind'[136] are right. Foucault might, for example, have been able to sketch out a theory of interiorization which offered insight into the mechanisms of subjectivization and at the same time showed under what conditions one could speak of a divergent, 'repressive' *subjectivization*. Such an expressly normative theory would perhaps have allowed him to explain to what extent the specifically Christian and modern techniques of subjectivization necessarily entail a kind of 'individualization' which 'separates the individual, breaks his links with others ... forces the individual back on himself and ties him to his own identity *in a constraining way*'.[137] Instead of postulating the connection between subjectivization and subjection and associating this arbitrarily with a particular tradition, Foucault would have been able – by a further reflection on the specificity of the procedures of confession for example – to investigate whether the technologies of the self associated with this may have been dependent on mechanisms which prematurely close off the function of verbalization and thus lead to the kind of fixation of identity he has in mind.[138]

Whatever results such an approach may have produced, it is clear that he would have had to undertake something along these lines to answer those who, like Rorty, feel that Foucault 'does nothing to show that there is something wrong with whatever networks of power are required to shape people into individuals with a sense of moral responsibility'[139] or who, with Habermas, take the view that 'the model of repression developed by Marx and Freud in the tradition of the Enlightenment' cannot be replaced by a 'pluralism of successive, intersecting strategies of power, which cannot be judged in terms of criteria of validity, as was the case with conscious versus unconscious conflict resolution'.[140] On the basis of this criticism and others of a similar kind,[141] Foucault would *seem* to be forced to formulate a kind of criterion which would rescue his work from the danger of a 'crypto-normativism'[142] and connect the task of the critical intellectual once again with the formulation of a normative framework. But this would mean striking out along a path he had always wanted to avoid. The idea of a normative foundation, which Habermas and others have demanded from him, was rejected by Foucault because he associated such a project with the role of the 'left intellectual', who, as 'master of truth and justice',[143] prescribes to others what they have to do, instead of confining himself to 'show[ing] people that they are much freer than they feel, that people accept as truth, as evidence, some themes which have been built up at a certain moment during history, and that this so-called evidence can be criticized and destroyed'.[144] The intellectual, as Foucault conceives him, would abandon his old prophetic function.[145] He would, for example, avoid a normative theory of subjectivization in order not to impinge on the creativity of those who, ultimately, have to turn their own lives into a work of art. He would confine himself to a 'nominalistic critique, formulated ... by way of a historical analysis'[146] and show that 'a great number of postulates, evidences of all sorts, institutions and ideas we take for granted'[147] are more recent than we think. It is not the aim of the critical philosophy he always strove after 'to say that things are not good as they are', but to see what 'self-evidences [évidences] ... the practices we accept rest on'.[148] 'What is could have been different'[149] – for Foucault, the 'theoretico-political function'[150] of genealogy does not seem to consist in any more than this: 'I believe the intellectual can, if he wants to, contribute important elements to the perception and criticism of things; elements from which, later, if people so desire, a particular political choice emerges *quite naturally*.'[151]

One may disagree with his position here and take the view that analyses, which merely point to the possibility of changes without at the same time, even crudely, laying down a direction for change, are simply evidence of the 'young conservative' abdication of the intellectuals.[152] Alternatively, one may argue that such analyses introduce a 'new, performative model' of critique, 'within which truth claims are assessed on the basis of the role they play in a practical learning process' which creates an experience in the person concerned that may be different from that of the author.[153] But whatever attitude one takes here, it is a fact that Foucault was never content with 'the Nietzschean realization that everything is possible'.[154] Like Nietzsche, he also wanted to use genealogy as an argument against particular possibilities that had become realities. Foucault not only wrote an arresting history of the emergence of the human sciences, of individualization, disciplining, normalization and 'sexualization', he also used his genealogical insights to query the value of these phenomena. And even the later Foucault by no means confined himself to pointing out the constant correlation between increasing individualization and the reinforcement of a political totality such as that of the State.[155] He was also of the opinion that *'liberation'* can only come from 'attacking' the 'very roots' of a 'political rationality'[156] which has saddled us with a 'double-bind' of individualization and totalization.[157] There can, admittedly, be no doubt that it is important to ask what factors have characterized political thinking and what form of rationality has been involved in it.[158] But appealing to the possibility of a liberation, to the need 'to refuse what we are', and calling for the promotion of 'new forms of subjectivity' that would renounce the 'kind of individuality which has been imposed on us for several centuries'[159] seems, none the less, to presuppose more than an analysis which casts light on 'the historical arbitrariness of states of affairs' and shows 'how and why things have got to be as they are'.[160] If Foucault's genealogy had merely been confined to this, not only would it have been unable to lead to the political consequences he sought to attach *directly* to it, it would also have given those who do not share its political commitment an argument by which to evade Foucault's critical intentions without becoming politically suspect. For why should we refuse what we are? Why not simply acknowledge it? Why should we not accept Rorty's call for a frank ethnocentrism[161] or merely admit, with Charles Taylor, that 'what we have become' here in the West 'counts for us' and determines what we understand by 'humanity' and 'politics'?[162] 'Can we really step outside the identity we have developed in Western civilization . . . ? Can we toss aside the whole tradition of Augustinian inwardness?'[163] What is more, is it worth the trouble? Genealogy can clarify for us the nature of the reason we are employing and the historical consequences of that reason. It can perhaps point to its 'limits' and, possibly, to the 'dangers' associated with it ('normalization' etc) and, in so doing, it is certainly not its aim to have us believe that everything was better in the past.[164] But, by allowing us to see that every age has its dangers,[165] does it not arouse the suspicion that it is not perhaps worth the trouble of 'doing violence to our minds and bodies in order to become something different?'[166] If Foucault wanted us to give up one danger for another, did he not owe it to us to provide a criterion whereby we could see what makes one kind of danger 'more xx x

dangerous than another'?[167] And if genealogy falls short of this task and if Foucault's continual recourse to a metaphysics of origins can be seen as an indicator of its inadequacy in this regard, doesn't this mean it can 'only function meaningfully within a wider analytico-theoretical framework and a normative-critical perspective'?[168]

Foucault sometimes gives this impression himself. For example, a number of passages in *Discipline and Punish* seem to wish to condemn the effects of power on the grounds of the asymmetry involved,[169] and one can easily understand why many a reader has taken this as hinting at the possibility of transposing Foucault's analyses of power into the terms of a normatively 'better'-founded investigation of systematically distorted communication.[170] However, the few texts in which he does undertake a systematic analysis of the phenomena of power would seem, rather, to thwart such attempts to assimilate his thinking directly to Critical Theory. In those texts, Foucault turns his back on a tradition which has been concerned primarily with power in the sense of domination (*Herrschaft*), in order to focus on a kind of power which can be met 'throughout every social field'.[171] Power relations of this kind differ from domination in that in the latter they are '*fixed* in such a way that they are *perpetually* asymmetrical'.[172] It seems that he wishes, for this reason, to bring into play against relations of domination a kind of criterion of reversibility: his problem is not that he wishes to dissolve power relations, but that he wants to allow them to be able to function with a 'minimum of domination'. This resistance to domination is not prompted by a regard for communicative symmetry (for example), but by a concern to rescue the play of existing asymmetries from a state of congealment.[173] The 'free play of antagonistic reactions', which is constantly being arrested by the 'stable [power] mechanisms' by which 'one can direct ... the conduct of others', must under no circumstances come to a halt.[174]

Foucault has obviously manoeuvred himself here into a rather uncomfortable position: in no sense does he wish to restrict his critique to structures of domination and he must, therefore, prevent his assertion that 'there cannot be a society without power relations' from being read as an argument for the 'necessity' of existing relations.[175] Instead of having recourse here to a criterion of symmetry, he now transposes the problematic on to an ontological level and sees the asymmetry which is characteristic of power relations as an indication of their reversibility. The continued existence of power is, for Foucault, always extremely precarious.

There is no power without the possibility of resistance, and this — resistance is guaranteed by the freedom present in every power relation. Power can only be exerted over free subjects and can only be exerted in so far as they are free. If this freedom disappears, then we must speak, rather, of violence: a slave in chains is not being subjected to power but to physical compulsion. Violence reduces the other to a thing; it applies to something passive. Power, by contrast, presupposes that the person on whom it is exerted be recognized as an active person: it is 'an action upon an action'.[176] With this emphasis on the intrinsically relational character of power, Foucault rejects the false conception that power excludes freedom. Freedom is precisely the condition of existence of power. It does not disappear where power is exercised, but makes power what it is and distinguishes it from the compulsion of violence. Such a freedom can be minimalized in particular power relations (domination), but without it the exercise of power is inconceivable: 'At the very heart of the power relationship, and constantly provoking it, are the recalcitrance of the will and the intransigence of freedom.'[177]

Foucault's philosophy of power may perhaps be a philosophy of freedom,[178] but the question remains whether this recourse to freedom resolves the problems of genealogy or, rather, is precisely an expression of its problematic situation. He has, admittedly, now anchored the possibility of resistance in the nature of power relations themselves, but he would seem also to feel relieved thereby of the task of thinking the 'legitimacy of this resistance'.[179] The difficulties of his theoretical commitment are thus shifted on to the problems facing the addressees of his commitment. The 'lack of orientation' attaching to Foucault's genealogy also seems to characterize his concept of freedom.[180] It remains 'formalistic' because it merely 'considers the possibility of distancing oneself from what exists' and neglects other features such as 'self-possession' and 'self-realization'. Foucault's inability to account for the commitment he associates with his genealogy is, as a consequence, repeated in his concept of freedom, in which, strictly speaking, 'all the positions which can be taken up by a free human being are, ultimately, equally valid' and no substantive orientation is present.

In one of his late articles – on Kant's 'What is Enlightenment?' – Foucault formulated this difficulty very precisely. He writes there, once again, of the need for 'a philosophical life in which the critique of what we are is at one and the same time the historical analysis of the limits imposed on us and an experiment with the possibility of going beyond them'. He clarifies this mission by calling it 'a patient labor giving form to our impatience for liberty'.[181] A mission of this kind, which doubtless gave form to his own life and bolstered his commitment, would seem, however, to presuppose more than he was able to express in his theoretical work. A freedom which would consist only in the possibility of 'making everything equally questionable',[182] as in genealogy, distancing oneself from everything and refusing all determination,[183] without having much idea why or to what ends, would not just make this mission an arbitrary commitment ('Why?'), but would also leave it without the orientation necessary to 'enlighten' the patience it demands.

Given all these considerations, must we then conclude that a genealogical critique which wishes to remain genealogical can only develop into a discourse in which, as Foucault once put it, 'truth functions as a weapon for a partisan victory'?[184] Does genealogy really only have a choice between basing its criticism on elements alien to it (a broader, normative scaffolding) – and which perhaps even infringe it (a metaphysics of origins) – and being transformed into a *machine de guerre*, as Paul Veyne will have it?[185] Is it, as genealogy, condemned to remain the counter-history which demonstrates ever anew that the 'blinding light of power ... is a light which divides, which illuminates one side, but leaves another part ... in shadow'?[186] Does its attempt 'to emancipate historical knowledges from ... subjection' by 'the hierarchical order of power associated with science'[187] simply attest to 'the arbitrary *partisanship* of a criticism that cannot account for its normative foundations'?[188]

The foregoing discussion has perhaps created this impression. However, it moved at the level of an empirical-descriptive analysis (of power) which Foucault claimed as his own[189] and which is also ascribed to him by his critics. Such an analysis, which increasingly gains the ascendancy in Foucault's later texts, is not really concerned with the question of how it turns out that power *can* be exercised, but concentrates on the problem of *how* power is exercised. It seeks merely to show that 'what is given to us as universal, necessary, obligatory' can, in reality, be traced back to 'arbitrary constraints',[190] *but it does not really pose the problem of whether the existence of constraints is itself arbitrary.* Nor has the discussion of Foucault's work concerned itself with this question. It has, admittedly, clearly shown that the commitment involved in an analysis which confines itself to exposing the arbitrariness of constraints is itself in danger of becoming arbitrary, but *the real problematic* to which a concept like that of the productivity of power referred has remained in the background in this debate. Thus, Habermas shares with the Foucault of the quotation marks the conviction that power entails an avoidable repression and that an analysis of power must reveal that repression in all its arbitrariness. Hence the meaning of the term 'power' for Habermas is already fixed. He does, admittedly, refer to a 'systematically ambiguous use' of the term by Foucault,[191] but, on closer inspection, he would seem to mean by this that Foucault burdens an *already known* empirical phenomenon with a transcendental function: 'Foucault abruptly reverses power's truth-dependency into the power-dependency of truth'.[192] If Habermas were correct in his assertion that Foucault's genealogy 'naturalistically' reduces the problematic of the 'ought' to that of the 'is' of power,[193] then genealogical historiography would have to 'abstain' from 'the question of whether some discourse and power formations could be more legitimate than others'.[194] Such historiography could only be a description of 'meaningless kaleidoscopic changes of shape in discourse totalities that have nothing in common apart from the single characteristic of being protuberances of power in general'.[195] But where does all this get us? Is it not too easy simply to see here the 'internal contradictions' into which all attempts at an 'argumentative liquidation of reason', from Nietzsche to Foucault, have become embroiled?[196] Can one speak here of 'a theory of the Eternal Return of power',[197] without running the risk of prematurely empiricizing that theory and distorting its problematic *in the same way Foucault's quotation marks have done*? What if there were, between 'is' and 'ought', an 'intermediate region' to which the theoretico-constitutive aspect of power, pointed out, but neglected, by Habermas referred?[198] Would this not offer a way out of a discussion which was led astray not just by the exemplary, but, as remains to be shown, systematic character of Foucault's quotation marks? We reach a point here where we can no longer evade the question of the possibility of a critique of objectivism.

The Systematic Character of 'Foucault''s Quotation Marks

What of the Foucault debate? The establishment of an aporia: a 'radical' critique of reason itself no longer has rational criteria at its disposal[1] – genealogy becomes a *machine de guerre*. The outcome of the reading we have carried out? Repeated hesitation: 'Perhaps ...', 'Foucault would seem to think ...', 'one gets the impression that ...'. Whence this stubborn refusal to follow those who apparently possess the means to overcome this indecisiveness? Who, *intentione recta*, push on through to what an author does, instead of endlessly asking what it is that he seems to be doing. Who are, ultimately, so logically consistent as to refute him where necessary, even if that refutation entails rejecting his project in its entirety. What sense is there in this boundless deconstruction which apparently leads nowhere and spurns obvious conclusions? Would it not have been better to leave out this string of maddening subjunctives and drop all the phrases which merely cast doubt on the force and firmness of the conclusions, which are, curiously enough – though still too cautiously – formulated from time to time? Why this indecision?

Doubtless, this is anything but an elegant way of concealing a state of thorough embarrassment. But was there any possible alternative? One could, admittedly, have smoothed out the folds in Foucault's text and presented the transition from one work to the next as the product of a carefully thought out architectonic structure which time alone would reveal in all its glory.[2] And one could, without too much trouble, have pushed the contradictions in his text to extremes and presented these as an effect of that 'paradoxical linking of a positivist attitude with a critical claim' which Habermas sees as characteristic of Foucault's works.[3] No contradictions, no hesitation or, alternatively, just the one basic contradiction and the entire programme left in ruins. Such a reading would perhaps have been more attractive and, at any rate, *less obscure*.* *But it would never have been able to raise the problem of Foucault's quotation marks*. It would have had either to ignore them or regard them as a direct expression of the aporia in which his work finds itself.[4] Either approach would have meant granting Foucault's text a consistency it does not possess. It would have meant seeing him either as a writer who had had the good fortune, at an early stage, to hit upon a problematic which could be developed without difficulty or as someone who was on the wrong track from the start and who, in spite of all his changes of direction, never managed to surmount a basic contradiction.[5] Either he had seen everything in two or three phases or he had seen nothing. He was either in total control of his problematic or he was controlled by it. From this perspective there is no reason whatever to distinguish, as Merleau-Ponty would have, between Foucault's problems 'such as [he] thought them' and the problems 'which really move' him 'and which *we* formulate'.[6] One is either for or against; there is no other choice. But in both cases one would have to start out from the tacit idea that, as regards its structure and effect, a text must – and can – be reduced 'to what its presumed author wanted to say, to the *vouloir-dire* of a so-called unique and identifiable "signatory"'.[7]

In order to avoid this alternative between a radical rejection and a triumphant, but equally denunciatory[8] acceptance, one must drop this assumption. The point is not to go to the other extreme and assert that a text or a work cannot be understood as the 'expression' of an author, that it is only assigned to an author in a process of ascription which is anything but self-evident. Nor is it a question of declaring the concept of author dead[9] or of pluralizing it and asserting that a text does not come from a *single* hand, that the contradictions in the *oeuvre* or even in one of the works clearly show that there are many Foucaults and hence, also, one cannot say that 'he' contradicts 'himself', since this would presuppose that there is *one* internally contradictory body of thought, the supposed unity of which gives meaning and reference to the name of the

---

* Translator's note: This is an allusion to Habermas (1985b) (*Die neue Unüber-sichtlichkeit*), the central essay of which, 'The New Obscurity', is translated in Habermas (1989), pp. 48–70.

author, instead of being, itself, its constantly threatened effect.[10]
Interesting as such reflections may be, they do not contribute to our
acquiring an understanding of all these hesitations and constant
changes of position within Foucault's texts. These hesitations
cannot be understood by neglecting them, as Deleuze does, or
transforming them, like Habermas, into theses. But one gains no
more understanding of them either by regarding them as the effect
of a kind of polylogue between the various Foucaults supposedly
dwelling even within a single work. The problem with Foucault's
constantly recurrent quotation marks is that they are neither
accidental nor necessary. They are connected with his problematic,
but do not seem to be a direct expression of it. They occupy a place
in his work which is anything but marginal, but they are not
coextensive with that work. The effect they have would seem rather
to be that Foucault's entire *oeuvre* – and also each individual work
– contains a kind of fissure, as a result of which it splits into two
apparently equivalent, but incompatible positions. Thus, for example, *Histoire de la folie* appears at one and the same time to
anticipate genealogy and to fall short of it. And, with the ideas of
power-knowledge and the productivity of power, *Discipline and
Punish* introduces a theoretical framework which is irreconcilable
with the implications of a metaphysics of origins generated by the
quotation marks which occur in the same book. What is going on
here? Can we simply say that Foucault contradicts himself? Must a
reading of his work confine itself to drawing attention to these
contradictions, conscious that each further step presupposes a
decision on which the work can in no way whatever exert a
determining influence? What is the nature of these inconsistencies?
What is actually the place of the quotation marks in his work and,
most importantly, what place do they make Foucault assume in his
work?

Our reading could not evade these questions. Nor could it avoid
answering them. Hence the hesitation, the constant concern with
what Foucault 'could be said' to be doing or 'seems' to be doing. All
these forced turns of phrase should indicate how difficult it was to
speak of the work 'of' Foucault, how problematic it was to privilege
a particular position by giving it the last word and thus suggesting
that the same 'Foucault' who gave the impression of wishing to
adopt a new standpoint now either contradicts himself or belies that
impression. In order to deal with these difficulties without resorting
to speaking of 'many Foucaults', we might at this point introduce a

stipulative definition of the author 'Foucault' as that instance in his text which prevents a problematic that repeatedly appears within it from unfolding fully. The quotation marks with which he has, so to speak, 'signed' his texts, and which make his texts recognizable as *his*, could then be understood as an 'answer' to a problematic which seems to be at stake in his work, but which, precisely because of this 'answer' can never break through as such. The 'answer' distorts the problematic and withholds it from the field of vision of the author within whose work it emerges.

Such a conception of the author may seem artificial, but it offers significant advantages. By assigning the author to a particular position in 'his' text, by understanding him as an instance which signs and distorts 'his' problematic in a particular way, one is no longer obliged to regard his text as a linear, one-dimensional structure in which everything that is said has the same weight, because it is said by the same individual. To operate with such a linear model would mean being obliged to take all the contradictions in a text literally: one would be dealing with contradictory standpoints taken up by the same individual. However, if one's starting point is the idea that a text, even when it is the work of a single individual, is not made 'all of a piece', but consists of various different strata, and is constantly interpreting itself and seeking to give itself a coherence which creates the impression that it consists of only one stratum, then these contradictions show up in a different light.[11] They no longer have to be attributed to two contradictory standpoints of one and the same external author, but can be related to the conflict between what he, as external author, wanted to say and what he, as internal author, is able to say.

This idea brings a dual e-mancipation (in the etymological sense of doing away with a *mancipium*). The text is accorded a materiality it would not have had if it were merely regarded as the inscription of what someone intended to say. And the (external) author is also liberated once one realizes in what way the text limits his freedom. For example, the position which Foucault adopts in his text as internal author, as he presents a particular interpretation of his problematic, prevents him from ascribing to particular concepts the meanings he, as external author, would have liked to associate with them. Hence the apparently blatant contradictions to which concepts like the 'productivity of power' and 'power-knowledge' lead. These concepts cannot be reconciled with the interpretation 'Foucault' offers of his problematic. It is not so much that they are in contradiction with the rest of the text, as Habermas and others imply, but they belong to another layer of the text. In reality, they are not even anomalies that can only be understood from the perspective of a different problematic.[12] They are 'slips' which show up the extent to which Foucault's quotation marks truss up 'his' problematic. If one wishes to get beyond Foucault's problems (4.1) and connect his problematic with the programme of a critique of objectivism (4.3), then one has not only to release it from this predicament but also to understand how and why it came to be embroiled in it (4.2).

4.1. From the problems to the problematic

1. A review of the argument

One of the reasons – if not the reason – why it was so hard for Foucault's genealogy to make headway lies in the fact that it only seemed capable of putting its critical intentions into practice by dressing itself up as a genealogy of oppression. It wanted to discover the interpretation which lies at the base of every truth,[13] but it seemed compelled, itself, to appeal to a kind of ontological truth which decides the value of any and every interpretation. The protest by which madness disturbed the peace of psychiatric reason and the 'revolt of the body' against the power which had to discipline it were, in Foucault's view, arguments against a history which had suppressed the *truth of madness* and deprived the body of its *original spontaneity*. All the apocalyptic pathos of the 'history of madness' depended on this idea of a historically datable, avoidable exclusion of madness. And it was not merely in *Histoire de la folie* that Foucault appealed to the sublime truth of madness 'itself' to found his critique of the scientificity of psychiatry and psychology. We have seen how, in *Discipline and Punish*, his critique of science only becomes comprehensible when a similar argument is developed: his doubts regarding the 'scientificity' of the human sciences presuppose that one subjects disciplining as a bodily technique, i.e. as a technique which oppresses 'the body *itself*', to criticism. And lastly, the aporias in which the history of sexuality became entangled were of the same kind. It proved impossible to think subjectivization and subjection together without being led off into a critique which was structured, once again, on the quotation-mark model ('science'). It became clear that the difficulties with

Foucault's critique of the human sciences were of an exemplary character. The question how power brought 'subjectivity' and 'sexuality' into being is indistinguishable in terms of structure and implication from the question: 'How did the power exerted on insanity produce psychiatry's "true" discourse?'[14]

It is clear that this cannot mean that, contrary to their stated intentions, Foucault's 'genealogies' were simply variations on the theme of *Histoire de la folie* and that they did not succeed in leaving behind the theoretical model with which he operated in that work. If it seemed that Foucault was constantly being compelled to resort again to such a model, concepts like power-knowledge or the productivity of power indicated that what we have here are relapses back beyond his problematic. The idea that power does not repress or alienate, but produces was motivated by the intention to rule out any possible appeal to an ontological truth which would unmask the products of power as forms of alienation. And what was interesting or surprising in a concept like power-knowledge was that it seemed to belong to a different conception of truth – one which did not see the presence of power as an obstacle to knowledge. Truth and knowledge could be said to be 'thing[s] of this world' which are only produced 'by virtue of multiple forms of constraint'.[15] The fact that knowledge is bound up with power does not prevent one from knowing. Knowledge would not thereby become less 'true'. On the contrary, the hyphen seemed explicitly directed against the impulse to put knowledge or – as in the quotation at the end of the last paragraph – truth in inverted commas.

Yet neither of the two concepts succeeded in establishing itself. It will be remembered that only by stressing the hyphen between power and knowledge were we able to protect the concept of the 'productivity of power' from being taken over once again by the theory of power's repressiveness. But the opposite was also the case: the hyphen was constantly under threat because it seemed that Foucault had a tendency to cling to the old connotations of the power concept. Moreover, these difficulties are not confined to concepts like 'the productivity of power' or 'power-knowledge'. They re-emerge whenever Foucault speaks of power. Thus, for example, he writes in this same period of a ' "regime" of truth' and a ' "political economy" of truth', meaning by this that ' "truth" is linked in a circular relation with systems of power which produce and sustain it, and to effects of power which it induces and which extend it'.[16] It is clear that such a link between truth and power is subject to the same constraints as that between power and knowledge. If this were merely to relate to the fact that truth gives rise to particular power effects or that it can only establish itself when based on a system of power which stimulates and uses it to its own advantage, then it would remain an external link. In both cases, the idea of a circular relation between truth and power would merely connect two pre-given systems with one another and, as in the case of power-knowledge, we would again be faced with the difficulty that an internal connection between truth and power can only be achieved if we succeed in displacing the meaning of one of the two terms (and hence, also, of the other). At first sight, the prospects for such an attempt are not very good. If it were to succeed, it would at best allow us to see the power-truth[17] concept as a special case of power-knowledge. Yet it would not bring us one step nearer to an understanding of what Foucault means by 'power'.

There is a chance, however, that an internal connection of this kind between power and truth could put us more directly on the tracks of Foucault's problematic than the power-knowledge concept. Interestingly, Foucault does not attempt here to shift the burden of proof for the internal nature of the link on to the 'productivity of power'. He introduces a stipulative definition of truth which, as will become clear, implies a conception of power to which the power-knowledge concept had given up – or been forced to give up – access: 'By truth, I do not mean "the ensemble of truths which are to be discovered and accepted", but, rather, "the ensemble of rules according to which the true and the false are separated and specific effects of power attached to the true".'[18]

Though dating from the time when Foucault introduced the power-knowledge concept, from a systematic point of view this definition is older. It can only be properly understood if we turn our attention from the parallel with the power-knowledge concept, naturally suggested by the chronology, and relate what we have decided to call, in the light of the above definition, the power-truth concept to Foucault's conception of order.

2. Order, truth, power

Foucault's idiosyncratic definition of truth goes back to a number of ideas he first formulated in an explicit way in his inaugural lecture at the Collège de France. He points out there, for example, that 'for a proposition to belong to botany or pathology, it has to fulfil certain conditions, in a sense stricter and more complex than pure and simple truth'.[19] This remark is general in character: before a decision can be made about the truth of a proposition, it must already be 'in the true' (*dans le vrai*).[20] In this case, entirely in the spirit of the definition given above, truth is understood as (or equated with) a discursive régime, i.e. as a set of conditions which a statement must satisfy in order to be susceptible of verification or falsification in the usual sense. In order to belong to a discipline or science, a statement must address itself to a determinate plane of objects, using particular concepts and metaphors and rejecting others, and must move within a fixed theoretical horizon.[21] It must follow the 'rules of a discursive "policing"' and continually 'reactivate' those rules.[22] Foucault will say later that it must conform to the 'internal régime of power' which controls statements of the same type.[23] In *The Order of Discourse*, he sees 'what effects of power circulate among [*inter alia*, R.V.] scientific statements'[24] as the consequence and expression of the *internal procedure* by which a discourse (that of science, for example) orders itself.[25] Such an 'order of discourse' creates its own disorder: by a string of rules, it establishes a profile of normality which functions as an exclusion mechanism and assumes the existence of 'a whole teratology of knowledge'.[26] Those who do not keep to these rules disqualify themselves. Their speech is neither true nor false because it is located outside 'the true'.[27]

Whatever conditions have to be met for something to qualify for the distinction between true and false, these conditions will only give a particular form to that distinction.[28] In order to be capable of being judged either true or false, a statement must not only obey particular rules of pertinence but must first be governed by this true/false distinction. It must 'want to know' or, to put it another way, it must desire truth.[29] For Foucault, this is by no means a self-evident point: truth is itself a mechanism of exclusion. In *The Order of Discourse*, he sees this 'constraint of truth'[30] as one of the *external procedures* by which discourse is ordered: 'Between Hesiod and Plato a certain division was established, separating true discourse from false discourse: a new division because henceforth the true discourse is no longer ... the one linked to the exercise of power. The sophist is banished.'[31] This conflict was, in Foucault's view, decisive for the development of Western knowledge. But it is not only significant in its historical uniqueness. It is prototypical of a situation in which there is no authority, no judicial power which can decide which party is right or wrong. The one being right entails the other being wrong, because the dispute concerns two incommensurable positions. It is not a dispute in the usual sense, in which one is agreed on criteria of judgment and procedures, but a conflict in which these criteria themselves are in question. It is not a litigation *within* an order, but a conflict *between* principles of ordering.[32]

Whether these principles of ordering relate to external or internal ordering procedures, the result remains the same for Foucault: 'truth' is a political question. In order to be accepted, it must force others to accept it and give up their own external and/or internal rules of ordering. One can, in fact, resist the régime of truth or a particular truth-régime, but – and this is decisive – one cannot base oneself in this resistance on a truth lying 'outside power'. According to Foucault, it can never be 'a matter of emancipating truth from every system of power ... for truth is already power'.[33]

This linking of truth and power amounts to *de-substantivizing* truth. It is (the name for) the *event* in which the distinction between true and false breaks through and a determinate form is given to this distinction. The first aspect refers to the power effects which, according to Foucault's definition quoted above,[34] are associated with the true. It reminds us that the triumph of science, which is tied up with the power of the distinction between true and false, entails the 'marginalization' of other forms of discourse.[35] But 'truth' does not possess power solely by virtue of a historically contingent, *external ordering* of discourse. It also exercises power by imposing an *internal order* on discourse, in terms of the definition given above: by fleshing out the true/false distinction in a determinate way by introducing an 'ensemble of rules according to which the true and the false are separated'.[36]

On a first inspection, it follows from this definition of 'power-truth' in terms of the concepts of external and internal discourse procedures that the hyphen between the two terms here has a wholly different meaning from that later reserved by Foucault for the power-knowledge concept. The 'power of truth'[37] is here related to the historical privileging of a particular conception of truth (external order), which also seems predisposed to various forms of elaboration (internal order). Truth and power are not related here by power 'creat[ing] and caus[ing] to emerge new objects of knowledge',[38] as in the case of 'power-knowledge', but because 'truth' cannot be detached from a series of 'internal' and 'external' rules of exclusion by which we must be guided in our relations to things. At this stage in Foucault's thinking, the hyphen between truth and power does not (yet) refer to the light with which power produces a referent of knowledge, but to the fact that the truth itself is a kind of light, which *generates* a particular relationship to things (true/false) and depicts that relation in a particular way (internal procedures). The two hyphens seem to perform different functions. In the case of 'power-knowledge', the aim is to avoid – by the idea of productivity of power – the consequences of an ontological conception of truth. Power is not alienating but productive; its intervention does not mean that knowledge loses its object, but that it gains an object. The equally internal connection which, in *The Order of Discourse* and beyond, is posited between truth and power, is located at another level. The question is not one of ascribing a truth to things (ontological truth) or denying it (power-knowledge). The conflict between a 'repressive' conception of power shaped by the critique of ideology ('alienation') and a productive conception does not arise here, since, as Paul Veyne so aptly puts it, 'in the belief that they are seeking after the truth of things, men succeed only in establishing the rules by which what is said comes to be regarded as true or false'.[39] The ontological conception of truth is not subjected to a direct critique here. It is supplanted by what we might call, drawing on this passage from Veyne, a regulative theory of truth.[40]

All this gives the impression that we are dealing in *The Order of Discourse* with a transitional text. The link posited there between truth and power does indeed 'break' with the ontological conception of truth which, from *Histoire de la folie* onwards, kept embroiling Foucault in an archeo-eschatological model of critique. But this break is not the result of a direct confrontation with that model, as will be the case with the 'power-knowledge' concept. The 'power-truth' concept does not yet take account of the insights by which Foucault will later attempt to break free of archeo-eschatology. In an interview with Lucette Finas, he mentions, for example, that the mechanism of power in *The Order of Discourse* was still conceived too much in terms of exclusion/rejection and that the ideas which were developed in *Discipline and Punish* and later works (productivity of power etc) run contrary to the analysis which identifies the relations between power and discourse with negative selection mechanisms.[41] This self-criticism seems convincing: in *La Volonté de savoir*, Foucault does not in fact analyse the repression or exclusion of sexuality, but its production *in and by* discourses. What is striking about this criticism, however, is that he not only suggests that, in such an analysis, the idea of a repressive power must be abandoned, but also that everything which was said about procedures of exclusion in *The Order of Discourse* could be said to be incompatible with the theory of power.

We may ask whether Foucault is not 'mistaken' here and whether his association of 'repressiveness of power' with 'negative selection mechanisms' is not the cause of all his subsequent difficulties. While, in *Discipline and Punish*, he no longer has at his disposal a concept of 'repression' which does not immediately strike at the heart of everything he asserts about the productivity of power, in *The Order of Discourse*, he seems to have in mind a form of productivity which comes into being *in and by* a repression and an exclusion: thus, he argues emphatically that the 'positive' role of the procedures of ordering cannot be understood 'if we do not take into consideration their restrictive and constraining function'.[42] The exclusion procedures he analyses there are not purely negative selection mechanisms, but bring something into being: without selection, no order is possible; and selection is only productive because it represses other possible orders.

Curiously, no trace is to be found in *Discipline and Punish* of such a theory, which not only postulates the productivity of power but seems able to explain it or, at least, to begin to do so. Moreover, we have seen that the absence of this connection between productivity and repressiveness seemed to be responsible for Foucault being forced to retain the customary connotations of the power concept and, finally, for his having to concede, with Deleuze, that power produces before it represses. Foucault could only have avoided this *displacement* of the repression hypothesis, which explains the quotation marks in his later work, if he had, in some way, taken into account the insights in *The Order of Discourse* on the connection between productivity and repressiveness. The fact that he did not do so – or could not, or would not – requires careful interpretation. It was not, perhaps, necessary that Foucault should associate repressiveness with selectiveness, yet neither was it accidental. We must understand this if we wish to gain insight into the kind of 'decision' which prevented him from formulating a critique of objectivism.

4.2. From the problematic to the problems

1. Problems with the concept of order

Although Foucault points in *The Order of Discourse* to the internal connection between productivity and repressiveness, in the further course of this inaugural lecture, he seems interested mainly in the fact that the emergence and continued existence of an order depends on a series of principles of *exclusion*. The role of these principles is, admittedly, not purely negative – they bring an order into being – but it is negative none the less: 'the negative action of a carving out and a rarefaction of discourse'.[43] The accent here is not so much on the *productivity* of the internal and external principles of ordering, which bring about such a rarefaction of discourse, but on a *repressiveness* which is always assumed in this productivity and makes it possible. This shift of emphasis explains the critical pathos which characterizes *The Order of Discourse* no less than Foucault's other texts. The fact that particular statements come to lie outside of a particular 'truth' or even outside the order of 'truth' as such, in order that others may lie within that 'truth' or within 'truth', seems sufficient for Foucault to endow an analysis of this *'imposed scarcity'*[44] with a critical character.[45]

Within the logic of *The Order of Discourse*, this 'criticism' seems connected solely with the contingent character of the exclusion mechanisms which it brings to light. Thus, for example, every 'régime of truth' is dependent on a number of principles of ordering which, ultimately, merely originate in a selection from all conceivable principles, by which the other possible or actually existing rules of ordering are repressed, pushed aside or 'excluded'.[46] It is clear, however, that the discovery of this selectiveness and exclusiveness can only be termed critical in a very restricted sense. Both processes are *necessary*, in Foucault's view, for an order of any kind to come into being. To put it in the form of a paradox, the contingency he seeks to point out in his critique is a necessary one. It can in no sense be adduced as an argument against a particular order of truth, since Foucault has made the concept of an order of truth itself dependent on the existence of principles which owe their legitimacy *wholly and solely* to the fact that they make such an order *possible*. Whatever reasons Foucault may have for claiming the status of critique for his analyses, it should at once be clear that such a 'critique' finds itself in an uncomfortable position: it can never 'relativize' the validity of a particular order of truth without at the same time protecting that

117

validity from the charge of relativism. Foucault's concept of order *appears* to render a possible attempt to criticize a particular order impossible by no longer allowing any room for a standpoint outside that order, from which it might be criticized. The fact that the order has, so to speak, 'internalized' its own conditions of validity seems to condemn any attempt at criticism from the outset to be merely a deep, but empty sigh that 'what is might also be otherwise'.[47] Neither Foucault himself, nor his critics are prepared to leave it at such a sigh, however. The concept of order leads us back once again to the centre of the Foucault debate. But it also allows us to reduce this whole discussion to the analysis of *one* concept and the consequences that go with it – at least if we are able to convey the basic ideas of Foucault's archaeology and genealogy in that concept. This is not especially difficult so far as archaeology is concerned, since the concept of order which Foucault presents in *The Order of Discourse* is still clearly archaeological in character.[48]

2. The archaeological order of discourse

As we have already shown, Foucault's analysis of the human sciences in *The Order of Things* did not start out from man as object, but from a determination of the 'archaeological' conditions on which he could emerge as an object of the human sciences. Unlike in his later genealogy, Foucault did not as yet connect these conditions with the existence of different kinds of processes of subjectivization and individualization. He was not writing the history of mechanisms by which man was formed into a subject or individual, or constituted 'himself' as the subject of a sexuality. Nor was his intention that of an *archè-ology* which, like *Histoire de la folie*, related a history in which an original self-presence was alienated from itself. Foucault sought to understand the discourse of the human sciences without asking whether an original truth of humanity was being suppressed in that discourse and whether the human being about which the human sciences speak with such apparent ease is not rather the product of a historical process in which they themselves are not entirely uninvolved. This archaeology of the human sciences, which was no longer archè-ological, but not yet genealogical either, was primarily a systematic reflection on the epistemo-logical conditions which made it possible for what was said from a particular point about human beings *to be said*.

This astonishment at the fact that something can be said is, as

Foucault later explained, characteristic of the archaeological approach in general. This makes it 'a quite different history of what men have said'.[49] Instead of questioning 'things said as to what they are hiding',[50] it rejects all forms of interpretative method and confines itself to an archaeological 'description that questions the already-said [*déjà-dit*] at the level of its existence'.[51] What was said does not concern it on account of its content but because it was *this* which was said instead of all the other things which could, in principle, have been said in its place. Hence the archaeologist is no sleuth with a spade. Nor is he driven by a blind collecting mania which wants to preserve everything that has been said precisely because it has been said. His archaeology is an an-archaeology which simply questions 'things said' with the aim of determining 'what it means to them to have come into existence'[52] and thus seeks 'the law of what can be said'.[53]

In order to understand that law and to understand that not everything which 'one could say correctly in a particular period (according to the rules of grammar and those of logic) . . . is actually said',[54] one must take discourse seriously. And for Foucault this means that we must stop regarding it as a mere inscription of what was thought elsewhere or a reflection of what was present elsewhere, as though thinking or 'things' merely used discourse to express themselves rather than discourse imprinting itself upon thinking or things.[55] Discourse is not 'a surplus which *goes without saying*', a completely diaphanous medium which 'does nothing else except to say what is said'.[56] Nor is it the ever unreliable translation which lacks the words to match up to the richness of the original – the deep murmur of things, the inner dialogue of the mind.[57] In order to remain 'at the level of discourse itself',[58] one must stop looking behind or beneath what is said for a deeper or more comprehensive discourse. The manifest discourse is not 'the repressive presence of what it does not say'.[59] It is not a group of signs referring to something else.[60] In discourse itself, something takes place.[61] Discourse is a *practice* which cannot be reduced to a function of reference or expression. Rather than refer to pre-given objects, it brings its own objects into being.[62] Rather than document the originality of thinking subjects, it binds them to a set of rules which makes their thought and their originality possible.[63] And rather than offer them a boundless space in which everything can be said, it consists of a series of conditions of existence for an 'essentially incomplete [*lacunaire*]' and 'limited' space.[64] It is neither the object of a semiology of reference nor of a hermeneutics of the unsaid or the unthought, nor yet of a formalism of the sayable.[65] It is the object of an archaeology, i.e. of an analysis which reveals a 'systematic organization [*systematicité*]'[66] in thinking and speaking which is neither logical nor linguistic, but discursive in nature: an order of discourse.

One does not need to be familiar with the mostly technical details of Foucault's attempt to specify such an 'order of discourse' to understand his difficulties. Let us confine ourselves to the essential elements. Foucault defines discourse as an active principle. It is the difference between 'what could be said correctly ... and what is actually said'.[67] Or, more precisely, it is the instance which is responsible for that difference. It consists of a set of rules, later to be termed the principles of ordering, 'in accordance with which its objects, statements [*énonciations*], concepts, and theoretical options' are formed.[68] Its identity derives from those rules, not from what is regulated by them. It is not, for example, particular privileged objects which make nineteenth-century psychiatric discourse what it is, but the way it itself forms its objects.[69] Such a constitution of its objects presupposes, in Foucault's view, that 'discourse' satisfy a series of conditions which make it possible for an object to appear: it must specify a series of relations between institutions, socio-economic processes, behavioural patterns and systems of norms and classifications.[70] Foucault terms such 'discursive' relations – somewhat exaggeratedly – rules of object formation. 'Discourse' is a host of such relations – a *'mise en relation'*[71] which makes it possible to 'say something new'[72] and enables a *'discursive* object' to appear. The conditions under which such an object appears coincide with the 'historical conditions required if one is "to say something" about it'.[73] But what is more – and here the restriction inherent in the archaeological approach clearly shows up: the discursive object which appears under these conditions coincides with what is said about it. Thus, for example, in Foucault's view, mental illness 'was constituted by all the statements that named it, divided it up, described it, explained it, traced its developments, indicated its various correlations, judged it, and possibly gave it speech by articulating, in its name, discourses *that were to be taken as its own*'.[74]

One can see that Foucault gives the problem of *Histoire de la folie* a very wide berth here, but one can also see that the detour is not great enough to escape that problem. On the one hand, in the passage cited, he seems to understand mental illness as a kind of internal reference point of psychiatric discourse – an 'object of knowledge' which only comes into being in this discourse and in no sense pre-exists it: 'the object does not await in limbo the order that will free it ... it does not pre-exist itself ... It exists under the positive conditions of a complex group of relations.'[75] Yet, on the other hand, he seems to wish at the same time to keep open the possibility that the discourse on mental illness ('internal reference') is *only* a discourse which is carried out *in the name of* this mental illness ('external reference'; 'discourses that were *to be taken* as its own'). Strictly speaking, however, his archaeology no longer possesses the means to test the validity of the claims of a particular discourse to be indeed what it presents itself to be: a discourse of 'mental illness itself'. Foucault expressly forbade archaeology any further involvement with a 'history of the referent' in the style of *Histoire de la folie*.[76] In order to avoid ending up once again with an 'archaeology of alienation',[77] he jettisoned not just the concept of alienation, but also the problematic which it tried to express. In contrast to archè-ology, an-archaeology must now 'dispense with "things"'. It must define its objects without referring to the 'things themselves' (*les 'choses mêmes'*). 'For the enigmatic treasure of "things" anterior to discourse', it substitutes 'the regular formation of objects that emerge only in discourse'.[78]

The motive for this 'farewell to things' is clear. To define discourse independently of things or, as he later put it, to 'conceive discourse as a violence which we do to things ... as a practice which we impose on them'[79] is a way of preventing it from being trivialized by being regarded merely as the expression of a pre-given 'order of things'. And to search in this practice it imposes upon things for the 'principle of ... regularity' of the events of discourse[80] is a way of thinking an 'order of discourse' which does not supervene later, but comes about in and by that discourse. But the price to pay for this *démarche* would seem to be that, instead of (for example) 'undermining the order of psychiatric discourse', such an archaeological concept of order can only describe it and, indeed, even seems compelled to legitimate it. Instead of an order which violates the truth of things and is really nothing more than a 'field of alienation'[81] an order now emerges which has to do violence to things and is thus thrown back on itself in such a way that there seems no longer any point at which critique can obtain a purchase.

Foucault's embarrassment is easily understood: an archaeology of this kind could only make his critique of the human sciences the more difficult. [82] And one can perhaps understand now why he was so ready in his later genealogy to go back to the model of *Histoire de la folie*. In the archaeological period, the problems of archè-ology were only deferred: they could not but reappear with the same intensity when Foucault once again took on, in *Discipline and Punish*, the problem of a history of the referent of knowledge. We may therefore also expect to meet once again in the genealogical concept of order the traces of a problematic which archaeology had skirted around.

3. The concept of order in genealogy

At first sight, Foucault's genealogical power problematic can be translated without any great difficulty into the terms of the concept of order developed earlier. The body, for example, is in a certain sense 'ordered' by determinate bodily techniques which, like all ordering procedures, are selective and exclusive: discipline is a possible bodily technique, i.e. a technique which imposes a particular order on the body which 'excludes' or *represses* other possible orders. [83] Foucault's criticism of discipline was not, however, related to *this* repression. In order to safeguard his critique of science, he had to subject discipline to a critique which did not portray it as *one* bodily technique among others, but was able to reject it *as* bodily technique. [84] For this purpose, he went back to an archè-ological model which shrinks back from the consequences of the concept of order and – unlike archaeology – plays off the violence which the order 'do[es] to things' against that order itself: the *decision* to take the part of 'the body itself' (*le corps lui-même*) against discipline amounts to arguing that, in its attempt to order the body, not only discipline, *but any other form of bodily technique*, is suspect and unjust from the outset. The rejection of discipline is based on the fact that it imposes *an* order on the body, not that it imposes any *particular* order. This leads to the body having to be regarded as a kind of original, 'pre-ordinal', self-sufficient entity and, consequently, to *any* bodily technique *whatever* having to be interpreted as an offence against its intactness.

As has already been argued repeatedly, such a way of proceeding is incompatible with a genealogy which expressly wished to jettison the 'naturalistic' presupposition that, 'under power with its acts of violence and its artifice, we should be able to rediscover the things themselves in their primitive vivacity'.[85] If 'everything is already interpretation',[86] then there is no original interpretandum that could be known without having to go through these interpretations and that would constitute an internal check on interpretability. It is, however, clear that such a 'strictly' genealogical point of departure can no more satisfy Foucault either: if one considers the order of discipline as an interpretation which 'inscribes' itself in the body and if, like Foucault, one also rejects every external, normative criterion permitting us to evaluate that interpretation in relation to others,[87] then it seems one is able only to demonstrate the *relative* validity of this form of bodily ordering. Discipline is, then, a bodily technique which allows particular actions and experiences to take place and prevents others. As a result, Foucault is faced with an aporia: a non-genealogical starting point condemns all forms of ordering of the body; a strictly genealogical standpoint does not condemn a single one. In order to avoid this aporia, he would either have had to revise his 'anti-naturalistic' premises and prove that *particular* 'interpretations' or *particular* ways of ordering the body come into conflict with an internal 'normativity' of life (or of the body); or he would have had to keep to his general rejection of every form of 'metaphysics of origins' and would no longer have been able to seek support for his critique in something like the original spontaneity of the body.

Instead of deciding between them, Foucault combines the two positions. From Nietzsche he takes over a nominalism which explains every identity as an 'equating [of] the unequal'[88] and – unlike Nietzsche – he seeks in this 'distortion' *itself* an argument against the order established by it.[89] Individuality, for example, then appears as a *product* of a power which classifies the heterogeneous and imposes an order upon it: 'disciplinary tactics ... allows both the characterization of the individual as individual and the ordering of a given multiplicity'.[90] But this individuality is, at the same time, the product of a *power* which one must resist: 'What is needed is to de-individualize.'[91] This critique of individualization, of discipline (etc), seems borne along by a kind of nostalgia for an anonymity which must have preceded individualization. Thus Foucault speaks, for example, of the 'joy of a non-identity' which the hermaphrodite knew before being deprived of the 'pleasure of having no sex'.[92] And the pain and suffering of the person who has to confess to his 'true sex' is not, for Foucault, an argument against the way we – or our institutions – relate to the symbolic order of sexuality, but an argument against that order itself: the body does not have one or two sexes, but has none and, consequently, 'modern, Western society' is making a mistake when it 'obstinately seeks to deploy the criterion of "true sex" in an order of things in which one might have thought that *only the reality of bodies and the intensity of their pleasures count*'.[93]

'The reality of bodies and the intensity of pleasures' – instead of breaking with a binary order (man/woman), as Foucault would have liked to do, this formula feeds on another binary order (no sex/a sex) beneath which, once again, the model of *Histoire de la folie* can be seen emerging. Disciplinary bodily techniques, confessions and individualization hold their objects captive in the black light of an original eclipse. Identity casts its shadow over the non-identical. The order of the human sciences, which arises in this darkness, is based on an avoidable reduction of the heterogeneous: 'The man described for us ... is already in himself the effect of a subjection much more profound than himself. A "soul" inhabits him and brings him to existence ... *the soul is the prison of the body.*'[94] The 'examination' in the human sciences, 'still caught up in disciplinary technology',[95] is *violence itself*, because it introduces concepts for what is not to be grasped in terms of concepts: man can only be recognized as 'the object-effect ... of this domination-observation'.[96] Instead of coinciding with all that is said about him,[97] he is the product of 'power and knowledge relations that invest human bodies and subjugate them by turning them into objects of knowledge'.[98] He only appears within an order which is, ultimately, repressive and whose repressiveness is reinforced by what is said about him in the human sciences. This at least is the conclusion a genealogical critique, which has made itself dependent upon an archè-ological concept of order, threatens to produce. In order genuinely to break with the idea that 'power is bad' and 'what power is exercised upon is right, good and rich',[99] this concept of order will have to be recast. But such an emendation can only succeed if Foucault's quotation marks ('science', 'soul', 'subject') are dropped and another kind of critique developed.

4.3. An emendation

1. An overview of the difficulties

Let us summarize. Whereas the problem of archaeology was that it could no longer think an inauthentic order, an archè-ological-'genealogical' critique threatened to turn every order into an inauthentic order: into a 'field of alienation' which must disappear if one wishes to restore contact with the truth of madness or of the body. In the case of archaeology one must refrain from any criticisms of an order; in the case of archè-ology and 'genealogy', every order must be put in inverted commas. Consequently, Foucault's concept of order only seems compatible with a type of critique which we also met in his analysis of the human sciences ('science'). Indeed, it seems to be presupposed in these analyses. The archè-ological-'genealogical' critique of order *as such* has its counterpart in a critique of the scientificity of the human sciences as such: their claim to scientificity is seen as illegitimate because they become possible only on the basis of an initial process whereby something is suppressed which deprives them of their proper referent ('madness itself') or provides them with a pseudo-referent ('the soul' etc). On the other hand, the lack of an archaeologically-based critique of order means that, in *The Order of Things*, Foucault can only reject the human sciences' claims to scientificity by introducing an external criterion of scientificity which is not susceptible of further analysis.

We have seen from the analyses above that Foucault was only able to introduce these quotation marks ('order', 'science') by failing to match up to his own initial positions. This was the case with 'genealogy', which was obliged to resort to the 'naturalism' it had precisely sought to avoid. And the enthusiasm with which Foucault set about analysing mechanisms of order as *exclusion* mechanisms stands in stark contrast to the 'critical' consequences he could properly have associated with this. One can, of course, see in discourse a 'principle of control' which imposes limits on what is said 'by the action of an identity which takes the form of a permanent re-actuation of the rules'.[100] But even if these rules are ascribed to the intervention of a 'discursive policing',[101] the existence of such a 'police' control is not adequate as an argument against the legitimacy of the order which comes about as a result of its action. Such control makes order possible and it would be mistaken to attribute a direct political significance to the mechanisms of exclusion it sets in place. As Foucault has repeatedly stressed, the alternative to an order of discourse is not a chaos in which anything can be said, but another order. The 'rarefaction' associated with every discourse is unavoidable; it is, admittedly, imposed, but not in such a way as to impoverish some original richness of discourse. Every order of discourse puts restrictions in one way or another on what can be said, but Foucault nowhere makes clear that these restrictions prevent other orders from imposing their own restrictions. The philosophical order of 'truth', for example, to a certain extent excludes the order of sophistry, but this does not prevent the order of sophistry from introducing its own principles of ordering. Philosophy and sophistry can only come into conflict because they start out from different principles of ordering. Whatever standpoint one wishes to take in this conflict, it is clear that one cannot reject the philosophical order of discourse wholly and solely because it is a *philosophical* order of discourse which, as a consequence, can be said to 'repress' other orders. Or, to take another example, the instruments, techniques and discourses of contemporary physics in a certain sense exclude their Newtonian precursors, but that exclusion is, none the less, distinct from a 'repression' which would have a direct political significance. If one neglects this, then one confuses, as Peter Dews has rightly remarked, 'a *politically enforced silence*' with 'a silence or absence which is merely the reverse side of the positivity of a given cultural formation'.[102] The concept of the political is trivialized if one makes every definition into an exclusion that is an effect of the exercise of power. To be able to speak of a 'politics' of truth, to make truth a political problem and to take the view that we must free ourselves from the order of truth in which we find ourselves[103] more solid arguments are required than the mere assertion that 'truth' can be traced back to 'the play of a primary ... falsification which erects the distinction between truth and falsehood'.[104] The fact that, by this falsification, an order of 'truth' is introduced which can itself be neither true nor false because it is what initially makes possible the distinction between truth and falsehood,[105] does not mean that truth is *only* the effect of a trial of strength, the result of which can *only* be arbitrary and repressive. Even if a particular order necessarily engages in a trial of strength, in order to be able to impose itself and acquire a right to existence, and even if, as an order, it is internally incompatible with other already existent or possible orders, then it still does not follow that this kind of exclusion would deprive it of its legitimacy. To resist an order because (like every other order) it 'excludes' other possible orders amounts, unavoidably, to making that resistance dependent on a decisionism for which there can only be strictly political grounds. One is entitled to expect more from a critical *theory*. Instead of *simply* coming out on the side of repressed knowledge and making that choice dependent only on a 'theoretical-political' decision,[106] Foucault would have had to show, as Derrida remarked immediately after the publication of *Histoire de la folie*, that there is, associated with the order in which we find ourselves, not merely an exclusion but a *specific* exclusion.[107]

2. A special form of relativism

If the criticism of an order cannot base itself on the fact that that order excludes others (which is contrary to the premises of archaeology), and cannot appeal, either, to the fact that it violates the non-identity of a pre-ordinal, self-sufficient entity (which is contrary to the premises of a genealogy *stricto sensu*), then the 'primary and always reconstituted falsification, which erects the distinction between truth and falsehood'[108] cannot be a falsification in the normal sense of the word. Such a falsification in reality falsifies nothing. It is necessary in order that something like the order of truth can arise. The 'equating [of] the unequal' and the 'exclusion' of other possible orders is inevitable and, in itself, provides no argument against the order of truth brought into being thereby. Or, to put it another way, to interpret is not 'only' veiling or concealment. It is 'at the same time also revealing, discovering, creating meaning'.[109]

Even when, in such a perspective, one no longer has means to judge the truth of an order of truth, an order which can only come into being on the basis of a preceding interpretation or 'falsification', this does not directly imply that one is thereby surrendering to a primitive form of relativism. In fact, Foucault nowhere defends a simple relativism with regard to truth or validity.[110] He brackets out (in the sense of Husserl's *epoché*), the question of truth and refrains from appealing to expressly normative criteria,[111] but he does not assert that no practical or theoretical truth (in the usual sense) exists. Rather than defend a relativism with regard to truth or validity, he investigates the conditions of validity and truth. The order 'of truth' – or a particular order of truth – forms a framework within which particular truth-claims can be made. In the same way, one might envisage a framework – one may term it a 'lifeworld', as Waldenfels does,[112] or, with Wittgenstein, speak of a 'form of life' – which permits determinate normative validity claims to be made: 'What people accept as a justification – is shewn by how they think and live.'[113] These frameworks make particular attempts at foundation possible, but they can no longer themselves be founded or legitimated by that which they make possible.[114] They are characterized by an insurmountable 'positivity': 'order *exists*'.[115] Selective and exclusive as such orders must be, they cannot without loss of meaning be traced back to a kind of common ground or referred to a common horizon. The specificity of these orders would disappear if one were to bracket out the selectiveness and exclusiveness which makes them what they are and relate them back to a 'founding order' or integrate them into an overarching 'general order'.[116] One fails to grasp, for example, the specificity of the various orders of truth (internal principles of ordering) if one merely sees them as variants of a general order of truth and takes the view that an analysis of the external principles of ordering which underlie the order of truth as such is sufficient, while the significance of the internal principles, which differentiate truth itself, can be neglected.[117] And one may, similarly, ask whether it is *at all* the same body which is 'captured' in discipline or in another bodily technique and whether it makes sense in general to focus on this substrate, since, by so doing, one abstracts precisely from the specific nature of the various bodily orders.[118] A critique of discipline and a critique of the (or a) truth which also wishes to take the concept of order seriously must forgo recourse to a common ground or to the universality of a common horizon.

But doesn't this mean that there is no possibility of such a critique? That it cannot be carried out and, indeed, not even conceived? Doesn't a 'relativistic' programme of this kind contradict its own intentions? Doesn't it in fact always and in principle show the relative validity of the order in which it finds itself and the impossibility of lending credence, in a non-decisionistic way, to 'the task of transforming' the order in which we find ourselves?[119] Doesn't this 'relativism' of conditions of validity have to be supplemented by a hard concept of truth or by a normative criterion no longer dependent on the 'particularistic' conditions of validity which seem to be presupposed here? If one admits that the selectiveness and exclusiveness of orders is not to be confused with 'power', isn't the only chance of still using such a conception of power meaningfully, without lapsing back into the rejected naturalism of a repressive concept of power, to be found in introducing a normative framework?[120] Is it true that 'productive' power is always bent on exclusion, discipline and the like? Mustn't an 'exercise of power on the basis of other norms' be presupposed, 'if critical knowledge is to have an effect' and is not to condemn itself from the outset to be the agent of another system of power or exclusion (in the usual sense)?[121] Lastly, if one wishes to use the concept of power in a sense different from normal usage and to link selectiveness/exclusiveness with the 'productivity' of 'power', will one not be faced once again with the alternative of either refraining from all further criticism and describing the effect of 'power' positivistically or founding one's criticism in explicitly normative terms by adopting a criterion that makes it possible to evaluate orders, which are always in some measure both enabling and constraining, in terms of their relative performance?[122]

All these questions revolve around the problem of whether a form of critique is still possible if we continue to adhere strictly to Foucault's archaeological-genealogical premises. Is a critique of power possible which doesn't already presuppose a critique of order *as such*? Is a critique of the order of truth or the order of the body, or the order of the human sciences possible which doesn't get caught in the undertow of a repressive conception of power? Could Foucault have given up his 'politics of quotation marks'[123] or was he forced to retain these marks on pain of being reduced to silence not only as a critical philosopher but also as a 'citizen'? Could he have identified with the programme of a critique of objectivism?

3. The prospects for a critique of 'objectivism'

One way of preventing the concept of order having itself to be abandoned along with the critique of order might be to subject not order *as such* but its self-interpretation to criticism. Instead of looking in the constitutive conditions of an order for arguments against that order itself, Foucault could have criticized particular orders for objectivistically misrecognizing their conditions of possibility. Such a critique would relate not to selectiveness/exclusiveness itself, but to its misrecognition. It would not draw its pathos from the ambiguity of concepts like 'exclusion', 'discursive policing', 'control' etc, but would attempt to show that particular orders can only function because they conceal the exclusion which *makes them possible*. It would have to show that, alongside control in terms of discursive policing, such a legitimation strategy introduces a non-discursive 'police power' which is not necessary, but avoidable and to be avoided. Instead of casting suspicion on every order because it can only constitute itself in and by an 'exclusion', it would have to investigate how orders relate to this process of constitution. For example, discipline would not have to be condemned *qua* bodily technique; it would not be 'bad' because it subjects the body as such nor because, by its existence, it takes the place of another, possible but not simultaneously realizable, technique. Foucault could have investigated whether the specificity of the disciplinary bodily technique – and the reasons why it seems instinctively repellent – is not so much to do with its being not only, like all other bodily techniques, selective and exclusive, as with the fact that the corporeal order it brings into being can only remain in force because it misrecognizes its own selectiveness and exclusiveness, and imposes itself upon the body or justifies that imposition *as though* it were the only conceivable order.

The practical relevance of such a research *hypothesis* is obvious. To regard discipline as a bodily technique which must misrecognize its character as bodily technique in order to be able to function could allow Foucault to examine whether it is not *this misrecognition* which enables it to bind the body to *one* norm and to make the application of other bodily norms more difficult or exclude them altogether.[124] The rigidity and irreversibility[125] characteristic of disciplinary processes would then be related to – or would follow from – the way they are elaborated and legitimate themselves. The critique of the disciplinary order would then consist not in exposing it as *an* order, but in exposing its forgetting that it is an *order*.

It is, at first sight, surprising that Foucault's 'genealogy' did not develop a critique of this type, since his archaeology seemed to provide scope for it. It would not seem to be such a great step from the insight that a discourse presupposes a 'rarefaction' and can only exist on the basis of a necessary 'unsaid'[126] to the supposition that it may be in the interest of such a discourse to conceal this fact – and, hence, its own discursivity – a step which, incidentally, the commentators have made without much difficulty.[127] It would, for example, be possible for discourses – those of the human sciences, for instance – to wish to deny their discursive character because this would allow them to divert attention from the fact that their referent is not simply delivered up to them ready-made by reality.[128] One can see the plausibility of such an objectivist interest, if one looks at the self-referential structure of law or of mathematicizing economics. That the law understands human beings as always already juridical beings – as legal subjects – and dismisses the construction of the juridical by recourse to the distinction between 'brute facts' and 'institutional facts';[129] that economics has taken great pains to project the economic back into the beginnings of all culture and already sees an embryonic *homo economicus* in the primitive;[130] that, lastly, 'metaphysics' in its various forms, as Derrida's analyses show, always obeys a 'logic of the supplement' which produces a strict separation between inside and outside, fact and essence, nature and culture all indicates that discourses – or particular discourses – may feel threatened by their discursiveness, by their limitation. Whether they then attempt to universalize themselves self-referentially and, by so doing, to sweep away their limits or at least to blur them or, conversely, seek to stress those limits the better to control them, in both cases they seem to wish to forget the ordering to which they owe their specificity and the delimitation which makes them *possible*. In the first case, limitation is denied; in the second, there is an effort to control it, since the aim is to ground the limitation which makes one's own discourse possible in that discourse itself. In both cases, the *ordering* of one's own discourse is denied or misrecognized.

Whatever the value of these proposals, Foucault's archaeology cannot permit itself to neglect the problem which prompts them. Since the possibility cannot be excluded that discourses – or particular discourses – strive systematically to hide from view the occurrence of ordering to which they owe their identity, an archaeology which makes the identification of discourses dependent on the discovery of a series of 'recognizable' rules or principles of ordering, must be extremely careful if it wishes to avoid its effort at identification coming to duplicate the self-understanding of those discourses. That the problem is not an imaginary one was clear from the difficulties, already discussed above, with which Foucault's identification of the dimensions of the 'trihedron of knowledge' had to contend in *The Order of Things*. As we have seen, that identification was caught up in a vicious circle: Foucault was operating with a concept of 'anthropologization' which really should only have emerged as the product of his construction. The construction of the trihedron of knowledge was to enable him to establish the specific status of the human sciences and to determine the scope of the attendant 'anthropologistic' danger. But he was faced with the problem that the non-human-scientific disciplines, which were supposed to form the dimensions of his trihedron, might always be infected *de facto* by an anthropological supplement. He was, as a result, compelled to purge the disciplines in question of such anthropologisms, even before he could determine the nature and scope of the danger. And he could determine neither the nature nor the scope of that danger without first making a strict distinction within the empirical sciences (including economics) between the central core of those disciplines and their anthropologistic supplement – a procedure which could not be sure of being free of arbitrariness or of avoiding a trap set by the empirical sciences themselves when they asserted that they were not human sciences. To separate economics out from the human sciences and assert that the impure anthropologizing discourse with which it has been associated since its mathematicization can play no role in the determination of its epistemological specificity is entirely consonant, as we have shown elsewhere,[131] with the *self-understanding* of a self-mathematicizing economics.

This should have made Foucault wary – economics being for him one of the model sciences to which he referred in contesting the human sciences' claim to scientificity. But was such a reference justified? What if the anthropologism within economics were only apparently a parasitic supplement; what if, with regard to what it was allegedly added to, this supplement were not so external, as the non-anthropologizing 'central' core of economics suggests? And what if this were also the case with the other empirical sciences? How serviceable then is the criterion implicitly being applied here to enable us to speak of human 'sciences'? Is it *at all* meaningful, within the limits of the archaeological method, to seek to judge the scientificity of particular disciplines? Shouldn't Foucault have backtracked here too and, as with genealogy, developed another type of criticism? A criticism which neither subordinates the sciences to philosophy nor does the opposite, but which finds a niche for itself in the margins of scientific discourse as a kind of 'indirect speech' (Merleau-Ponty) and analyses the internal discourse which particular discourses carry on about themselves, in order to remind them that it is not they who have control of the light within which they flourish, but that that light comes from elsewhere, that their ordering presupposes a more originary event which lets something appear within discourses, but also leaves a lot in the dark?

A problem still remains in all this, and here we must confess our ignorance. We do not yet seem to have met all the conditions to be able properly to speak of a *critique* of objectivism. Even if one is prepared to take seriously the proposition that the power associated with disciplinary technique finds the conditions of possibility of its 'productivity' in the selectiveness and exclusiveness of that bodily technique and that it would only become power in the normally accepted sense if it misrecognized these conditions of possibility and hence misrecognized its own productivity, and even if one is convinced that the problem of the human sciences perhaps lies not so much in their claim to scientificity as in the *authority* they derive from that scientificity, the question still remains whether one can simply assume that an order is actually able to take stock of its own selectiveness and exclusiveness. What if every order were, to a certain extent, characterized by the blindness which comes from such a 'mis'recognition? And why should an order not be allowed to 'forget' its selectiveness/exclusiveness? Why should it not be permitted to 'deny' its origins and 'shut itself up in itself'?[132] These are in no sense assertions disguised as questions, but questions which continue to be due an answer. Within the premises of an amended Foucaultianism, it seems difficult – if not perhaps impossible – to decide on what basis it should be possible to distinguish an authentic from an inauthentic order. Unlike the later Husserl or the early Habermas, Foucault does not possess the rigorous means of a transcendental philosophy *stricto sensu* which would permit him to locate, in the *forgetting* of the operations of a transcendental subjectivity, the possibility of a crisis of knowledge. Unlike the later Heidegger, he does not work in a conceptual framework within which one can distinguish between the 'autism' with which particular orders, e.g. 'enframing' (*Gestell*) turn away from a more originary occurrence of Being and from the co-origination of concealment and unconcealment which applies to every 'destiny'.[133] The distinction between an authentic and an inauthentic relation to the event of ordering or of truth – the distinction between the blindness of technique and *releasement* (*Gelassenheit*) – cannot, so far as we can see, be thought here in its totality.[134] But whether one looks for an answer to the question 'what pushes an order beyond itself' in Heidegger or (like Waldenfels)[135] in Merleau-Ponty, this much is clear: the meaning of the transgression Foucault dreamed of, the meaning of the *se déprendre*[136] ('the getting free of oneself'), which he proposed as an ideal, depends on the answer to this question. In this sense, these pages which were initially intended to form a kind of 'Afterword to Transgression' now turn out to be a Preface, even if it is one inspired by a different pathos than the sort we encounter in Foucault's *Préface à la transgression*.[137] When the smoke has cleared, all that remains is the patient work in and at the limit, a 'think[ing] differently'[138] perhaps, which does not attempt to think something new, but seeks to take up a new relation to thinking. By *working* at this relation, it will eventually become clear whether or not the concept of 'transgression' is still appropriate.[139]

* * *

We would have preferred to shed the responsibility for these last few pages. At the time when they were written, they constituted for us the 'outside' of our thought. And one knows how difficult it is to free oneself from a system of thinking and how long that effort can last, how much patience it requires. Which is why at that time, and at this point, this text which perhaps, in its naïveté, was meant to lay the ground for an 'other' philosophy 'of' 'the' 'crisis' had to be broken off. As Foucault's discourse was growing fainter and gradually falling silent, and as we in our turn were swept away by a new passion which we did not yet understand, but which no longer made it possible for us to listen to the sound of his fading words, at that point, then, when there was nothing left for us to do but lose ourselves once again – and for a long time – we had to leave it – as we have to now in a language not our own – to others to confront us with these dying words. The philosopher, like the lover, is condemned to live with an exteriority which he can never incorporate, but which, none the less, does not leave him unmoved. Like Emily L., he is 'someone who's unfaithful'.[140] He sees always in others the embodiment of the unknown in himself, of this 'place' which he must keep 'where one can be alone' and he always needs others who, for a spell, become the 'outside' of his thinking, the 'side' he 'never sees', and which constantly eludes him. This is perhaps the reason why, in philosophy, there can only be eternal beginners. It is, in this regard, no different from life, in which one must 'set aside a place in oneself to wait ... to wait for a love, perhaps for a love without a person attached to it yet, but for that and only that. For love.' But in life one does the impossible, one says to someone that he or she is what one has waited for and one knows or learns that there is no point going back on this. Philosophy's is a different freedom. It is dependent on dialogue, but never coincides with it.

Abbreviations and References

For the works by Foucault which we quote most frequently the following abbreviations are used (details of editions can be consulted in the Bibliography).

AK *The Archaeology of Knowledge.*

BC *The Birth of the Clinic.*

DP *Discipline and Punish. The Birth of the Prison.*

FD *Folie et déraison. Histoire de la folie à l'âge classique.*

HF *Histoire de la folie à l'âge classique.*

HS1 *The History of Sexuality,* vol. 1.

HS2 *The Use of Pleasure. The History of Sexuality,* vol. 2.

HS3 *The Care of the Self. The History of Sexuality,* vol. 3.

MIP *Mental Illness and Psychology.*

NGH 'Nietzsche, Genealogy, History', *Language, Counter-Memory, Practice: Selected Essays and Interviews.*

OD *The Order of Discourse. Untying the Text.*

OT *The Order of Things. An Archaeology of the Human Sciences.*

P/K *Power/Knowledge. Selected Interviews and Other Writings 1972–77.*

RC *Résumé des cours 1970–1982.*

Other works by Foucault are cited in the Notes by their (short) titles. Works by other authors are identified by short references (author's name, publication date). Full details may be found in the Bibliography.

Notes

Introduction

1. 'Resistance – for this was a resistance on my part – often indicates the sensitive point in a reading, the point of incomprehension that organizes it' (J. Derrida, 1989a), p. 14.
2. J. Derrida (1982), p. 4.
3. NGH, p. 139.
4. HF, p. 121. Cf pp. 315, 446.
5. DP, pp. 22, 24, 185, 256, 295–6, 308.
6. M. Foucault, 'Two Lectures', P/K, p. 84 (translation modified).
7. The context makes clear that it is psychiatry which is chiefly being referred to here.
8. M. Foucault, 'L'Extension sociale de la norme' (1976), p. 16.
9. M. Foucault, 'Two Lectures', P/K, p. 85.
10. Ibid, pp. 84–5.
11. Ibid, p. 82.
12. Feyerabend has pointed out that one can understand this concept either descriptively or prescriptively in P. Feyerabend (1981), p. 198.
13. OT, p. 366.
14. J. Derrida (1978), p. 38.
15. M. Foucault, 'Truth and Power', P/K, p. 109. Foucault explains here why, in HF, he analysed a discipline with a 'low epistemological profile': 'Couldn't the interweaving of effects of power and knowledge be grasped with greater certainty in the case of a science as "dubious" as psychiatry?'
16. M. Foucault, 'Two Lectures', P/K, p. 83: 'Genealogies are therefore not positivistic returns to a more careful or exact form of science. They are precisely anti-sciences.'
17. B. Waldenfels (1986), pp. 30–31.

Chapter 1

1. This text dates from 1962 and is based on Foucault's revision of *Maladie mentale et personnalité* (1954) after the appearance of HF in 1961. See Macherey (1986), pp. 753–4. Chapter 5 is a summary of HF (MIP, pp. 64–75).

2. On this argument, see MIP, p. 73.

3. Ibid.

4. HF, p. 548.

5. We have pointed out above that Foucault uses these terms 'unsystematically' (see especially MIP, pp. 64–75, where Foucault speaks of 'psychology' and 'psychiatry' without distinguishing between the two). For this reason we confine ourselves in what follows to the former term unless Foucault's text determines that we act otherwise.

6. See e.g. HF, pp. 235, 396 (on Pomme and Bichat, cf BC); HF, pp. 346, 469, 521 (cf DP); pp. 97, 103 (cf HS1) and many anticipations of OT (passim).

7. HF, p. 548.

8. Ibid, p. 176.

9. MIP, p. 87.

10. According to Merquior, HF represents a counter-history, which does not aspire to be anything more than that. The only question which must be put, in his view, is 'Does Foucault get his history right?' (Merquior, 1985, p. 26). This is not our approach here, not because it is unimportant, but because it relates only to the execution of a programme, whereas it is the philosophical validity of that programme that is at issue here. For a discussion of the facts, see also Gordon (1990), Midelfort (1990), Porter (1990) and Scull (1990) in the special number of *History of the Human Sciences* devoted to HF.

11. HF, pp. 120, 124.

12. MIP, p. 64.

13. HF, p. 132.

14. Ibid, p. 483.

15. Ibid, pp. 93, 132.

16. MIP, p. 64 (my emphasis, R.V.). Cf HF, p. 74n.

17. HF, p. 93.

18. We shall return to the example of the insane (*'les insensés'*) below.

19. Mental illness (*'maladie mentale'*) – we have already pointed out this oddity.

20. HF, p. 93.

21. I am referring to the possibility and not the actuality of such a psychology, since the existence of an object independent of its constitution by psychology does not mean that psychology has knowledge of that object. What we have here is a necessary, but not a sufficient, condition for a realist interpretation. Admittedly, this argument lends support to psychology's claim that it *is able* to know an independent object, yet it remains conceivable that the psychological constitution of the object annuls this independence of the object (see below). On the other hand, the refutation of this argument does not imply *ipso facto* a refutation of psychology's claim, since it remains conceivable that the object is indeed co-existent with the constitution of psychology, but still independent of it.

22. HF, p. 231; see also HF, pp. 131, 150, 291.

23. By analogy with Merleau-Ponty's '*kosmotheoros*': 'a thought that looks at being [for being, read 'illness', R.V.] from elsewhere, and as it were head-on' (Merleau-Ponty, 1968, p. 113).

24. NGH, p. 152.

25. HF, p. 124.

26. We take this expression from Habermas's commentary on Foucault (J. Habermas, 1987, p. 249).

27. HF, p. 144.

28. This pair of concepts comes from G. Berthoud and F. Sabelli (1976), pp. 106, 116.

29. HF, pp. 132, 137–8, 446 and passim.

30. NGH, p. 148. We attempt here, with the aid of a later text (1971), to clarify

the argument of HF (1961). Whether what we have here is a true anticipation of the later text is a question we shall discuss at a later stage.

31. NGH, p. 142. Cf HF, p. 132.
32. NGH, p. 148.
33. R. Bernet (1986), p. 95.
34. DP, p. 31.
35. HF, pp. 138–9.
36. The genealogical method, which Foucault introduces later, distances itself expressly from this pair of concepts (NGH, pp. 154, 161 and HF, p. 120 on identity and continuity).
37. HF, pp. 120, 359.
38. Ibid, p. 238.
39. Ibid, p. 177.
40. Ibid.
41. Ibid.
42. Ibid, pp. 458, 471.
43. See the analysis ibid, p. 137. The term 'non-contemporaneity' is taken from Althusser (1970), pp. 91 ff.
44. MIP, p. 65 and HF, p. 147. This concept is, however, ambiguous (see below).
45. HF, p. 139.
46. Ibid, pp. 75, 94 and the second chapter of Part I ('Le Grand Renfermement'), ibid, pp. 56–91.
47. This episode is described in the fourth chapter of Part III: 'Naissance de l'asile' (ibid, pp. 483–530, especially pp. 487 ff.).
48. Ibid, p. 93.
49. Ibid.
50. Ibid, p. 132.
51. Ibid, p. 135.
52. Ibid, p. 124.
53. Ibid, pp. 96, 124, 147, 176.
54. Ibid, p. 96.
55. Ibid, p. 176 (my emphasis, R.V.).
56. Ibid, p. 125; MIP, p. 67.
57. The comprehensive term for this 'colourful population' (HF, p. 116) is, literally, 'those who have lost their senses' (ibid, p. 151: 'Bargedé est insensé' and the whole of Chapter 5 of Part I ('Les Insensés') (ibid, pp. 150–77).
58. Ibid, p. 117 ('a coherence which is neither that of a right nor that of a science; the more secret coherence of a *perception*').
59. Ibid, p. 125 ('*sur un autre ciel*').
60. Ibid, p. 96.
61. It would perhaps be no exaggeration to say that Foucault's entire philosophy is encapsulated in this manoeuvre: we are dealing here not with a philosophy of discontinuity, but with a philosophy for which discontinuity is a problem (cf M. Foucault, 'Truth and Power', P/K, pp. 111–12).
62. HF, pp. 73, 100, 106 ('*une étrange révolution morale*'), 121, 177.
63. Ibid, p. 519 and also p. 346.
64. MIP, p. 71; HF, pp. 515, 521.
65. MIP, p. 69. The fact of confinement not only expresses a moral rejection of madness, but its undifferentiated character also leads, beyond this, in a peculiar process of moral osmosis, to a further ethical disqualification of madness: 'It [the classical age] brought together a whole set of *condemned* behaviours, forming a kind of halo of *guilt* around madness' (HF, p. 106; my emphasis, R.V.).
66. HF, p. 521.
67. MIP, p. 72.

68. HF, pp. 520–21 (Foucault is quoting Pinel).
69. MIP, p. 72; see also HF, pp. 315, 359–60.
70. HF, p. 159; cf also HF, p. 165: 'This negative fact, that "the madman is not treated like a human being" has a very positive content.'
71. NGH, p. 146.
72. MIP, p. 73.
73. NGH, p. 141. In the original French text of NGH, Foucault uses this expression to refer to Nietzsche's 'first philosophical writing exercise [*Schreibübung*]' (*On the Genealogy of Morals*).
74. Ibid, p. 160.
75. HF, p. 528 and MIP, p. 72 for a similar passage in which Foucault uses the term 'psychology'. We shall continue to use this latter expression in what follows (see above, note 5).
76. HF, pp. 291–2 and, above: 'the fool', '*les insensés*'.
77. Ibid, p. 174.
78. Ibid, p. 93.
79. We have already referred in note 21 to the difference between the possibility and the actuality of a realist interpretation. A minimal requirement for the possibility of realism is the existence of an independent object. The plausibility of this assumption is frequently defended by psychology in a 'strong version', which presupposes not only the independence, but also the universal presence of the object. A genuine refutation of the possibility of realism requires not only that the thesis of the historical pre-existence of the object is refuted, but also that of its independence.
80. HF, p. 139.
81. Ibid, p. 547; cf p. 445.
82. Ibid, p. 548.
83. Ibid, p. 528 (my emphasis, R.V.).
84. Ibid, p. 121; see also MIP, p. 73 ('"objective" or "positive" or "scientific" psychology') and FD, p. ix.
85. See, e.g., MIP, p. 73: 'None of this psychology would exist without the *moralizing sadism* in which nineteenth-century "philanthropy" enclosed it, under the hypocritical appearances of "liberation".'
86. Ibid, p. 74.
87. Ibid, p. 76 (Foucault's emphasis!); cf HF, pp. 458, 547–8.
88. MIP, p. 72; HF, pp. 514 ff.
89. MIP, p. 73; see also HF, pp. 106, 525; MIP, p. 71. From time to time – no doubt echoing Nietzsche's 'On Truth and Falsity in Their Ultramoral Sense' – Foucault introduces variants of this viewpoint: psychology discovers what it has itself put into things – HF, p. 525; cf Nietzsche (1911), p. 183: 'If somebody hides a thing behind a bush, seeks it again and finds it in the self-same place, then there is not much to boast of, respecting this seeking and finding.'
90. HF, p. 528.
91. MIP, p. 74; cf HF, pp. 175–6, 557.
92. HF, pp. 132–3 (my emphasis, R.V.).
93. See quotation at note 70.
94. FD, p. vi; HF, pp. 39, 46, 184.
95. HF, p. 46.
96. Ibid, pp. 40, 174, 359; MIP, p. 65.
97. HF, pp. 56, 177, 525; MIP, p. 87.
98. HF, pp. 56, 119, 183, 537; MIP, p. 69. Madness is also 'torn' (*arrachée*) from its freedom (HF, p. 91) and its truth (HF, p. 118), 'objectified' (HF, pp. 39, 119 and passim), 'reduced' (HF, p. 40 and passim) and 'exiled' (HF, p. 58).
99. HF, p. 189 (my emphasis, R.V.).

100. Ibid, p. 39.
101. Ibid, p. 119.
102. Ibid, p. 120 (my emphasis, R.V.). Foucault sees this crisis foreshadowed in the contrast between a tragi-comic and a critical-moral consciousness. In the course of the Renaissance, this contrast steadily intensifies (ibid, pp. 38 ff.) and ultimately imposes itself – to the advantage of the latter term, thereby 'disarm[ing]' madness (ibid, p. 39).
103. FD, p. vii (my emphasis, R.V.).
104. HF, p. 463, 'madness is alienated *from itself*' (my emphasis, R.V.).
105. MIP, pp. 87–8 ('And when, in lightning flashes and cries, it [madness] *reappears*, as in Nerval or Artaud, Nietzsche or Roussel ...' [my emphasis, R.V.]) and HF, pp. 40, 530, 554 ff. and passim, where Hölderlin, Sade, Goya and Van Gogh are all brought in to support the argument.
106. HF, p. 118. Confinement, for Foucault, is merely an *expression* of this primal alienation (ibid).
107. J. Derrida (1978), p. 40.
108. MIP, p. 76 (my emphasis, R.V.).
109. FD, p. ix.
110. MIP, p. 87 (Foucault uses quotation marks again a few lines further on).
111. Ibid, p. 69.
112. Ibid, p. 76 (see the quotation in the main text referenced at note 87).
113. HF, p. 174.
114. Ibid, p. 119. It might be said that such a discourse imposes on madness a form incompatible with its essence. The problem would then lie not only in the reduction of the *poly*morphous but in the *morphé* itself. Foucault's alienation thesis thus seems to presuppose the possibility of a genuine, exhaustive 'form'.
115. As is suggested by the title of Chapter 5 of MIP: 'The Historical Constitution of Mental Illness'.
116. HF, p. 133.
117. Ibid, p. 40.
118. Ibid, p. 359.
119. J. Derrida (1978), p. 41 (Derrida's emphasis).
120. P. Macherey (1986), p. 764.
121. See the first quotation referenced at note 31.
122. HF, p. 551 (my emphasis, R.V.).
123. Compare, for example, what we have written about psychology in the passages on the mad and the insane with the following quotation from Foucault: madness is 'liberated in the sense that it is released from the old forms of experience in which it was *caught up*' (my emphasis, R.V.), HF, p. 439.
124. MIP, p. 75 and P. Macherey (1986), pp. 773–4.
125. HF, p. 10 (from the second preface).

Chapter 2

1. FD, p. x.
2. HF, p. 94.
3. Foucault is aware that the 'historical totality – notions, institutions, juridical and police measures, scientific concepts' which he investigates 'holds captive a madness the wild state [*état sauvage*] of which can never in itself be restored' (FD, p. vii). In his view, there are, however, only factual reasons, not reasons of principle why we 'do not have that inaccessible, primal purity' (ibid) and this does not prevent him from formulating the archaeo-eschatological project of a 'history of madness

itself' (ibid: *histoire ... de la folie elle-même*) and thus introducing a conceptual framework which takes into account the factual, but not the theoretical limitation of that project.

4. HF, p. 265.

5. 'Réponse au cercle d'épistémologie', *Cahiers pour l'analyse*, 1968, 9, p. 19. This text is a first draft of the methodological work, *The Archaeology of Knowledge*, which appeared one year later, in which this passage recurs not literally, but in substance (AK, pp. 7, 138–9).

6. Dreyfus and Rabinow (1983), p. 12; and also Dreyfus (1987), pp. xxvii ff.

7. BC, pp. xvi–xvii (critique of 'exegesis').

8. The orthogenesis of knowledge actualizes a possibility which was already present from the beginning. It is only a genesis in that it removes the obstacles which stand in the way of that actualization. Corresponding, in Foucault's work, to this archeo-teleology in which the *telos* adds nothing to the *archè* (except clarity of view) is an archeo-eschatology, based on a logic which has already been analysed.

9. The symmetry with the dating in *Histoire de la folie* is striking: the classical period begins in 1656 (the year in which Velasquez painted his 'Las Meninas' (OT, pp. 3–16) and also the date of the edict on the building of the Hôpital général (HF, p. 75) which led to the 'Great Confinement'). It ends, more or less, with the French Revolution (Foucault assumes a transitional period (OT, pp. 217–49) with a definitive breakthrough to the modern age (OT, pp. 250–387) between 1795 and 1800 (OT, p. 221). The discussion of the classical period (OT, pp. 46–214) is also preceded here by a sketch of the Renaissance (OT, pp. 17–45).

10. Ibid, p. 365.

11. Ibid, pp. 310, 311, 344, 348, 349, 355 (inverted commas and/or explicit doubting or denial of their scientificity. The expressions 'human sciences' and the 'sciences of man' are equivalent.)

12. Ibid, pp. 250 ff.

13. Ibid, p. 348. It is striking that there is no third '-ism' here, to which a third human science might correspond, 'the study of literatures and myths' which, following Seitter (1980), we shall designate simply by the term 'cultural science'. Kwant's suggestion that 'linguologism' (=linguisticism) should be introduced as a third term is based on the misconception that Foucault includes the 'sciences of language' in the human sciences – Kwant (1975), pp. 315–17. See, however, OT, pp. 347, 359–60, 381–2.

14. The significance of this terminology which is taken from Derrida will become clear later – Derrida (1976), pp. 141–64, 'That Dangerous Supplement'; see also Moyaert (1986), especially pp. 47 ff.

15. OT, p. 348.

16. This 'trihedron' of knowledge (ibid, p. 344: the French, '*Le Trièdre des savoirs*', is rendered as 'The Three Faces of Knowledge') must be conceived as a pyramid with three edges with an infinitely thin skin stretched over it. Any in-curving is fatal: it means that one leaves the intermediary planes between the axes and ends up in the space of the human sciences (by contrast, in a pyramid with four edges, contact with a non-adjacent axis would *necessarily* take one through that space. Foucault's figure is well thought out.)

17. Ibid, pp. 347–8, 356–7, 358–9.

18. Ibid, p. 348; cf pp. 354, 356, 358, 364, 366.

19. Ibid, pp. 354, 358.

20. The danger can be avoided so long as one remains on the intermediary plane of economics and mathematics (ibid, p. 348).

21. Ibid, pp. 348–51.

22. Ibid, p. 351 and, for what follows, pp. 351–3, 355–6.

23. Ibid, p. 354.

24. For what follows, see ibid, pp. 356–8, 362–3.

25. Ibid, pp. 356–7.

26. Foucault says expressly that the human sciences take over 'models or concepts' from the empirical sciences (ibid, pp. 347, 356, 357) and it is clear that he is referring to the pairs of concepts mentioned here (ibid, pp. 357–60). But can one say that sociology takes the concepts of 'conflict and rule' from economics (which presupposes, indeed, that these concepts are already operative in economics)? Function and norm could surely not be said to be a biological model in the same way as conflict and rule are an economic model. Foucault seems to want to show that, at bottom, sociology operates with an economic model, i.e. with a model for which the economy, with the conflicts contained in needs and interests (though these are not investigated by economics), itself provides the model. But this is in no sense the same as asserting that sociology *takes over* an economic model.

27. Ibid, p. 362; cf p. 352. We shall come back to this point.

28. Ibid, pp. 357, 358–9, 362.

29. What characterizes the modern period is that the finite is no longer conceived on the basis of the infinite. It is no longer his *'inadéquation à l'infini'* which explains why man is compelled 'to live an animal existence, to work by the sweat of his brow, to think with opaque words'. Man discovers his finitude because life, work and language seem to bend back upon themselves and have a history and laws of their own – ibid, p. 316 and Deleuze (1988), pp. 88, 127. But this language which has a history of its own and which is always threatening to slip away from me (the philological discovery), this economy in which I work and yet which, in its crises (Marx) or its pursuit of stability (Ricardo), follows its own laws, the functions and mechanisms of this life by which I feel carried along (Cuvier) – all these determinations which hold man down to a finitude which he cannot escape and the regularities of which are analysed in disciplines which do not have man as their object (philology, economics, biology) are related by philosophy, in an 'analytic of finitude', to the being of man himself: to his corporeality, to the yawning of his desires, to the temporality of his language. The way man exists has to provide the ground for all that refers to his finitude. His finitude is not imposed on him from without, but rests on himself (ibid, pp. 312–18, 340–43 and passim).

30. Ibid, p. 362.

31. Namely 'the "cogito" and the unthought' (pp. 322–8), 'the retreat and return of the origin' (pp. 328–35) and 'the empirical and the transcendental' (pp. 318–22).

32. OT, p. 348.

33. Ibid, pp. 354, 371–2.

34. Ibid, p. 362.

35. Ibid, p. 364.

36. Ibid.

37. Ibid.

38. Ibid.

39. Ibid (my emphasis, R.V.).

40. Ibid, p 366 (Foucault's emphasis).

41. Ibid, p. 355.

42. Ibid, p. 366.

43. Ibid, p. 366 (my emphasis, R.V.).

44. Ibid, pp. 365–6.

45. The *epistemè* is not something other than this trihedron, but it is also not this trihedron itself. It is what makes the trihedron a trihedron, but it does not lie outside it. Foucault will later drop this peculiar concept which is, in many respects, reminiscent of Althusser's 'structural causality' (compare AK, p. 16 with OT, p. 168).

46. OT, p. 364.

47. Ibid, p. 347.

48. Ibid, pp. 354, 364.

49. See the emphasis in the passages referenced at notes 39 and 43. Foucault only cites 'characteristics of objectivity and systematicity' (ibid, p. 365) as criteria of scientificity, without it being clear what is intended, nor to what extent or why the human sciences cannot meet these criteria. One may conclude from the context of argument that Foucault takes these criteria in the first place from the empirical sciences.

50. Apart from some vague allusions (see note 49), taken up in the methodological deliberations of *The Archaeology of Knowledge* but not further elaborated: 'Only propositions that obey *certain* laws of construction belong to a domain of scientificity' (my emphasis, R.V.), AK, p. 183. See also AK, pp. 181–4.

51. As explained above, sociology for Foucault is, principally, an analysis in terms of the basic concepts of conflict and rule. The determination of this basic model contains a formal criterion for the identification of sociology (OT, pp. 357–8). It may be combined with secondary models (function/norm etc), but in Foucault's view such a combination indicates a 'psychologizing' (and not, as one would expect, that sociology, like psychology, is here employing a biological model. It is clear that Foucault, who finds himself confronted with a proliferation of models within the various human sciences, decides rather than demonstrates that he possesses, in the concept of 'basic model', a formal criterion of identification.)

52. Ibid, p. 352 ('the requisite of a function').

53. Compare: 'need and desire withdraw towards the subjective sphere – that sphere which, in the same period, is becoming an object of psychology. It is precisely here that in the second half of the nineteenth century the marginalists will seek the notion of utility' (ibid, p. 257). Must we deduce from this that economics, at least from the point at which it begins to develop the 'demand side' theoretically, shares its basic concepts with psychology? And can we sustain the suggestion of a perversion, which is implied in the concept of 'psychologism', without at the same time concerning the whole of post-classical economics to inauthenticity? We begin to see here how high can be the price which Foucault must pay for starting out from a de-anthropologized economics.

54. This is documented in Visker (1988).

55. OT, p. 353.

56. On this formulation, see Derrida, *Speech and Phenomena*, Chapter 7. For an elaboration of this idea of an originary supplement, taken from Derrida, in which a distinction is made between the *content* of such an impure discourse and the fact that it accompanies 'pure economics' like a shadow, see Visker (1988), pp. 179–82, 195–6. The concept of an 'originary supplement' presupposes that one show that the supplement is a necessary (and not just an accidental) 'addition' (it is what makes possible that to which it is added. It must be there not merely by chance, but on principle.) In what follows, the significance of this concept for Foucault's problematic will only be hinted at.

57. We cannot go into the demarcation of biology and linguistics from the human sciences here ('the *effort* to constitute . . . a pure linguistics' [my emphasis, R.V.], OT, p. 353). In contrast to what is suggested by the structure of OT, these problems seem to us to be specific to each discipline.

58. Ibid, pp. 366–7 (Foucault's emphasis).

59. Chapter 4 of Part III of HF bears the title 'Naissance de l'asile'.

60. See e.g. DP, pp. 185–6 on the hospital and DP, pp. 198–9 for a theoretical sophistication of the exclusion model which HF had uncovered behind the 'Great Confinement'.

61. '*Il s'agit en somme d'un chapitre dans l'histoire de la "raison punitive"*' (M. Foucault, 'La Poussière et le nuage', *L'Impossible Prison. Recherches sur le système pénitentiaire au XIXe siècle réunies par Michelle Perrot. Débat avec Michel Foucault*, Paris, 1980, p. 33).

62. DP, p. 24 (translation modified). Note the inverted commas. In retranslating *'assujetissement'* as 'subjectifying subjection', we are following De Folter (1987), p. 126.

63. DP, pp. 22–3.

64. M. Foucault, 'Body/Power', P/K, p. 61.

65. 'Power and Sex: an Interview with Michel Foucault' (1977), p. 158.

66. DP, pp. 232 ff. This self-evidence does not exclude the possibility of a constant critique of the prison (see below). What is involved here is a 'second best solution', for want of a 'first best': 'It is the detestable solution which one seems unable to do without' (ibid, p. 232).

67. Ibid, pp. 19, 23.

68. Ibid, pp. 264–8.

69. Ibid, p. 234.

70. For the historical evidence that this was a (relatively) new penal technique, see ibid, pp. 117 ff. (Foucault here reminds us, among other things, of the old adage *'ad continendos homines, non ad puniendos'*.)

71. Ibid, pp. 114, 119–20.

72. Ibid, p. 117 (Foucault is quoting from the 'Archives Parlementaires' – quotation abbreviated by me, R.V.).

73. Ibid, p. 117; cf p. 231.

74. Ibid, p. 99.

75. Ibid, p. 113.

76. Ibid, p. 111.

77. Ibid, p. 128.

78. Ibid, pp. 244 ff.

79. Ibid, p. 247.

80. Ibid, pp. 125, 236–48.

81. Compare ibid, p. 240, where Foucault cites Julius: 'a habit that is at first purely external, but is soon transformed into a second nature'.

82. DP, pp. 130, 236.

83. Ibid, p. 233.

84. Ibid, pp. 10, 255, 304.

85. DP begins with a detailed and now celebrated account of the quartering of Damien – an extreme example of the extraordinary brutality of the physical punishments which are analysed in the first part of DP ('Torture').

86. DP, p. 16 ('the non-corporal nature of the penal system').

87. Ibid, pp. 125–6.

88. Ibid, p. 249.

89. Thus prisoners were stimulated to write their autobiographies (ibid, p. 252). One example of this which has become very well-known is that of Pierre Rivière – *I, Pierre Rivière, having slaughtered my mother, my sister and my brother ... A Case of Parricide in the 19th century*, Harmondsworth, 1978.

90. DP, p. 255.

91. Ibid, p. 253.

92. On these quotation marks, compare ibid, pp. 254–5 and also the references in note 5 to the Introduction and the interview with Brochier, 'Prison Talk', P/K, pp. 47–8.

93. DP, pp. 17–23.

94. Ibid, p. 256.

95. From the blurb to the original French edition, signed by Foucault.

96. In so far as Foucault does not seek to question the referential structure of law and the judicial system, but into the basis of this alloreferentiality itself, it seems natural that he wishes to formulate a critique of the human sciences. By contrast with the earlier works, he has here an external motive for this critique. But this motive seems compelling because he problematizes *allo*referentiality, not allo*referentiality*.

97. See Part III of DP, 'Discipline', pp. 133 ff.

98. In this connection, see the last paragraph of DP: 'At this point, I end a book that must serve as a historical background to various studies of the power of normalization and the formation of knowledge in modern society' (p. 308). Cf OD, p. 71.

99. DP, pp. 18, 21.

100. Ibid, p. 27; cf DP, pp. 249 ff. for examples. In what follows, we are not so much concerned with the way this thesis is presented in terms of concrete content – Foucault is not, in fact, very explicit – but about its right to exist.

101. Ibid, p. 305.

102. G. Raulet (1983), p. 210: 'If they [power and knowledge] were identical, I would not have to study them ... The very fact that I pose the question of their relation proves clearly that I do not *identify* them' (Foucault's italics).

103. DP, p. 305 (my emphasis, R.V.). In the last chapter of Part IV of DP, Foucault introduces the concept of the 'carceral'. Alongside other (semi-)total institutions, the prison is presented as a privileged part of the 'carceral network' (ibid, p. 298).

104. Thus it is uncertain whether the expression '*pouvoir-savoir*' should be rendered as 'power-knowledge'. IJsseling (1979, p. 91) rightly points out that the term '*pouvoir*' also connotes 'to be able'.

105. Where this distinction between problems and problematic is concerned, we have taken our inspiration from Althusser, *Reading Capital*, pp. 13–69, 155 and passim. This implies a problematization of the author concept to which we shall return below.

106. DP, p. 27 and 'Prison Talk', P/K, p. 51, where this tradition is summarized as follows: 'only those who keep their distance from power, who are in no way implicated in tyranny, shut up in their Cartesian *poêle*, their room, their meditations, only they can discover the truth'.

107. DP, p. 27 (my emphasis, R.V.).

108. Ibid.

109. Foucault has repeatedly declared that he is not concerned with 'power in general' ('*le* *pouvoir*'). On this problematic of nominalism, see S. IJsseling (1979). The various distinctions which Foucault elaborates within the framework of an 'analytics of power' (HS1, pp. 82, 90) – power is not a property and not a possession but a strategy or a strategic relation etc (HS1, pp. 92–102) – do not go to the heart of the problem we are raising here. As we shall see, there is a more deep-lying 'plurivocity' in the power concept.

110. DP, p. 226 and RC (1971–2), pp. 19–25.

111. DP, p. 226 (my emphasis, R.V.).

112. Ibid (my emphasis, R.V.).

113. RC (1971–2), pp. 20–21.

114. Ibid.

115. Following the German translation of DP, we use the terms 'soil' and 'model' to explicate matrix in 'technical matrix' (DP, p. 226).

116. For example, an *a priori* 'internal' history of science in the sense of the late Husserl (see 'The Origin of Geometry', Appendix III to *The Crisis of European Sciences* ...) or a transcendental pragmatics in the style of Habermas – Habermas (1987), p. 272, where the argument is directed against Foucault, and the afterword to Nietzsche's epistemological writings in Habermas, ed., (1968) – or an immanent reflection on the proper scope of genealogy – see M. Donnelly (1986), p. 25.

117. The confusion on this point in Dreyfus and Rabinow's *Michel Foucault* seems to me symptomatic: on the one hand, the human sciences are characterized as pseudo-sciences (pp. 160, 177), whereas, at another point (pp. 161 ff.), it is suggested they misunderstand themselves (critique of the interpretation of scientificity) and, at yet another, that they are in principle possible as sciences, but only on the basis of

a misconception (they require an objectivism in order to be able to function, pp. 182 ff.).

118. On this concept, which has a technical significance and is directed against all forms of thinking in terms of origins (*Ursprungsdenken*), see NGH passim.

119. L. Althusser (1970), p. 28 (we shall come back to this point).

120. NGH, p. 146 (my emphasis, R.V.).

121. Ibid, p. 157.

122. DP, p. 191.

123. RC (1971–2), p. 20.

124. Habermas, for example, writes as follows: 'Once again, functionalist modes of argumentation are supposed to establish what they cannot establish – namely, that technologies of power constitute the domain of scientific objects and *hence also* prejudice the criteria of validity for what is considered true or false within scientific discourse' (1987), p. 416 (my emphasis, R.V.). The thrust of the following commentary will problematize this 'hence also'.

125. DP, p. 226 (my emphasis, R.V.).

126. 'Body/Power', P/K, p. 59.

127. DP, p. 227 (my emphasis, R.V.).

128. Ibid, p. 305.

129. Cf AK, Part IV, Chapter 6, pp. 178–95.

130. Ibid, p. 185 and perhaps DP, p. 185 for a late (less precise) echo.

131. See above, 2.1(3): The 'neutrality' of archaeology.

132. Above, subsection (ii): What is at stake in the power-knowledge concept.

133. The expression occurs repeatedly: DP, pp. 185, 191, 224.

134. Ibid, p. 186.

135. Ibid, p. 144.

136. Ibid, p. 185.

137. Ibid, p. 148.

138. Ibid, p. 149.

139. Ibid, p. 218.

140. Ibid, p. 191 and BC, p. 170.

141. DP, p. 191.

142. Ibid, p. 224.

143. Ibid. Foucault here mentions clinical medicine, psychiatry, child psychology, educational psychology and the rationalization of labour all in the same breath and suggests – wrongly, as will become clear – that the same kind of link between power and knowledge is involved in all of these.

144. This expression, reminiscent of Popper (1975: 'the searchlight theory of science'), was suggested by Foucault himself in one of his finest texts: 'In order that something of this should come across even to us, it was nevertheless necessary that a beam of light should, at least for a moment, illuminate them . . . What rescues them from the darkness of night . . . is an encounter with power' and, further on, 'the lightning flash of power'. M. Foucault, 'The Life of Infamous Men' (1979), pp. 79, 81.

145. DP, p. 184.

146. Neither in BC nor in DP did Foucault seek to cast doubt on the scientificity of medicine.

147. Thus, for example, the expression, 'another power, another knowledge' is very misleading – or, more precisely, it camouflages a confusion (see the titles of the third, fourth and fifth subsections).

148. AK, p. 164.

149. DP, p. 191.

150. Ibid, pp. 190–91.

151. Ibid, p. 211.

152. This is, for example, the case with the unfortunate farm hand who, 'as history would have it ... was named Jouy'. Caught in intimacies obtained from village girls, he is brought before a judge and tried. His brainpan was measured and his anatomy inspected for possible signs of degenerescence (HS1, pp. 31–3). But Pierre Rivière (see above, note 89) and *Herculine Barbin, dite Alexina B.* (see *Herculine Barbin ...*, New York, 1980) are also examples of this infamy, which gives individuals a name.

153. DP, p. 194.

154. Ibid, p. 24.

155. Ibid, p. 126.

156. Ibid, p. 296 (my emphasis, R.V.).

157. Ibid (translation modified).

158. Ibid, p. 250 (Foucault is quoting Ducatel, *Instruction pour la construction des maisons d'arrêt*, Paris, 1841).

159. Bentham's 'panopticon', an annular building with cells into which light falls through windows on the outside and with a watchtower in the middle, can be seen as an architectonic de-metaphorization of this metaphorics of light (ibid, pp. 200 ff. and 'The Eye of Power', P/K, pp. 146–65): 'Visibility is a trap' (DP, p. 200).

160. DP, p. 281: 'the appearance of the card-index and the constitution of the human sciences'.

161. Ibid, p. 194 (my emphasis, R.V.) and cf M. Foucault, 'Questions on Geography', P/K, pp. 73–4:"The individual is not a pre-given entity which is seized on by the exercise of power. The individual, with his identity and characteristics, is the product of a relation of power, exercised over bodies, multiplicities, desires, forces.'

162. DP, p. 155 (my emphasis, R.V.).

163. Ibid, p. 211 and the whole of Part III ('Discipline').

164. Ibid, p. 255.

165. Ibid, p. 29 ('This is the historical reality of this soul, which, unlike the soul represented by Christian theology, is not born in sin and subject to punishment, but is born rather out of methods of punishment, supervision and constraint.')

166. Ibid, p. 101; cf pp. 295–6, 305.

167. Ibid, p. 29.

168. Ibid, p. 102.

169. Ibid, p. 183.

170. Ibid, p. 251.

171. Ibid. (But strictly speaking, this is a tautology: the delinquent is nothing other than an 'individual to know' – he is the product of this movement and does not precede it.)

172. Ibid, pp. 102, 183, 255.

173. Ibid, p. 277.

174. Ibid, p. 256.

175. Ibid, p. 101. The French term '*doubler*' also has the meaning of 'lining' (e.g. a garment).

176. Ibid, p. 305 (already cited in passage referenced at note 101).

177. Ibid.

178. P. Boncenne, 'Du Pouvoir. Un entretien inédit avec Michel Foucault', *L'Express*, 13 July 1984 (nr 1722), p. 61.

179. The expression only occurs once or twice in DP – e.g. p. 29, where '*découpé*' is rendered as 'carved out'. It is interesting that '*découper*/to carve out' seems to take the place of '*repérer*/locate or identify', '*champ de repérage*/fields for ... mapping' (AK, p. 163), terms which also mean to 'mark out' and to 'mark with guide marks' and which might support the assertion that the 'first model' (pro-ductivity) is more an archaeological hangover than a specifically genealogical starting point.

180. DP, p. 255 (translation modified).

181. There might be a kind of affinity between particular forms of power and particular forms of knowledge (e.g. between the 'examination' and the human sciences) which is neither random nor in a position to establish the context of application of knowledge with the quasi-transcendental necessity of knowledge-constitutive interests (Habermas, 1978).

182. A trivial critique would base itself upon a stipulative definition: science presupposes a referent which does not come into being in a process that can be uncovered genealogically (for example, the 'strong version' of realism, which Foucault ascribed to psychology – see above).

183. DP, p. 185 and RC (1971–2), pp. 19–20.

184. On this list, see DP, p. 194.

185. We have spoken above of a systematic *plurivocity* of the power concept because we are dealing with *two* models (see above, Second and Third attempts at differentiation, in which the power concept of the second model, as will immediately become clear, is itself *ambi*guous).

186. All quotations from J. Habermas (1987), p. 274.

187. Ibid. As will become clear later, this quotation from Habermas *in no way* obliges us to follow him in his Foucault critique.

188. G. Deleuze (1988), p. 29.

189. See the quotation referenced at note 64 above: the ambiguity of the term 'invest' is not accidental.

190. DP, pp. 30, 91, 155, 156, 221.

191. Ibid, pp. 25, 26, 103.

192. Ibid, p. 26 (translation modified); NGH, pp. 147–8. In this connection, see also J. Rajchman (1978), especially pp. 101 ff.

193. DP, p. 26 (my emphasis, R.V.). The parallel with the expression to which we referred previously – 'madness itself' – is striking.

194. See above, Introduction to this chapter.

195. All these terms recur several times. See, e.g. pp. 25–6, 221, 305.

196. See the quotation referenced at note 153 above.

197. DP, p. 155 (my emphasis, R.V.). Already quoted at note 162 above.

198. Ibid, p. 30. Note the quotation marks around 'soul'.

199. Ibid, p. 295; again there are quotation marks.

200. M. Foucault, Preface to Deleuze, Guattari, *Anti-Oedipus* (1977), p. xiv.

201. DP, p. 191.

202. See quotation at note 198.

203. See above, end of section 2.2(1).

204. DP, pp. 136 ff.

205. M. Foucault, 'What is an Author?' (1977), pp. 113–38.

Chapter 3

1. See, for example, the famous passage in AK, p. 17.

2. 'Le Philosophe Masqué' (1984), p. 22.

3. The question is covered in detail in M. Foucault, 'What is an Author?' (1977), pp. 113–38.

4. On intertextuality as a theoretical limitation to any such attempt at interpretation, see IJsseling (1986), pp. 251–9.

5. The objection goes too far. In *The History of Sexuality I*, we still find a chapter with the heading 'Scientia Sexualis' (pp. 51–73), which, in Dreyfus and Rabinow's view, offers a kind of genealogy of the hermeneutic sciences (1983, pp. 178 ff.).

Although the quotation marks have not disappeared here (*The History of Sexuality*, vol. I, pp. 5, 57 [in the latter case, the translator has omitted the quotation marks Foucault placed around the word 'science' in the original French edition: *La Volonté de savoir*, Paris, 1976, p. 76, Tr.]), we shall not concentrate in what follows on the problematic of science, in order to avoid unnecessary repetition.

6. HS1, p. 10.

7. Various writers have pointed out that it is not clear whether the concept 'productivity of power' applies only to modern power or to all forms of power. While the passages in DP tend to suggest the latter (see, e.g., DP, p. 194), the plan of HS1 argues, rather, for the former (pp. 88 ff. – although Foucault seems to have doubts: see the formulations in HS1, p. 10). On this question, see Fraser (1981), p. 285 and De Folter (1987), pp. 91, 121–2.

8. HS1, p. 4 ('untrammeled sex') and p. 152 ('rude sex'). Cf also HS1, p. 152.

9. Ibid, pp. 3–13 and the last sentence: 'The irony of this deployment is in having us believe that our "liberation" is in the balance' (p. 159).

10. See the title of Part Two, 'The Repressive Hypothesis' (ibid, pp. 15–49).

11. HS2, p. 5 (this text was written eight years later. We shall return to the question of the extent to which we can speak of a 'turn' here.)

12. See, *inter alia*, C. Honegger (1982).

13. HS1, pp. 8–9.

14. Ibid, p. 35.

15. On the logic of the secret, see the very fine work by Descombes (1977), especially pp. 27 ff.

16. It simulates that it is concealing something, but it is concealing nothing, except perhaps the fact that it is concealing nothing. (On the concept of the *simulacrum*, see Van Gils, 1986.)

17. HS1, p. 27.

18. Ibid, p. 73.

19. Ibid, pp. 105, 108, 114 and passim.

20. Ibid, p. 11 (power-knowledge-pleasure); on the concept of 'instrument-effect', see pp. 48, 101.

21. On this circular movement, see ibid, pp. 90–91.

22. Foucault does not introduce a distinction between these terms until the end of volume 1 of the *History of Sexuality*. Before that, he used the two interchangeably. This has led to repeated problems of translation, particularly where the second term ('*le sexe*') is concerned.

23. Ibid, pp. 4–5 ('triple edict of taboo, nonexistence, and silence').

24. Ibid, p. 69.

25. Compare, for example, ibid, pp. 7 ff. with pp. 122 ff.

26. Ibid, p. 17 ('discursive explosion') and the passage quoted at note 17 'not one but many silences'. Cf ibid, pp. 18, 30, 32.

27. Ibid, p. 32.

28. Ibid, p. 117.

29. For a remarkable analysis of sexuality as specific intentionality, see Merleau-Ponty (1968), Part One, Chapter 5 ('The Body in Its Sexual Being').

30. The projected later parts of the history of sexuality were to have gone deeper into these themes. They were never written. Instead, there appeared studies on Greece and Rome (see below).

31. HS1, p. 34 ('a dispersion of *centers from which discourses emanated*' – my emphasis, R.V.). ['Centers' is used here by Foucault's translator to render the French term '*foyer*', Tr.]

32. HS1, pp. 27, 30.

33. 'Des Caresses d'homme considerées comme un art' (1982), p. 27.

34. See HS1, p. 157. Here and in what follows we treat of homosexuality only in

so far as it is exemplary of one of the many 'sexualities' to which Foucault gives expression.

35. Expressions like 'solidification', 'solidify' are repeatedly found. See ibid, pp. 44, 48, 53 etc. They seem to play the role of 'root metaphors' (S. Pepper) in Foucault's analyses.

36. Paul Veyne attributes this comment (about madness) to Foucault in 'Foucault révolutionne l'histoire' (1978): '*il faut dire ... que la folie n'existe pas, mais qu'elle n'est pas rien pour autant*' (p. 229).

37. To return to the metaphors in the preceding paragraph, light is not regarded as simply illuminating something pre-given, but it none the less does not illuminate nothing. One should think here, rather, of a beam which develops something (in the photographic sense). Foucault's problem, however, is that what one comes to see is not established in advance. The light does not realize a given possibility, but sets in train a process of emergence. This is what we take Paul Veyne to mean, when, drawing on Duns Scotus, he writes: '*la matière à folie existe réellement, mais pas comme folie ... Il faut qu'un homme soit objectivé comme fou pour que le référent prédiscursif apparaisse rétrospectivement comme matière à folie*' – ibid (1978), p. 229 – Veyne's emphasis.

38. We here transpose what Foucault says of the relations between the subject and object of a knowledge, in a conversation with Duccio Trombadori, to the relation between discourse and the object of discourse – see *Remarks on Marx. Conversations with Duccio Trombadori* (1991), pp. 70–1.

39. HS1, p. 60 ('their constitution as subjects in both senses of the word').

40. Ibid, p. 46 ('a network of pleasures and powers').

41. Ibid, p. 68 ('A *dispositif* [which Foucault's translator generally renders as 'deployment', Tr.] is a totality of verbal and material elements, i.e. statements, stories and laws, on the one hand, and institutions, such as the family or the health care system or practices like building [e.g. the construction of dormitories – R.V.] on the other'); H. Achterhuis (1988), p. 271.

42. HS1, p. 43 (translation modified).

43. Ibid.

44. Ibid, p. 59.

45. M. Foucault, 'The Battle for Chastity' (1985), p. 25: 'if there is subjectiviza-tion, it also involves an indefinite objectivization of the self by the self' (translation modified).

46. HS1, p. 45 (my emphasis, R.V.).

47. Ibid.

48. Ibid, p. 47 (with this idea, Foucault refutes the repressive hypothesis in the proper sense of the word: something is being produced, not repressed – however, see below).

49. For this list, see ibid, p. 43.

50. Ibid, pp. 47–8 (translation modified).

51. Ibid, p. 48 (my emphasis, R.V.).

52. See the overall problematic of subjectifying subjection and the 'falling back short of genealogy' (above, 2.2 (3, vi).

53. '[Power] is the name that one attributes to a complex strategical situation in a particular society' (HS1, p. 93).

54. Ibid, p. 45 (my emphasis, R.V.). An anticipation of this idea is found in DP, p. 27 (though the French '*prendre appui sur*' – to rest on, to support itself on – is mistranslated there as 'to exert pressure on' and 'to resist'). See *Surveiller et punir*, pp. 31–2 for original text.

55. HS1, pp. 44–5 (quotation p. 44).

56. Ibid, p. 45.

57. J. de Wit and J. François (1984), p. 53.

58. HS1, p. 23 [the passage in question is mistranslated in the English version: the reader should consult *La Volonté de savoir*, p. 33, Tr.].

59. This expression comes from Horkheimer's late work; see Horkheimer (1970).

60. On this criticism, see Peter Dews (1984), p. 93.

61. HS1, p. 157 (my emphasis, R.V.).

62. Ibid, p. 152.

63. Ibid, pp. 44 ff.

64. Pierre Macherey, 'Towards a Natural History of Norms', in: *Michel Foucault, Philosopher*, p. 187.

65. In DP and HS1, the concept of 'body' occurs repeatedly as a grammatical subject ('the body confesses' etc), but this is more a rhetorical camouflaging of the problem than an answer to it (see e.g. DP, pp. 42, 47 etc).

66. HS1, p. 159.

67. M. Foucault, *Howison Lecture on Truth and Subjectivity* (1980), Part I, p. 4.

68. M. Foucault, 'Une Esthétique de l'existence' (1984), p. xi.

69. 'The Return of Morality', *Politics, Philosophy, Culture: Interviews and Other Writings, 1977–1984* (1988) p. 243.

70. 'Une Esthétique de l'existence', p. xi.

71. '[S]omething which can eventually change, which is of course politically important,' M. Foucault and R. Sennett (1981) pp. 4–5.

72. The expression is taken from Schürmann (1986), p. 294. In what follows, 'subject' is to be understood as *practical* subjectivity.

73. 'The Return of Morality', p. 243.

74. HS2, p. 6.

75. See M. Foucault, 'On the Genealogy of Ethics: an Overview of Work in Progress', in: P. Rabinow (1984), pp. 340–72.

76. M. Foucault, 'The Ethic of Care for the Self as a Practice of Freedom' (1984), p. 113.

77. HS2, pp. 5–6.

78. The terms italicized here refer respectively to the formal, final and acting cause of ethical subjectivization – on this terminology, see Deleuze (1988), p. 104. In this connection, Foucault deals with ascetic or technological, teleological and deontological aspects of the relation to the self (see, for example, HS2, p. 37).

79. HS2, pp. 188 ff.

80. M. Foucault, 'The Concern for Truth', *Politics, Philosophy, Culture* (1988), p. 257.

81. HS2, p. 4.

82. HS3, p. 144.

83. See, for example, HS2, pp. 3–4; 'On the Genealogy of Ethics', p. 352; Preface to the *History of Sexuality* (vol. II) in Rabinow (1984), p. 333: 'an effort to treat sexuality as *the correlation* of a domain of knowledge, a type of normativity and a mode of relation to the self' (my emphasis, R.V.).

84. Announced by this title (*Les Aveux de la chair*) upon the publication of the second and third volumes. Foucault died shortly afterwards.

85. HS2, p. 5.

86. *Truth and Subjectivity* II, p. 20.

87. On this expression, see *Truth and Subjectivity* I and II, passim.

88. HS1, p. 20.

89. M. Foucault, R. Sennett (1981), p. 5.

90. In *this* sense, one could not speak of a sudden prohibition of many and varied forms of sexuality (HS2, pp. 14 ff.; HS3, pp. 39, 143–4, 239–40), although Foucault concedes that 'some of the prohibitions are much stricter and more rigorous in Christianity than in the Greek period' ('On the Genealogy of Ethics', p. 355).

91. HS2, pp. 30, 138.

92. Ibid, p. 32; see also HS1, pp. 18–19.

93. HS2, p. 251.

94. In the relation to women, to one's own sex and to the body and health, Foucault sees 'three austerity themes of the code' ('On the Genealogy of Ethics', p. 356). These themes re-emerge in the structuring of HS2 and HS3.

95. HS2, pp. 143 ff.; HS3, pp. 147 ff.

96. HS3, p. 184.

97. HS2, p. 250.

98. 'On the Genealogy of Ethics', p. 356.

99. HS2, p. 251.

100. M. Foucault, 'The Battle for Chastity' (1985), p. 17.

101. In 'Sexuality and Solitude', Foucault analyses Augustine's conception that the uncontrollable movement of the genitals must be seen in relation to the Fall: 'Sex in erection is the image of man revolted against God' (p. 5).

102. M. Foucault, 'Technologies of the Self' in: L.H. Martin *et al.* (eds) (1988), pp. 47–8.

103. HS2, p. 92; HS3, p. 36.

104. HS3, p. 67; 'On the Genealogy of Ethics', p. 356.

105. *Truth and Subjectivity* I, pp. 9 ff.; 'Technologies of the Self', pp. 33–4; HS3, pp. 60 ff.

106. Cf HS3, pp. 142–3.

107. *Truth and Subjectivity* II, p. 13.

108. 'The Battle for Chastity' (1985), p. 23.

109. J. de Wit and J. François (1984), p. 48.

110. HS2, p. 6.

111. See M. Foucault and R. Sennett, 'Sexuality and Solitude' (1981), p. 6.

112. See note 101.

113. 'Technologies of the Self', pp. 35, 38.

114. *Truth and Subjectivity* II, p. 18; cf HS2, p. 89.

115. HS1, p. 20.

116. HS2, p. 35.

117. *Truth and Subjectivity* II, p. 20 (my emphasis, R.V.).

118. 'On the Genealogy of Ethics', p. 343 and, above, on Foucault's conception of an 'aesthetics of existence', a conception which is, in fact, contested: 'In Platonism, and also in Epicureanism and Stoicism ... it is a question not of a construction of a self as a work of art, but of a surpassing of the self, or at least of an exercise by which the self is situated in the totality and feels itself part of that totality' (P. Hadot, 1987, p. 232).

119. 'On the Genealogy of Ethics', p. 350.

120. 'The Return of Morality', p. 253.

121. *Truth and Subjectivity* II, p. 20 ('the politics of ourselves'). See above, quotation in note 71.

122. See above quotation referenced at note 80.

123. Cf HS2, pp. 38–52.

124. HS1, p. 117.

125. Ibid, pp. 152–3.

126. Ibid, p. 157.

127. Ibid, p. 154 ('fictitious unity').

128. HS2, p. 42.

129. HS1, p. 153.

130. HS2, p. 42.

131. Ibid, p. 42 and 'On the Genealogy of Ethics', p. 359.

132. This is the difference between an 'identity technology of the self' and a 'sacrificial technology of the self' (*Truth and Subjectivity* II, p. 19).

133. HS2, p. 42.

134. See, for example, the interpretation by C. Jambet (1992), p. 240: 'Individuals are therefore the matter on which the work of subjectification is to be carried out. They do not really have any being outside this work, previous to it, or in the absence of the form in which ethical . . . experience shapes them.' Cf, however, above, the end of section 3.1(2) for a more sophisticated version of this model (the form *seduces* the matter).

135. We take this terminology from Jambet (1992), pp. 240 ff.

136. N. Fraser (1981), p. 283.

137. M. Foucault, 'The Subject and Power' (1983), pp. 211–12 (my emphasis, R.V.).

138. This construction is, of course, hypothetical and it suggests no answer to the question of the specificity of Christian and modern techniques of subjectivization. The idea is as follows: *if* Foucault were right to assert that such confessional techniques lead to a fixation of identity and, if, on the other hand, psychoanalysis were right to assert that the nature of the verbalizing 'confession' in analysis leads precisely to breaking down an imaginarily fixed identity, then one would have to be able to demonstrate how this difference comes into being in actual verbalization. This requires a theory of verbalization which takes into account – as Foucault does not do – the particular nature (and difficulties) of the psychoanalytic situation, but also asks what it, as a verbalizing confessional procedure, might have in common with other similar procedures and whether, on the basis of *these* shared features, the effect of modern confessional techniques can be interpreted as 'oppressive'. [Note to English edition: This point has since been taken up and developed by Van Haute (1993).]

139. Richard Rorty (1992), p. 332. (In Rorty's view, this is even a plus point of Foucault's analyses which, regrettably, escaped his notice.)

140. J. Habermas (1983), p. 426.

141. See, *inter alia*, M. Walzer (1986), p. 61.

142. J. Habermas (1987), pp. 276 ff.

143. M. Foucault, 'Truth and Power' (1980), p. 126.

144. 'Truth, Power, Self: an Interview with Michel Foucault', in: L.H. Martin *et al.* (1988), p. 10.

145. 'Power and Sex' (1977), p. 161.

146. 'Questions of Method: an Interview with Michel Foucault', *I & C*, no. 8 (Spring 1981), p. 14.

147. 'The Political Technology of Individuals', in: L.H. Martin *et al.* (1988) p. 161.

148. 'Is It Really Important to Think?' (1982), p. 33.

149. P. Veyne (1978), p. 204.

150. 'Questions of Method: an Interview with Michel Foucault', p. 6.

151. 'L'Intellectuel et les pouvoirs' (1984), p. 338.

152. This is what Habermas would seem to mean when he refers to 'young conservatives'. See his much-discussed lecture, 'Modernity – an Incomplete Project', in: Hal Foster (ed.) (1985a), pp. 3–15; cf N. Fraser (1985), pp. 165–84.

153. On this argument, see H. Kunneman (1986), pp. 347 ff. (quotation from p. 365).

154. D.R. Hiley (1985), p. 77.

155. 'The Political Technology of Individuals', in: L.H. Martin *et al.* (1988), p. 162.

156. M. Foucault, 'Omnes et Singulatim: Towards a Criticism of "Political Reason"' (1979), in: McMurrin (ed.) (1981), p. 254 (I emphasize '*liberation*', R.V.).

157. 'The Subject and Power', p. 216.

158. 'The Political Technology of Individuals', p. 161 and 'Omnes et Singulatim', p. 254.

159. 'The Subject and Power', p. 216.
160. J. O'Higgins (1988), p. 302.
161. R. Rorty (1985), p. 166: 'It would be better to be frankly ethnocentric', a
recommendation which is also offered to Foucault (p. 172).
162. C. Taylor (1986), pp. 96–7.
163. Ibid, p. 99.
164. M. Foucault, 'Space, Knowledge and Power', in: P. Rabinow (1984),
pp. 248–9.
165. 'On the Genealogy of Ethics' (1984), p. 343.
166. Dreyfus and Rabinow (1983), p. 304.
167. Ibid, p. 307.
168. R. Devos (1987), p. 298.
169. See, for example, the passage which is also quoted by Kunneman (1986),
p. 368: 'he is the object of information, never a subject in communication' (DP,
p. 200); similar passages passim.
170. J. Habermas in an interview with A. Bolaffi (1978). Reprinted in Habermas
(1981), p. 507. Cf also I. de Haan (1987) and the important discussion which took
place in the journal *Krisis* between Josef Keulartz, Harry Kunneman (1983, 1984)
and Rudi Laermans (1984).
171. M. Foucault, 'The Ethic of Care for the Self as a Practice of Freedom (1984),
p. 123 and 'The Subject and Power' (1983), p. 224.
172. 'The Ethic of Care for the Self as a Practice of Freedom' (1984), p. 123 (my
emphasis, R.V.).
173. Ibid, p. 129, where Foucault distances himself from Habermas: 'The thought
that there could be a state of communication which would be such that the games
of truth could circulate freely, without obstacles, without constraint and without
coercive effects, seems to me to be Utopia.' One might perhaps be inclined to object
to Foucault that, for Habermas too, 'domination-free dialogue' has a counter-factual
status – it is a fiction that is always operatively effective in every dialogue actually
conducted. As a result, all charges of utopianism would miss the mark since they fail
to grasp its status as an *anticipated* utopia. But this does not get us far. Foucault's
argument is not on the level of the achievability of such a 'utopia'; it is a *de jure*
argument which questions the concept of a counter-factual 'freedom from domination' itself.
174. 'The Subject and Power' (1983), p. 225.
175. Ibid, p. 223.
176. Ibid, p. 220.
177. Ibid, pp. 221–2.
178. For an enthusiastic defence of this point of view, see J. Rajchman (1985).
179. R. Devos (1987), p. 298.
180. For critical comment on Foucault's conception of freedom, see P. Jonkers
(1986), pp. 417–18. The following quotations are drawn from this article.
181. M. Foucault, 'What is Enlightenment?', in: Rabinow (1984), p. 50.
182. R. Devos (1987), p. 50.
183. F. Crespi (1979), pp. 104–8.
184. M. Foucault, 'War in the Filigree of Peace: Course Summary', *The Oxford
Literary Review*, 4, 2, p. 18. (This quotation occurs in a context where Foucault is
elaborating a kind of genealogy of his genealogy.)
185. P. Veyne (1986), p. 937.
186. M. Foucault, *Vom Licht des Krieges zur Geburt der Geschichte. Vorlesungen
vom 21. und 28.1.1976 am Collège de France*, Berlin, p. 35.
187. M. Foucault, 'Two Lectures', P/K, p. 85 (these lectures directly preceded
those referred to at note 186).
188. J. Habermas (1987), p. 276.

189. 'The Subject and Power' (1983), pp. 216 ff.
190. M. Foucault, 'What is Enlightenment?' (1984), p. 45.
191. J. Habermas (1987), p. 270.
192. Ibid, p. 274.
193. Ibid, p. 276.
194. Ibid, p. 282.
195. Ibid, p. 277.
196. J. Habermas (1985b), p. 124.
197. J. Habermas (1989), p. 52.
198. J. Habermas (1987), pp. 272 ff.

Chapter 4

1. On this formulation which encapsulates Habermas's critique of Foucault, see J. Habermas (1986), p. 171.

2. Deleuze (1988), p. 120, succeeds, for example, in forcing Foucault's *oeuvre* into a schema which is gradually built up as the works succeed one another, but never revised.

3. Habermas (1987), p. 270.

4. See, for example, Habermas (1987), pp. 284–6.

5. Compare, for example, the following statement by Deleuze with our arguments: 'If at the end of it [*The History of Sexuality*] Foucault finds himself in an impasse, this is not because of his conception of power but rather because he found the impasse in which power itself places us,' Deleuze (1988), p. 96 (translation modified).

6. Merleau-Ponty (1968), p. 199.

7. J. Derrida (1984), pp. 93–4.

8. Deleuze (1988), p. 90 ('new fools').

9. See, e.g., R. Barthes (1977), pp. 142–8. For a critique, see S. Weber (1987), pp. xv ff.

10. A series of remarks by Derrida on the '*Auseinandersetzung* between the Nietzsches and Martin Heidegger' (p. 68) might lead to such a – perhaps over-hasty – conclusion. See J. Derrida (1989b), especially pp. 61–2 (which we draw on here) and pp. 67–8.

11. We take our inspiration here from Derrida, 'From Restricted to General Economy: a Hegelianism without Reserve' in *Writing and Difference* (1978), pp. 259–60 and pp. 274–5.

12. Our interpretation here diverges from Althusser's 'symptomatic reading' (cf Althusser, *Reading Capital*, pp. 24–8).

13. M. Foucault, 'Nietzsche, Freud, Marx' (1969): '*L'interprétation que toute vérité a pour fonction de recouvrir*'.

14. M. Foucault, 'Power and Sex' (1977), p. 153.

15. M. Foucault, 'Truth and Power', P/K, p. 131.

16. Ibid, p. 133; p. 131 ('political economy' of truth).

17. This concept does not occur as such in Foucault's work. The parallel with the *power-knowledge* concept is, however, so striking that it is justifiable to introduce it.

18. M. Foucault, 'Truth and Power', P/K, p. 132.

19. M. Foucault, OD, p. 60.

20. Ibid.

21. Ibid. In *The Birth of the Clinic*, Foucault shows, for example, how the refusal of Bichat and others to use a microscope or other optical techniques which had long

been known is understandable if one analyses the discursive régime of anatomical pathology at the end of the eighteenth century: 'The only type of visibility recognized by pathological anatomy is that defined by everyday vision: a *de jure* visibility ... and not ... a *de natura* invisibility that is breached for a time by an artificially multiplied technique of the gaze' (BC, pp. 166–7).

22. OD, p. 61.

23. 'Truth and Power', P/K, p. 112.

24. Ibid.

25. OD, p. 56.

26. Ibid, p. 60.

27. Ibid, p. 61. ('*Mendel spoke the truth* but he was not "within the true" of the biological discourse of his period.' The passage italicized by me can only mean that, for Foucault, Mendel spoke the truth within *another* 'truth'. On this difference from epistemology, see R. Machado (1992) and AK, pp. 126–7.

28. OD, pp. 54–5.

29. For what follows, cf ibid, pp. 54–6. The expression 'the will to truth', reminiscent of Nietzsche, appears here repeatedly.

30. Ibid, p. 54.

31. Ibid.

32. We might, following Lyotard, term such a conflict a 'differend': 'As distinguished from a litigation, a differend [*différend*] would be a case of conflict between (at least) two parties, that cannot be equitably resolved for lack of a rule of judgment applicable to both arguments' – Lyotard (1988), p. xi.

33. 'Truth and Power', P/K, p. 133.

34. See above, quotation for note 18.

35. 'Questions on Geography', P/K, p. 66; 'Two Lectures', P/K, pp. 84–5.

36. 'Truth and Power', P/K, p. 132.

37. Ibid, p. 133.

38. M. Foucault, 'Prison Talk', P/K, p. 51.

39. P. Veyne (1986), p. 935.

40. We should point out that this in no way means that a problematic of truth (in the usual sense) in terms of correspondence is excluded. Foucault's regulative theory of 'truth' does not have – and does not claim to have – the same status as, say, a coherence theory of truth (in the usual sense). Cf D. Hoy (1979), p. 87: 'The way the world is may determine what is true or false, but that will still not explain what is actually said, or comes up for counting as true or false.'

41. M. Foucault, 'The History of Sexuality', P/K, p. 184.

42. OD, p. 61.

43. Ibid, p. 67 (translation modified).

44. Ibid, p. 73 (my emphasis, R.V.).

45. Ibid, pp. 70–71.

46. Cf 'History of Systems of Thought' (1977), p. 200 ('principles of exclusion and choice').

47. P. Veyne (1978), p. 204.

48. Foucault's use of the terms 'archaeology' and 'genealogy' is none too precise. In OD, for example, a so-called 'genealogical' analysis is outlined which, in reality, coincides with what he had previously done in AK (OD, pp. 70–71). For other examples, see also M. Lambrechts (1981), p. 543. It seems to us, *rebus sic stantibus*, less important to arrive at an exact definition of 'archaeology' or 'genealogy' than to be able to show what their common problematic might have been.

49. AK, p. 138.

50. Ibid, p. 109.

51. Ibid, p. 131.

52. Ibid, p. 109.

53. Ibid, p. 129.

54. 'Politics and the Study of Discourse', *Ideology & Consciousness*, 3 (Spring 1978), p. 18 (translation modified).

55. AK, pp. 42–3, 129, 209.

56. 'Politics and the Study of Discourse' (1978), pp. 17–18.

57. See 'Politics and the Study of Discourse' (1978), p. 16; AK, pp. 27–8, 48, 118–20.

58. AK, p. 48; cf p. 76.

59. Ibid, p. 25.

60. Ibid, p. 49.

61. Ibid, p. 209 ('to speak is to do something – something other than to express what one thinks, to translate what one knows, and something other than to play with the structures of a language'); 'Politics and the Study of Discourse' (1978), p. 18.

62. AK, pp. 32–3, 49 ('practices that systematically form the objects of which they speak').

63. Ibid, p. 209.

64. Ibid, pp. 67, 110 and 'Politics and the Study of Discourse' (1978), p. 16.

65. AK, pp. 25, 47–9, 109, 135; 'Politics and the Study of Discourse' (1978), p. 14.

66. 'History of Systems of Thought' (1977), p. 199.

67. 'Politics and the Study of Discourse' (1978), p. 18.

68. AK, p. 72 and above, section 4.1(2). For detail on this question, see AK, pp. 21–76.

69. AK, p. 44. We shall confine ourselves to this example.

70. Ibid, p. 45. Thus, for example, the 'pathologizing' of delinquency presupposes a number of relations between penal and psychological categories; between medical and penal authorities; between familial, sexual and penal norms of behaviour etc (ibid, pp. 43–4).

71. Ibid, pp. 47, 48. There is, once again, a mistranslation here and the reader is advised to consult the original French text: *L'Archéologie du savoir*, Gallimard, Paris, 1969, p. 64 (para. 1), p. 65 (para. 2).

72. AK, p. 44.

73. Ibid.

74. Ibid, p. 32 (my emphasis, R.V.).

75. Ibid, p. 45.

76. Ibid, pp. 47 ff. (an explicit critique of *Histoire de la folie*).

77. HF, p. 94 (also quoted above, Chapter 2, note 2).

78. AK, p. 47.

79. OD, p. 67. 'We must conceive discourse as a violence which we do to things.' AK was published in 1969 and the 'Inaugural Lecture', which forms the basis of *The Order of Discourse*, was delivered in late 1970.

80. OD, p. 67.

81. HF, p. 94.

82. We have already covered this matter: see above, 2.1(3).

83. DP, pp. 135 ff. In this connection, see also the classic text by M. Mauss, 'Body Techniques', *Sociology and Psychology*, London, 1979, pp. 95–122.

84. See above, 2.2(3, vi). Foucault does in fact start out from the idea that 'in every society the body is in the grip of very strict powers, which impose on it constraints, prohibitions or obligations' (DP, p. 136; translation modified), but, as we have argued, his critique of disciplinary bodily techniques did not, in the end, relate to their specificity, but to what they have in common with all other bodily techniques: constraint, prohibition and obligation. The possibility of a body without techniques is thus left open – see N. Fraser (1983), especially pp. 63 ff.

85. 'Power and Sex' (1977), p. 158 (quoted above at 2.2(1), last note).

86. M. Foucault, 'Nietzsche, Freud, Marx' (1969): 'If the interpretation can never come to an end, this is quite simply because there is nothing to interpret. There is nothing absolutely primary to interpret because, at bottom, everything is already interpretation' (p. 189).

87. See above, 3.2 *passim*.

88. Nietzsche, 'On Truth and Falsity in Their Ultramoral Sense', *The Complete works of Friedrich Nietzsche*, ed. Oscar Levy, vol. 2: *Early Greek Philosophy*, T.N. Foulis, London and Edinburgh, 1911, p. 179.

89. For Nietzsche, things only become interesting through falsification. It is this which allows things to be 'seen' and we cannot avoid it if we wish to 'see' something: 'That impulse towards the formation of metaphors, that fundamental impulse of man, which we cannot reason away for one moment – for thereby we should reason away man himself' – Nietzsche (1911), p. 188; cf also IJsseling (1973), p. 798: 'Nietzsche's critique of metaphysics is not that it is rhetorical, but that it refuses to recognize this.'

90. DP, p. 149 and above, 2.2(3, v).

91. M. Foucault, 'Preface to Deleuze and Guattari', *Anti-Oedipus* (1977), p. xiv. For the context, see the last pages of the second chapter.

92. 'Le Vrai Sexe' (1980), p. 622 ('the happy limbo of a non-identity') and the biography of Herculine Barbin: *Herculine Barbin, Being the Recently Discovered Memoirs of a Nineteenth-century Hermaphrodite*, trans. R. MacDougall, New York, 1980.

93. 'Le Vrai Sexe' (1980), p. 617 (my emphasis, R.V.). We would not wish to be misunderstood here: we are not arguing that Foucault was wrong to refrain from defining gender from the standpoint of biological conditions, but that it is not ‹ pertinent to play off the absence of such conditions against the symbolic (and *hence* unavoidably arbitrary) definition of sexual identity. Instead of setting a 'non-identity' against an identity, Foucault should have distinguished between a proper and an improper *relation* to such a symbolically imposed identity and should then have shown into which category 'modern, Western society' falls. In this connection, see R. Bernet (1988), pp. 231–47 and J.M. Broekman (1987a), pp. 103–15.

94. DP, p. 30 (my emphasis, R.V.).

95. Ibid, p. 227.

96. Ibid, p. 305.

97. See above, quotation for note 74 (there is a parallel here to what was said in that passage about mental illness).

98. DP, p. 28.

99. 'Power and Sex' (1977), p. 158.

100. OD, p. 61.

101. See above, quotation for note 22.

102. P. Dews (1986), p. 82. The example given is also taken from this article.

103. 'Truth and Power', P/K, p. 133: 'The problem is not changing people's consciousnesses ... but the political, economic, institutional régime of the production of truth ... The political question, to sum up ... is truth itself.'

104. 'History of Systems of Thought' (1977), p. 203.

105. See B. Waldenfels (1985), p. 51 and B. Waldenfels (1987), p. 150.

106. J. Habermas (1987), p. 278.

107. J. Derrida (1978), p. 42.

108. 'History of Systems of Thought' (1977), p. 203.

109. IJsseling (1973), p. 798.

110. B. Waldenfels (1986), p. 41.

111. AK, p. 126, and above, 3.2 and 4.1(2).

112. Cf the emergence of norms from the lifeworld, in Waldenfels (1985), especially pp. 139 ff.

113. L. Wittgenstein, *Philosophische Untersuchungen/Philosophical Investigations*, trans. G.E.M. Anscombe, Basil Blackwell, Oxford, 1968, para 325, p. 106^e.

114. A form of indirect foundation (*Begründung*) is not to be ruled out, however: even if every 'truth' were a fiction, an interpretation or a 'falsification', one could still argue that there are fictions which have preserved themselves 'species-historically [*gattungsgeschichtlich*]': 'Items of information are only "of service in life" ... when they *match up with something* in the reality objectified within the transcendental frame of possible technical disposition' (J. Habermas, 1968, p. 257 – my emphasis, R.V.). However, along with the objectivity of experience, Habermas seems to wish, at the same time, to rescue its identity. Yet it is not clear why one cannot speak of orders which make (diverse) experiences possible and still introduce a similar concept of truth. Habermas's arguments against simple validity-relativism/perspectivism do not seem to us an adequate refutation of a relativism of *conditions* of validity. [Note to English edition: I have further developed this point in Visker (1992).]

115. OT, p. xx.

116. B. Waldenfels (undated), p. 204.

117. See above, 4.1(2) for the distinction between internal and external principles of ordering.

118. On this argument, see N. Fraser (1983), p. 64 and Waldenfels (1985), pp. 23 ff. and 46 ff.

119. BC, p. xix.

120. As is argued, for example, by P. Dews (1987), pp. 169, 192.

121. F. Schipper, 'Review of De Folter' (1987), *Algemeen Nederlands Tijdschrift voor Wijsbegeerte*, 1988, 80 (4), p. 307 (my emphasis, R.V.).

122. S.K. White (1988), p. 145 and N. Fraser (1981), p. 286.

123. We take this expression from Foucault's essay, 'Powers and Strategies', P/K, p. 136 ('the politics of inverted commas' – Foucault's example is the frequently made comparison between real existing 'socialism' and true socialism).

124. These remarks were inspired by Canguilhem's observation that illness is a state in which one can admit of only one norm – Canguilhem (1978), p. 108.

125. For an example along these lines, see B. Waldenfels (1988), p. 208.

126. AK, pp. 110, 119, 192 and above, 4.2(2).

127. See, e.g., Parret (1979), pp. 102 ff.

128. Discourses are dependent on an external referent, which they do not form themselves but which it falls to them to transform into a discursive object (on the internal referent, see AK, pp. 163–4 and above, 4.2(2)). The denial of the fact that the internal referent has to be discursively constructed might also be accompanied by an attempt to conceal the genealogy of the external referent (cf here the role which realism played for psychology). The *conjunction* of the two processes can no longer be thought merely in terms of archaeology, nor indeed of genealogy. It requires a different model in which the internal and external referent co-constitute each other. This seems to be a form of 'power-knowledge' which was in fact already present in *Histoire de la folie*, though in a suppressed form: in this case, 'mental illness' might be said to be neither wholly and solely a 'discursive object', nor an external referent whose genealogy can be discovered by an analysis of power processes. It is not exclusively a product internal to discourse, yet it could not exist without these discourses. And it is not a product of power *tout court*, yet it presupposes the existence of a string of power mechanisms which must be related to knowledge. It is not clear, however, why such a co-constitution of power and knowledge should constitute an argument against (the scientificity of) that knowledge. On the other hand, such a history of the emergence of knowledge is not without significance: it uncovers a materiality in knowledge which prevents it from speaking with the distanced authority of realism (see above, 1.2(2) and our discussion of HS1 – especially at 3.1(2, i) – which pointed in this same direction).

129. Thus, among others, J.M. Broekman (1987b), pp. 231–42; see also Broekman (1979), pp. 135 ff. and Van Roermund (1983), pp. 13–56.

130. See Visker (1988).

131. See note 130.

132. For Waldenfels's treatment of this question, see (1987), pp. 34, 83.

133. We are playing here on Heidegger's distinction between the 'default of Being [*Ausbleiben des Seins*]' and the 'omission of the default of Being [*Auslassen des Ausbleibens des Seins*]' – cf, for example, Heidegger (1981), p. 367 and passim. [Note to English edition: I have further developed this point in Visker (1991).]

134. Perhaps because, 'with' Foucault, we have 'de-substantivized' truth (see above, 4.1(2) and spoken at times, in this sense, of a truth-event or ordering-event, without possessing the means to think the truth-*event* etc.

135. See note 132.

136. HS2, p. 8.

137. English version in *Language, Counter-Memory, Practice* (1977), pp. 29–52.

138. HS2, p. 9.

139. 'At the conclusion of a certain work, even the concepts of excess or transgression can become suspect', Derrida (1981), p. 12.

140. All the passages quoted are from Marguerite Duras, *Emily L.*, pp. 98–9.

Bibliography

ACHTERHUIS, H. (1988), *Het rijk van de schaarste. Van Thomas Hobbes tot Michel Foucault*, Baarn.

ALTHUSSER, L. and BALIBAR, E. (1970), *Reading Capital*, trans. B. Brewster, London.

BARTHES, R. (1977), 'The Death of the Author', *Image Music Text* (essays selected and translated by Stephen Heath), Glasgow, pp. 142–8.

BERNET, R. (1986), 'Differenz und Anwesenheit. Derridas und Husserls Phänomenologie der Sprache, der Zeit, der Geschichte, der wissenschaftlichen Rationalität', *Studien zur neueren französischen Philosophie (Phänomenologische Forschungen* vol. 18), Freiburg/Munich, pp. 51–112.

—— (1988), 'Sexualiteit en Subjectiviteit', *Tijdschrift voor Filosofie*, 50, 2, pp. 231–47.

BERTHOUD, G. & SABELLI, F. (1976), *L'Ambivalence de la production. Logiques communautaires et logique capitaliste*, Paris/Geneva.

BONCENNE, P. (1984), 'Du Pouvoir. Un entretien avec Michel Foucault', *L'Express*, 13 July 1984 (no. 1722), pp. 56–62.

BORGES, J.L. (1970), 'The Immortal', trans. James E. Irby, *Labyrinths*, Harmondsworth, pp. 135–49.

BROEKMAN, J.M. (1979), *Recht und Anthropologie*, Freiburg/Munich.

—— (1987a), 'De Man/Vrouw Differentiatie, Recht en Cultuur', *Rechtsfilosofie en Rechtstheorie*, 16, 2, pp. 103–15.

—— (1987b), 'Zur Ontologie des juristischen Sprechakts', in: W. Krawietz and W. Ott (eds), *Formalismus und Phänomenologie im Rechtsdenken der Gegenwart. Festgabe für Alois Troller zum 80. Geburtstag*, Berlin, pp. 231–42.

CANGUILHEM, G. (1978), *On the Normal and the Pathological*, trans. Carolyn R. Fawcett, Dordrecht/Boston.

CRESPI, F. (1979), 'Foucault o il refiuto della determinazione', *Aut Aut*, 170–71, pp. 104–8.

DE FOLTER, R. (1987), *Normaal en Abnormaal. Enkele beschouwingen over het probleem van de normaliteit in het denken van Husserl, Schütz en Foucault*, Groningen.

DELEUZE, G. (1988), *Foucault*, London.

DERRIDA, J. (1973), *'Speech and Phenomena' and Other Essays on Husserl's Theory of Signs*, trans. David B. Allison, Evanston.

—— (1976), *Of Grammatology*, trans. Gayatri C. Spivak, Baltimore/London.

—— (1978), *Writing and Difference*, trans. A. Bass, London.

—— (1981), *Positions*, London.

—— (1982), *Margins of Philosophy*, trans. A. Bass, Brighton.

—— (1984), *Otobiographies. L'enseignement de Nietzsche et la politique du nom propre*, Paris.

—— (1989a), 'Desistance', in: P. Lacoue-Labarthe, *Typography, Mimesis, Philosophy, Politics*, trans. C. Fynsk, Cambridge (Mass.)/London, pp. 1–42.

—— (1989b), 'Interpreting Signatures (Nietzsche/Heidegger): Two Questions', in: Diane P. Michelfelder and Richard E. Palmer (eds), *Dialogue and Deconstruction. The Gadamer–Derrida Encounter*, Albany, pp. 58–71.

DESCOMBES, V. (1977), *L'Inconscient malgré lui*, Paris.

DEVOS, R. (1987), 'Fragmenten voor een machtstheorie. Kritische analyse van de machtsproblematiek in M. Foucault "La volonté de savoir"', *Bijdragen, tijdschrift voor filosofie en theologie*, 48, 3, pp. 277–302.

DEWS, P. (1984), 'Power and Subjectivity in Foucault', *New Left Review*, 144, pp. 72–97.

—— (1986), 'The *Nouvelle Philosophie* and Foucault', in: M. Gane (ed.), *Towards a Critique of Foucault*, London/New York, pp. 61–105.

—— (1987), *Logics of disintegration. Post-structuralist Thought and the Claims of Critical Theory*, London/New York.

DONNELLY, M. (1986), 'Foucault's Genealogy of the Human Sciences', in: M. Gane (ed.), *Towards a Critique of Foucault*, London/New York, pp. 15–32.

DREYFUS, H.L. (1987), 'Foreword to the California Edition', in: M. Foucault, *Mental Illness and Psychology*, Berkeley/Los Angeles/London.

DREYFUS, H.L. & RABINOW, P. (1983), *Michel Foucault: Beyond Structuralism and Hermeneutics*, second edition, Chicago.

DURAS, M. (1989), *Emily L.*, London.

FEYERABEND, P. (1981), 'Consolations for the Specialist', in: I. Lakatos and A. Musgrave, *Criticism and the Growth of Knowledge*, pp. 197–213.

FOUCAULT, M. (AK), *The Archaeology of Knowledge*, London, 1972 [first French edition 1969].

—— (BC), *The Birth of the Clinic. An Archaeology of Medical Perception*, London 1973 [1963,[1] revised 1972].

—— (DP), *Discipline and Punish. The Birth of the Prison*, Harmondsworth, 1979 [1975].

—— (FD) *Folie et déraison. Histoire de la folie à l'âge classique*, Paris, 1961. This is the first edition, published by Plon, which contains a different preface from the editions subsequently published by Gallimard after 1972.

—— (HF), *Histoire de la folie à l'âge classique*, Paris, 1972.

—— (HS1), *The History of Sexuality. Volume I: an Introduction*, New York, 1978 [1976].

—— (HS2), *The Use of Pleasure. The History of Sexuality, volume 2*, London, 1987 [1984].

—— (HS3), *The Care of the Self. The History of Sexuality, volume 3*, London, 1990 [1984].

—— (MIP), *Mental Illness and Psychology*, New York, 1976 [1962].

—— (NGH), 'Nietzsche, Genealogy, History [1971], in: *Language, Counter-Memory, Practice: Selected Essays and Interviews* (ed. Donald Bouchard), Ithaca, 1977, pp. 139–64.

—— (OD), 'The Order of Discourse' (Inaugural Lecture at the Collège de France, given 2 December 1970), in: R. Young (ed.), *Untying the Text: a Post-Structuralist Reader*, Boston, London and Henley, 1981, pp. 48–78.

—— (OT), *The Order of Things. An Archaeology of the Human Sciences*, New York, 1971 [1966].

—— (P/K), *Power/Knowledge. Selected Interviews and Other Writings 1972–77* (ed. C. Gordon), New York, 1980.

—— (RC), *Résumé des cours 1970–1982*, Paris, 1989.

—— (1968), 'Réponse au cercle d'épistémologie', *Cahiers pour l'analyse*, no. 9, pp. 9–40.

—— (1969), 'Nietzsche, Freud, Marx', in: *Nietzsche* (Cahiers de Royaumont. VIIe colloque – 4–8 July 1964), Paris.

—— (1975), *Surveiller et punir*, Paris (otherwise referred to in English translation, DP).

—— (1976), 'L'Extension sociale de la norme' (interview with Pascale Werner), *Politique Hebdo*, no. 212, pp. 14–16.

—— (1976), 'Les Jeux du pouvoir', in: D. Grisoni (ed.), *Politiques de la philosophie*, Paris, pp. 155–74.

—— (1977), 'Power and Sex: an Interview with Michel Foucault', *Telos*, 32, pp. 152–61 [1977].

—— (1977), 'Preface to G. Deleuze, F. Guattari', *Anti-Oedipus*, New York.

—— (1977), 'What is an Author?', *Language, Counter-Memory, Practice*, pp. 113–38 [1969].

—— (1977), 'History of Systems of Thought', *Language, Counter-Memory, Practice*, pp. 199–204.

—— (1977), 'A Preface to Transgression', *Language, Counter-Memory, Practice*, pp. 29–52 [1963].

—— (1978), 'Politics and the Study of Discourse', *Ideology and Consciousness*, 3 (Spring), pp. 7–26 [1968].

—— (1978), *I Pierre Rivière, having slaughtered my mother, my sister, and my brother*, Harmondsworth [1973].

—— (1979), 'The Life of Infamous Men', in: Meaghan Morris, Paul Patton (eds), *Power, Truth, Strategy*, Sydney, pp. 76–91 [1977].

—— (1980), 'Body/Power', P/K, pp. 55–62 [1975].

—— (1980), 'Prison Talk', P/K, pp. 37–54 [1976].

—— (1980), 'Truth and Power', P/K, pp. 109–33 [1977].

—— (1980), 'The History of Sexuality', P/K, pp. 183–99 [1977].

—— (1980) 'Powers and Strategies', P/K, pp. 134–45 [1977].

—— (1980), *Herculine Barbin, Being the Recently Discovered Memoirs of a Nineteenth Century French Hermaphrodite*, New York [1978].

—— (1980), 'Two Lectures', P/K, pp. 78–108 [1976].

—— (1980), 'Questions on Geography', P/K, pp. 63–77 [1976].

—— (1980), *Howison Lecture on Truth and Subjectivity (I & II)*, Berkeley, 20–21 October 1980, manuscript (a published version of similar lectures delivered at Dartmouth on 17 and 24 November 1980 has recently become available: 'About the Beginning of the Hermeneutics of the Self. Two Lectures at Dartmouth', *Political Theory*, May 1993, vol. 21, 2, pp. 198–227).

—— (1980), 'Le Vrai Sexe', *Arcadie*, 27 (November 1980), pp. 617–25.

—— (1980), 'War in the Filigree of Peace: Course Summary', *The Oxford Literary Review*, 4, 2 [1975–6].

—— (1980), 'La Poussière et le nuage', *L'Impossible Prison. Recherches sur le système pénitentiaire au XIXe siècle réunies par Michelle Perrot. Débat avec Michel Foucault*, Paris.

—— (1981), 'Questions of Method', *Ideology and Consciousness*, 8 (Spring 1981), pp. 3–14 [1980].

—— (1981), 'Omnes et Singulatim: Towards a Criticism of "Political Reason"' (1979) in: S. McMurrin (ed.), *The Tanner Lectures on Human Values*, Salt Lake City/Cambridge, pp. 223–54.

—— (1982), 'Is It Really Important to Think?', *Philosophy and Social Criticism*, 9, no. 1, pp. 31–5 [1981].

—— (1982), 'Des Caresses d'homme considérées comme un art', *Libération*, 1 June, p. 27.

—— (1983), 'The Subject and Power'. Afterword to H. Dreyfus and P. Rabinow (1983), pp. 208 ff.

—— (1984), 'The Ethic of Care for the Self as a Practice of Freedom', *Philosophy and Social Criticism*, XII, 2–3, pp. 112–31 [1984].

—— (1984), 'Preface to *The History of Sexuality*', in: P. Rabinow, *The Foucault Reader*, London, pp. 333–9.

—— (1984), 'L'Intellectuel et les pouvoirs', *La Revue nouvelle*, 10 October, pp. 338–45.

—— (1984), 'Space, Knowledge and Power', in: P. Rabinow, *The Foucault Reader*, London, pp. 239–56.

—— (1984), 'What is Enlightenment?' in: P. Rabinow, *The Foucault Reader*, London, pp. 32–50.

—— (1984), 'On the Genealogy of Ethics: an Overview of Work in Progress', in: P. Rabinow, *The Foucault Reader*, London, pp. 340–72 [1983].

—— (1984), 'Une Esthétique de l'existence', *Le Monde aujourd'hui*, 15–16 July 1984, p. xi.

165

―――― (1984), 'Le Philosophe Masqué', *Entretiens avec* Le Monde. 1. *Philosophies*, Paris.

―――― (1985), 'The Battle for Chastity', in: Philippe Ariès, André Béjin (eds), *Western Sexuality: Practice and Precept in Past and Present Times*, Oxford [1982].

―――― (1986), *Vom Licht des Krieges zur Geburt der Geschichte. Vorlesungen vom 21. und 28. 1. 1976 am Collège de France*, Berlin.

―――― (1988), 'The Concern for Truth', *Politics, Philosophy, Culture: Interviews and Other Writings 1977–1984*, New York/London, pp. 255–67 [1984].

―――― (1988), 'The Return of Morality', *Politics, Philosophy, Culture: Interviews and Other Writings, 1977–1984*, New York/London, pp. 242–54 [1984].

―――― (1988), 'Technologies of the Self', in: L.H. Martin *et al.* (eds), *Technologies of the Self. A Seminar with Michel Foucault*, Amherst, pp. 16–49.

―――― (1988), 'Truth, Power, Self', in: L.H. Martin *et al.* (eds), *Technologies of the Self. A Seminar with Michel Foucault*, Amherst, pp. 9–15.

―――― (1988), 'The Political Technology of Individuals', in: L.H. Martin *et al.* (eds), *Technologies of the Self. A Seminar with Michel Foucault*, Amherst, pp. 145–62.

―――― (1991), *Remarks on Marx. Conversations with Duccio Trombadori* (1980), trans. R. James Goldstein and James Cascaito, New York.

FOUCAULT, M. and SENNETT, R. (1981), 'Sexuality and Solitude', *London Review of Books*, 21 May–3 June.

FRASER, N. (1981), 'Foucault on Modern Power. Empirical Insights and Normative Confusions', *Praxis International*, 1, 3, pp. 272–87.

―――― (1983), 'Foucault's Body-Language: a Post-Humanist Political Rhetoric', *Salmagundi*, 61, pp. 55–70.

―――― (1985), 'Michel Foucault, a "Young Conservative"?', *Ethics*, 96, 1, pp. 165–84.

GORDON, C. (1990), '"Histoire de la folie", an Unknown Book by Michel Foucault', *History of the Human Sciences* 3, 1, pp. 3–26.

de HAAN, I. *et al.* (1987), 'Habermas en Foucault ter beschikking gesteld. Kolonisering en disciplinering als analysemodellen', *Krisis*, 27, pp. 16–33.

HABERMAS, J. (1968), 'Nachwort', in: F. Nietzsche, *Erkenntnistheoretische Schriften*, Frankfurt am Main, pp. 237–61.

―――― (1978), *Knowledge and Human Interests*, trans. Jeremy J. Shapiro, London.

―――― (1981), 'Interview von Angelo Bolaffi mit Jürgen Habermas für die italienische Wochenzeitung Rinascita (1978)', *Kleine politische Schriften* (I–IV), Frankfurt am Main, pp. 491–510.

―――― (1983), 'Die Verschlingung von Mythos und Aufklarung. Bemerkungen zur *Dialektik der Aufklärung* nach einer erneuten Lektüre', in: K.H. Bohrer (ed.), *Mythos und Moderne. Begriff und Bild einer Rekonstruktion*, Frankfurt am Main, pp. 405–31.

―――― (1985a), 'Modernity – an Incomplete Project', in: Hal Foster (ed.),

Postmodern Culture, London/Sydney.

—— (1985b), *Die neue Unübersichtlichkeit. Kleine Politische Schriften V,* Frankfurt am Main.

—— (1986), 'Bemerkungen zur Entwicklungsgeschichte des Horkheimerschen Werks', in: N. Altwicker & A. Schmidt (eds), *Max Horkheimer heute: Werk und Wirkung,* Frankfurt am Main, pp. 163–79.

—— (1987), *The Philosophical Discourse of Modernity,* trans. Frederick Lawrence, Cambridge.

—— (1989), *The New Conservatism,* trans. Shierry Weber Nicholsen, Cambridge.

HADOT, P. (1987), 'Un dialogue interrompu avec Michel Foucault', *Exercices Spirituels et philosophie antique (Deuxième édition revue et augmentée),* Paris, pp. 229–33.

HEIDEGGER, M. (1981), *Nietzsche,* vol. II, Pfullingen.

HILEY, D.R. (1985), 'Foucault and the Question of Enlightenment', *Philosophy and Social Criticism,* 11, 1, pp. 63–83.

HONEGGER, C. (1982), *Uberlegungen zu Michel Foucaults Entwurf einer Geschichte der Sexualität* (manuscript), Frankfurt am Main.

HONNETH, A. (1985), *Kritik der Macht. Reflexionsstufen einer kritischen Gesellschaftstheorie,* Frankfurt am Main.

HORKHEIMER, M. (1970), *Verwaltete Welt? Ein Gespräch mit O. Hersche,* Zurich.

HOY, D.C. (1979), 'Taking History Seriously: Foucault, Gadamer, Habermas', *Union Seminary Quarterly Review,* 34, 2, pp. 85–95.

HUSSERL, E. (1970), *The Crisis of European Sciences and Transcendental Phenomenology,* Evanston.

IJSSELING, S. (1973), 'Nietzsche en de rhetorica', *Tijdschrift voor Filosofie,* 35, 4, pp. 766–99.

—— (1979), 'Michel Foucault en de strategie van de macht', *Denken in Parijs. Taal en Lacan, Foucault, Althusser, Derrida,* Alphen a.d. Rijn/ Brussels, pp. 69–93.

—— (1986), 'Intersubjektivität und Intertextualität', *Archivio di Filosofia,* 54, 1–3, pp. 251–9.

JAMBET, C. (1992), 'The Constitution of the Subject and Spiritual Practice', in: *Michel Foucault, Philosopher,* trans. Timothy J. Armstrong, New York etc, pp. 233–47.

JONKERS, P. (1986), 'Vrijheid en macht vanuit christelijk perspectief. Wijsgerige Kanttekeningen bij Rahners theologische antropologie', *Bijdragen, Tijdschrift voor Filosofie en Theologie,* 47, 4, pp. 395–420.

KARSKENS, M. (1989), 'Subjektiviteit en seksualiteit, een historische vergissing. Een kritische analyse aan de hand van de late Foucault', *Krisis,* 35, pp. 55–65.

KEULARTZ, J. & KUNNEMAN, H. (1983), 'Disciplinering en bevrijding in Habermas' maatschappijtheorie', *Krisis,* 12, pp. 28–53.

—— (1984), 'Kolonisering, disciplinering en onvergelijkbaarheid. Over de verhouding tussen Foucault en Habermas', *Krisis,* 17, pp. 85–93.

KUNNEMAN, H. (1986), *De waarheidstrechter. Een communicatie-theoretisch perspectief op wetenschap en samenleving*, Meppel.
KWANT, R.C. (1975), 'Foucault en de menswetenschappen', *Tijdschift voor Filosofie*, 37, 2, pp. 294–326.

LAERMANS, R. (1984), 'Foucault en Habermas. Een kritiek op de integratiepoging van Keulartz en Kunneman', *Krisis*, 15, pp. 86–92.
LAMBRECHTS, M. (1981), 'De archeologies-genealogiese methode van Michel Foucault', *Te Elfder Ure*, vol. 29 ('Foucault over macht'), Nijmegen, pp. 517–55.
LYOTARD, J.-F. (1988), *The Differend*, trans. Georges van den Abbeele, Manchester.

MACHADO, R. (1992), 'Archaeology and Epistemology', in: *Michel Foucault, Philosopher*, pp. 3–19.
MACHEREY, P. (1986), 'Aux Sources de l'"Histoire de la folie": une rectification et ses limites', *Critique*, 471–2, pp. 753–74.
—— (1992), Towards a Natural History of Norms', in: *Michel Foucault, Philosopher*, pp. 176–91.
MAUSS, M. (1979), *Sociology and Psychology. Essays*, trans. B. Brewster, London.
MERLEAU-PONTY, M. (1968), *The Visible and the Invisible: Followed by Working Notes*, trans. Alphonso Lingis, Evanston.
—— (1981), *Phenomenology of Perception*, trans. Colin Smith, London.
MERQUIOR, J.-G. (1985), *Foucault*, London.
MIDELFORT, H.C.E. (1990), 'Comment on Colin Gordon', *History of the Human Sciences*, 3, 1, pp. 41–5.
MOYAERT, P. (1986), 'Jacques Derrida en de filosofie van de differentie', in: S. IJsseling (ed.), *Jacques Derrida. Een Inleiding in zijn denken*, Baarn, pp. 28–89.

NIETZSCHE, F. (1911), 'On Truth and Falsity in Their Ultramoral Sense (1873)', *The Complete Works of Friedrich Nietzsche* (ed. O. Levy), vol. 2: *Early Greek Philosophy*, London and Edinburgh, pp. 173–92.
—— (1989), *On the Genealogy of Morals/The Birth of Tragedy*, trans. S. Whiteside, London.

O'HIGGINS, J. (1988), 'Sexual Choice, Sexual Act: Foucault and Homosexuality', in: Michel Foucault, *Politics, Philosophy, Culture. Interviews and Other Writings 1977–1984*, New York/London, pp. 286–303.

PARRET, H. (1979), *Filosofie en taalwetenschap*, Assen.
POPPER, K.R. (1975), 'The Bucket and the Searchlight: Two Theories of Knowledge', *Objective Knowledge. An Evolutionary Approach*, Oxford, pp. 341–61.
PORTER, R. (1990), 'Foucault's Great Confinement', *History of the Human Sciences* 3, 1, pp. 47–54.

RABINOW, P. (1984), *The Foucault Reader*, London.

RAJCHMAN, J. (1978), 'Nietzsche, Foucault, and the Anarchism of Power', *Semiotexte* III (1), pp. 96–107.
—— (1985), *Michel Foucault. The Freedom of Philosophy*, New York.
RAULET, G. (1983), 'Structuralism and Post-Structuralism. An Interview with Michel Foucault', *Telos. A Quarterly Journal of Critical Thought* 55, pp. 195–211.
RORTY, R. (1985), 'Habermas and Lyotard on Post-Modernity', in: R. Bernstein (ed.), *Habermas and Modernity*, Oxford, pp. 161–75.
—— (1992), Moral Identity and Private Autonomy', in: *Michel Foucault, Philosopher*, pp. 328–35.

SCHIPPER, F. (1988), 'Review of R. De Folter, "Normaal en abnormaal" ', *Algemeen Nederlands Tijdschrift voor Wijsbegeerte*, 80, 4, pp. 305–7.
SCHÜRMANN, R. (1986), 'On Constituting Oneself as an Anarchistic Subject', *Praxis International*, 6, 3, pp. 294–310.
SCULL, A. (1990), 'Michel Foucault's History of Madness', *History of the Human Sciences* 3, 1, pp. 57–67.
SEITTER, W. (1980), 'Ein Denken im Forschen. Zum Unternehmen einer Analytik bei M. Foucault', *Philosophisches Jahrbuch*, 87, pp. 340–63.

TAYLOR, C. (1986), 'Foucault on Freedom and Truth', in: D.C. Hoy (ed.), *Foucault: a Critical Reader*, Oxford, pp. 69–102.

VANDERMEERSCH, P. (1985), 'Michel Foucault: een onverwachte hermeneutiek van het christendom?', *Tijdschrift voor theologie*, 25, 3, pp. 250–77.
VAN GILS, W. (1986), *Realiteit en illusie als schijnvertoning. Over het werk van Jean Baudrillard*, Nijmegen.
VAN HAUTE, P. (1993), 'Michel Foucault: de psychoanalyse en de wet', *Tijdschrift voor Filosofie*, 55, 3, pp. 449–72 (English translation forthcoming in *Epoché. A Journal for the History of Philosophy*).
VAN ROERMUND, G.C.G.J. (1983), *Wetten en weten. 'Theorie van het recht': een wijsgerige kritiek*, Leuven/Louvain.
VEYNE, P. (1978), 'Foucault révolutionne l'histoire', *Comment on écrit l'histoire*, Paris, pp. 203–42.
—— (1986), 'Le Dernier Foucault et sa morale', *Critique*, 471–2, pp. 933–41.
VISKER, R. (1988), 'Marshallian Ethics and Economics. Deconstructing the Authority of Science', *Philosophy of the Social Sciences*, 18, 2, pp. 179–99.
—— (1991), 'From Foucault to Heidegger. A One-way Ticket?', *Research in Phenomenology*, XXI, pp. 116–40.
—— (1992), 'Habermas on Heidegger and Foucault. Meaning and Validity in "The Philosophical Discourse of Modernity"', *Radical Philosophy*, 61, pp. 15–22.
—— (1993), 'Raw Being and Violent Discourse. Foucault, Merleau-Ponty and the (Dis-)order of Things', in: P. Burke/J. Van der Veken (eds), *Merleau-Ponty in Contemporary Perspective*, Dordrecht, pp. 109–29.

WALDENFELS, B. (1985), *In den Netzen der Lebenswelt*, Frankfurt am Main.

—— (1986), 'Verstreute Vernunft. Zur Philosophie von Michel Foucault', *Studien zur neueren französischen Philosophie (Phänomenologische Forschungen* vol. 18), Freiburg/Munich, pp. 30–50.

—— (1987), *Ordnung im Zwielicht*. Frankfurt am Main.

—— (1988), 'Umdenken der Technik', in: W.C. Zimmerli (ed.), *Technologisches Zeitalter oder Postmoderne*, Munich, pp. 199–211.

—— (undated), 'Alltag als Schmelztiegel der Rationalität', *Amerikastudien*, 32, pp. 199–207.

WALZER, M. (1986), 'The Politics of Michel Foucault', in: D.C. Hoy (ed.), *Foucault: a Critical Reader*, Oxford, pp. 51–68.

WEBER, S. (1987), *Institution and Interpretation*, Minneapolis.

WHITE, St K. (1988), *The Recent Work of Jürgen Habermas. Reason, Justice and Modernity*, Cambridge.

de WIT, J. & FRANÇOIS, J. (1984), 'Interview met Michel Foucault', *Krisis*, 14, pp. 47–58.

WITTGENSTEIN, L. (1968), *Philosophische Untersuchungen/Philosophical Investigations*, trans. G.E.M. Anscombe, Oxford.

Index